Answering the Music Man

- Helps explain Thomas' 5 ways
- slavery, genocide, jealous · good rebuttal
- explains God's attributes - easy to understand

ANSWERING
the MUSIC MAN

*Dan Barker's Arguments
against Christianity*

Edited by
B. KYLE KELTZ
and TRICIA SCRIBNER

Foreword by
RICHARD LAND

WIPF & STOCK · Eugene, Oregon

ANSWERING THE MUSIC MAN
Dan Barker's Arguments against Christianity

Copyright © 2020 Wipf & Stock Publishers. All rights reserved. Except for brief quotations in critical publications or reviews, no part of this book may be reproduced in any manner without prior written permission from the publisher. Write: Permissions, Wipf and Stock Publishers, 199 W. 8th Ave., Suite 3, Eugene, OR 97401.

www.wipfandstock.com

PAPERBACK ISBN: 978-1-7252-5336-0
HARDCOVER ISBN: 978-1-7252-5337-7
EBOOK ISBN: 978-1-7252-5338-4

Manufactured in the U.S.A.   MAY 26, 2020

"Silly Putty." Trademark of Crayola Properties, Inc. Registration Number 0560758—Serial Number 71594970: Justia Trademarks. https://trademarks.justia.com/715/94/silly-71594970.html.

Scripture quotations taken from the ESV® Bible (The Holy Bible, English Standard Version®), copyright © 2001 by Crossway, a publishing ministry of Good News Publishers. Used by permission. All rights reserved.

Scripture quotations taken from the New American Standard Bible® (NASB), Copyright © 1960, 1962, 1963, 1968, 1971, 1972, 1973, 1975, 1977, 1995 by The Lockman Foundation Used by permission. www.Lockman.org

Scripture taken from the New King James Version®. Copyright © 1982 by Thomas Nelson. Used by permission. All rights reserved.

Contents

Foreword

—RICHARD LAND

KYLE KELTZ AND TRICIA Scribner have performed a valuable service for the scholarly world of Christian apologetics and philosophy by compiling, editing, and contributing to this book, *Answering the Music Man: Dan Barker's Arguments against Christianity.* This volume should help put to rest the old, hackneyed cliché promoted by its critics that Christianity is only for the uninformed and that Christians cannot deal with the philosophical and evidential questions generated by the compelling truth claims of the historic Christian faith.

Any objective reader of the chapters in this book will be impressed by both the erudition and scholarly research of each of the contributors. However, the volume's added bonus is the fact that these sometimes-difficult issues are explained in such a way that any serious lay reader will find each of them accessible and beneficial.

Albert Einstein is reported to have said, "If you cannot explain something simply, you do not understand it well enough." Clearly, each of this volume's authors understands his or her subject exceedingly well, and after you have read their chapters, you will too. The contributors also do Dan Barker the courtesy of taking his "arguments" seriously and dealing with them in a serious manner. Frankly, that in itself is an act of Christian charity in my opinion. Barker, a lapsed former minister and atheist advocate, understands just enough about Christianity and atheism to be dangerous, but not accurate.

Having the great privilege of serving as president of Southern Evangelical Seminary, I am extremely gratified that all of the contributors of this volume are SES graduates, with the exception of Richard Howe, who as Professor Emeritus at SES has invested in the lives of each contributor as his or her professor in some point in their educational pilgrimage.

Indeed, this book grew out of the responses by the contributors to a debate between Richard Howe and Dan Barker held at SES's annual National Conference on Christian Apologetics in 2017.

Answering the Music Man refutes Dan Barker's atheism, and while doing so, both encourages and edifies the bride of Christ, the church—a noble endeavor and a great accomplishment.

Richard Land, DPhil
President, Professor of Theology
Southern Evangelical Seminary in Matthew, NC.

Preface

—B. Kyle Keltz

The idea for this book originated at the 2017 National Conference on Christian Apologetics, which is the annual apologetics conference hosted by Southern Evangelical Seminary in Charlotte, North Carolina.[1] At the conference, which was held at Calvary Church in Charlotte, Dan Barker and Richard Howe debated the question "Is there a God who speaks?" and the debate was generally over the existence of God.[2] Of course, Dan Barker argued for the negative that theism is false (or at least that he lacks a belief in theism), and Howe argued for the affirmative that theism is true.

I had never heard Barker speak before, and I hadn't read any of his books, so without any specific expectations, I was anticipating a good debate. However, after the opening statements and the first round of cross-examinations, it became clear to me (and my fellow PhD-student friends sitting with me) that Barker didn't have well-reasoned arguments for his atheism, and he misunderstood the argument for God's existence that Howe presented. Not knowing much about Barker, it surprised me that Howe agreed to debate him (I didn't realize at the time that Barker is such a high-profile popular atheist).

After the debate, I was surprised to hear some of the comments made by people in the crowd as the sanctuary slowly emptied. I overheard a few groups of people saying they thought Barker had made a better case than Howe. This took me by surprise as it seemed to me that Howe easily bested Barker. Apparently, Barker wasn't the only one who didn't understand Howe's argument, which was admittedly a more technical argument from

1. https://conference.ses.edu.

2. Barker and Howe, "Is There a God Who Speaks?," https://www.youtube.com/watch?v=LD3-qK-2gu8&.

ix

Thomas Aquinas, one that most lay persons will need more than a quick debate to fully understand.

After the debate, myself and a few of my fellow PhD students thought it would be good to put together a book exposing Barker's poor arguments against Christianity. So, this book contains essays that answer Barker's main points he usually makes at debates and the arguments he included in his books *Life Driven Purpose: How an Atheist Finds Meaning*; *God: The Most Unpleasant Character in All Fiction*; *Mere Morality*; and especially *godless: How an Evangelical Preacher Became One of America's Leading Atheists*. In fact, the order of the topics of the essays roughly follows the order of the arguments found in *godless*.

This book, at times, contains some words directed at Barker that may seem harsh. However, I don't think anything said in this book is unwarranted. Barker is an atheist, and Scripture commands Christians to interact with nonbelievers with gentleness and respect (1 Pet 3:15). Yet Barker, a former evangelical pastor of all people, should know that preachers and teachers are judged with a stricter standard (Jas 3:1). So, our words in this book are not aimed at someone who has never heard the gospel, but at a brother who claims to have personally trusted in Jesus Christ for salvation. The contributors to this book and I have been praying for Barker throughout the writing and production of this book, and we hope that it will either have an impact on Barker (if he ever gets and reads a copy) or at the very least that it will help honest truth seekers who might have been led astray by him.

We chose to title this book *Answering the Music Man* in reference not only to the fact that Barker writes music, but also in reference to the musical *The Music Man*. For those who have not seen or heard the musical, it is a story about a traveling salesman named Harold Hill who travels throughout the American Midwest in the early 1900s. Hill travels from town to town, posing as a music professor and convincing the townspeople to buy sheets of music, musical instruments, and band uniforms with the promise that he will mold their children into musicians capable of forming proper marching bands. However, after he collects their money, and shortly before the children are scheduled to perform, Hill always skips town because, in reality, he knows nothing of music and couldn't form a marching band if he wanted.

I thought this was a fitting analogy for Dan Barker. Barker, despite his atheism and conviction that there is no objective purpose in life, finds pleasure in traveling the country, speaking, and trying to persuade people that God does not exist and that Christianity is untrue. Yet, Barker does not understand what he is selling. Like Hill, Barker may be a good speaker, but on closer examination, Barker's comprehension of Christianity is as poor as Hill's understanding of music.

This book was written to expose Barker for the pseudo-intellectual he is. I pray that it will help anyone who finds his arguments compelling to realize just how much they miss the mark and mischaracterize orthodox Christianity. Having said all this, I wish nothing but the best for Dan Barker. I pray that God will grant him grace and deliver him from the errors in which he has fallen.

B. Kyle Keltz

Contributors

Thomas Baker, PhD, Adjunct Professor at Southern Evangelical Seminary, and Associate Professor of Theology and Apologetics at Veritas International University.

J. Thomas Bridges, PhD, Associate Professor of Philosophy at Southern Evangelical Seminary.

Brett A. Bruster, MA, lay leader in the apologetic, equipping, and marriage ministries at Watermark Community Church in Dallas, Texas.

John D. Ferrer, PhD, Teaching Fellow at Equal Rights Institute, Concord, NC; and former Professor of Religious Studies at Texas Wesleyan University.

Richard G. Howe, PhD, Emeritus Professor of Philosophy and Apologetics, Southern Evangelical Seminary; Past President, International Society of Christian Apologetics.

B. Kyle Keltz, PhD, Assistant Professor of English and Philosophy at South Plains College. He currently lives in Lubbock, TX with his wife, Laci, and two sons, Thomas and Jack.

Steven Lewis, MA, PhD student in philosophy of religion at Southern Evangelical Seminary. He has a MA in apologetics from Southern Evangelical Seminary and a BS in Biblical studies from Welch College. He currently lives in Murfreesboro, TN with his wife, Rachel, and two sons, Corban and Dylan.

Jason B. McCracken, PhD, Adjunct Professor of Philosophy and Religion at Wilkes Community College.

Tricia Scribner, MAA, MSN, PhD candidate in Philosophy of Religion at Southern Evangelical Seminary. She is the author of *LifeGivers Apologetics: Women Designed and Equipped to Share Reasons for the Hope Within*, former Christian high school apologetics teacher and former RN.

1

Atheism New and Old
A Critique of Dan Barker's Brand of Atheism

—JOHN D. FERRER

Since I do not believe in a god, I am by default described as an atheist. . . .
Theists do not have a god: they have a belief. Atheism is the lack of theism, the
lack of *belief* in god(s).

—DAN BARKER[1]

WORDS EVOLVE OVER TIME, growing, losing, and changing definitions, all
depending on fickle social fashions. The word "atheism" is no exception. If
you haven't been tracking the history of this versatile little term, you may
not realize that, in the last ten to fifteen years, a new definition of the word
has grown in popularity, threatening to replace the classic sense of the word
"atheist." The change may not seem like much. It's subtle. It can go unno-
ticed by the untrained eye. But this recalibrated language is monumentally
different from its ancestor. And people like Dan Barker are benefactors.

Dan Barker ascribes to the *new* sense of the word "atheism." And this
new kind of atheism is most definitely deliberate. But, before addressing
that shift in terminology, it may help to have some situational context.
Barker's atheism is not simply a semantic issue, as if we can understand

1. Barker, *godless*, 130 (emphasis in original).

1

his nonbelief just by defining "atheism" properly. Barker is part of a wider culture of nonbelief.

Back in 1984, when Barker first went public about his deconversion from Christianity to atheism, it was an unpopular move.[2] Atheism didn't have the popular appeal back then as it does today. But times have changed, and his atheism sits comfortably within a large and growing culture of non-belief.[3] With some awareness of that culture, Barker's detour from the traditional sense of the word "atheism" appears downright fashionable. Is Barker just an intellectual hipster who can't stomach "old-fashioned" classics without a spritz of irony? He's in his seventies now, so "hipster" probably isn't the right term for him. Although, I'm sure he has rocked the tweed jacket and craft beer from time to time. Barker, however, is firmly entrenched in a new *socio-culture* of atheism known, ironically, as *New Atheism*.

THE "NEW ATHEISM"

In 2006, *Wired* magazine writer Gary Wolf introduced the world to the term "New Atheist," describing the likes of Richard Dawkins, Sam Harris, Daniel Dennett, and Christopher Hitchens.[4] These four characters, self-described as the "four horsemen" of atheism, were not *just* atheists, they were bull-horns of nonbelief. Well-published, eloquent, and adamant, their work has been a cross-continental campaign against theism, religion, and any bit of magic, mysticism, or superstition they can set their sights on. Even after the death of their British columnist, Christopher Hitchens (2011), the writing and influence of these four horsemen has marched on, undaunted. The four horsemen never typified all of modern atheism, however. Even among the New Atheists, they were never the only ones. They are, nonetheless, profoundly influential figureheads of a fierce new form of atheism.

The four horsemen have been like a rock-star boy band with a better education. Irreverent, self-assured intellectuals, their interviews are always laced with withering insults, witty comebacks, and an oppressing air of condescension. To be sure, the four horsemen did not represent the most intellectually sophisticated form of atheism (Dan Barker is no different). None of them have a PhD in theology, biblical studies, philosophy of religion, or any of the heavyweight fields that deal properly in questions of

2. Barker, *godless*, 40, 44.

3. Recent studies have shown growth in the numbers of religiously unaffiliated and self-declared atheists specifically. See Newport, "2017 Update on Americans and Religion"; and "2014 Religious Landscape Study."

4. Wolf, "Church of the Non-Believers."

God's existence (although Dennett comes close).[5] Rhetorically savage, they are always entertaining, provocative, and guaranteed clickbait, whether you love them or love to hate them. The four horsemen are popularizers. Their language is educated enough to suit the smart section of magazines and newspapers, but their argumentation favors sloganeering and flagrant exaggeration. It was never their rigor that made them famous; it was their rhetoric. For countless closeted atheists, this band of nonbelievers led the anthem in their coming-out party.

Compared to that band of four horsemen, Dan Barker has been like a solo artist promoting his songs of nonbelief since the mid-eighties. Barker never rose to the prominence of Dawkins, Harris, Hitchens, and Dennett. But, to be fair, he was a New Atheist before New Atheist was cool. Barker was never a member of the four horsemen, but their rise helped broaden the fan base for Barker's brand of music (i.e., evangelistic atheism).

It's still too early to tell how influential New Atheism really is and how it will ultimately relate to the rest of secularism and society. It is clear, however, that New Atheism is part of a larger phenomenon in the United States and much of the Western world. Many signs suggest a rising number of "nones" including atheists, agnostics, and nonreligious.[6] The popularity of New Atheism is undoubtedly helping to popularize nontheism and irreligion. In the shadow of that growth, it's not entirely clear whether the most aggressive edge in nontheism, the New Atheists, will dial back to something diplomatic and persuasive to the masses. In that event, New Atheists like Dan Barker would have to dull their blade a bit and learn to play nice with others. But it's also possible that the growing number of "nones" will continue to splinter into a variety of nontheist groupings with the New Atheists occupying only one tent in the camp. If that happens, Dan Barker and his *Freedom From Religion Foundation* (FFRF) will likely persist as militant as ever, competing for territory, and promoting nontheism, secularism, and irreligion with all the fervor of an evangelistic crusade.[7]

---

5. Sam Harris's PhD is in neuroscience, Dawkins's PhD is in zoology, and Christopher Hitchens never earned a PhD. Daniel Dennett, however, earned a PhD in philosophy, focusing on philosophy of mind and philosophy of science. Of course, a person doesn't have to be an expert on a subject to make a true claim about it. Their academic laurels don't prove anything about the truth or falsity of their claims (i.e., the genetic fallacy). Their academic standing does, however, testify to whether they are credible authorities, prima facia, when speaking as experts on questions of God's existence, the possibility of miracles, and so forth.

6. White, *Rise of the Nones.*

7. FFRF was founded in 1978 by Anne Nicole Gaylor. Barker became president of FFRF in 1987.

Dan Barker is more than just a New Atheist, but he is *at least* that much. He is not, for example, the quiet, respectful, public atheist who flies under the radar rather than drawing attention to himself. Nor is he the outlandish academic atheist squirreled away in his office in the biology department at some college in the 1970s.[8] New Atheism replaces peacemaking policies with verbal conquest; humble nonbelief becomes cocky secularism; timidity switches into boldness; and the pluralistic *se la vie* shifts to intolerant chants of "Stop that, or you're sued!"[9] The New Atheists are still the minority, culturally speaking, but their swagger and bravado is more like a majority culture. Atheists like Barker have ventured beyond the closed quarters of sterile classrooms. He's a public figure openly advocating for a world with less religious interference in public life. He writes books, gives interviews, frequents talk shows and podcasts and social media. He is regularly found on the debating circuit, arguing for atheism, promoting his books, and raising awareness about issues in church-state relations. And when you hear what he has to say, it's clear that he is not the peacemaker. He's an agitator, and not the unhinged combatant type either—like some Occupier or Antifa protestor.[10] Those are a flash in the pan compared to the sustained long-term culture shift at work in Barker, the FFRF, and New Atheism.

THE NEW "ATHEISM"

Besides that personality profile, Barker also aligns with the New Atheists in another important sense. The New Atheists define "atheism" a little different from its standard definition over the last 2,500 years or so. The New Atheists typically define "atheism" as "nonbelief," that is, "no belief in God," "lacking God-belief," or "no theism."[11] Barker follows this trend, saying, "It turns out

8. As Paul Vitz notes in *Faith of the Fatherless*, "Intense, self-avowed atheists tend to be found in a relatively narrow range of social and economic strata: in the university and intellectual world and in certain professions." Of these he notes a minority representation in government too. Nevertheless, "In general historians agree that explicit, systematic, and public atheism is a recent and distinctively Western phenomenon and that probably no other culture has manifested such a widespread public rejection of the divine." This shift suggests that "atheism has finally moved from relatively restricted intellectual and professional circles to a modest but significant mass-market level in today's society" (Vitz, *Faith of the Fatherless*, 3, xiii, xv).

9. The FFRF is well known for raising lawsuits over church-state issues.

10. "Occupier" refers to the 2011 Occupy Wall Street protests, and "Antifa" refers to self-declared anti-fascists beginning around 2017.

11. Smith, *Why Atheism?*, 18–19; Loftus, *Outsider Test of Faith*, 126–27; Carrier, *Sense and Goodness Without God*, 4; Ra, "You're Either Theist or A-theist; There Is No Agnostic Third Option!"; Dillahunty, "Atheist Debates: You're Not an Atheist, You're

that *atheism* means much less than I had thought. It is merely the lack of theism. It is not a philosophy of life and it offers no values. . . . Basic atheism is not a belief."[12]

In philosophical circles, this usage is known as "negative atheism" or, less commonly, "soft, implicit, or weak atheism."[13] This sense is in contrast to the classic (positive) sense of the term, which claims, "There is no god."[14] The New Atheist trend, however, has been to employ negative atheism as the default and normal sense of the word "atheism." In other words, atheism is interpreted as a statement about psychology (i.e., lacking an attitude of belief towards God) instead of a statement on metaphysics (i.e., no God exists).

This new usage departs from its historic sense. In the past, the term "atheism" has denoted a claim about reality beyond one's mind, namely, the claim that "no God exists."[15] Prominent atheist and philosopher William Rowe agrees with this classic sense: "Atheism is the position that affirms the nonexistence of God," and he adds a rebuttal to the New Atheists, saying that "[atheism] proposes positive disbelief rather than mere suspension of belief."[16] Another acclaimed atheist philosopher, Kai Nielsen, writing for the

Agnostic." Matt Dillahunty has been known to use the soft/negative/weak sense of atheism as the default sense but has shown awareness of the definitional dispute and is reasonably flexible on terminology.

12. Barker, *godless*, 97.

13. Martin, *Atheism*, 26.

14. Antony Flew helped establish this nomenclature of "positive" and "negative" atheism within philosophy of religion at least since 1984, although the concepts behind this distinction trace back further. He writes: "The word 'atheism,' however, has in this contention to be construed unusually. Whereas nowadays the usual meaning of 'atheist' in English is 'someone who asserts there is no such being as God,' I want the word to be understood not positively but negatively. I want the originally Greek prefix 'a' to be read in the same way in "atheist" as it customarily is read in such other Greco-English words as 'amoral,' 'atypical,' and 'asymmetrical.' In this interpretation an atheist becomes: someone who is simply not a theist. Let us, for future ready reference, introduce the labels 'positive atheist' for the former and 'negative atheist' for the latter" (Flew and Edwards, *God, Freedom, and Immortality*, 14).

15. Bunnin, *Blackwell Dictionary of Western Philosophy*, s.v. "atheism"; Audi, *Cambridge Encyclopedia of Philosophy*, s.v. "atheism"; *Cambridge Academic Content Dictionary*, s.v. "atheism"; Haldeman-Julius, *Meaning of Atheism*; Borchert, *Encyclopedia of Philosophy*, s.v. "atheism"; Stein, *Encyclopedia of Unbelief*, s.v. "atheism"; Ferm, "Atheism"; Honderich, *Oxford Companion to Philosophy*, s.v. "atheism"; Nielsen, "Definition of Atheism"; Nielsen, "Comprehensive Definition of Atheism"; *Random House Unabridged Dictionary*, s.v. "atheism"; Craig, *Routledge Encyclopedia of Philosophy*, s.v. "atheism"; Schellenberg, "Hiddenness Argument for Atheism"; Draper, "Atheism and Agnosticism"; and Smart, "Atheism and Agnosticism."

16. *Random House Unabridged Dictionary*, s.v. "atheism."

Encyclopædia Britannica, reiterates the point: "Atheism, in general, [is] the critique and denial of metaphysical beliefs in God or spiritual beings."[17] Still another nontheistic philosopher Paul Draper elaborates on *why* atheism is to be understood in the classic, positive sense of the word.

> "Atheism" is typically defined in terms of "theism." Theism, in turn, is best understood as a proposition—something that is either true or false. It is often defined as "the belief that God exists," but here "belief" means "something believed." It refers to the propositional content of belief, not to the attitude or psychological state of believing. This is why it makes sense to say that theism is true or false and to argue for or against theism. If, however, "atheism" is defined in terms of theism and theism is the proposition that God exists and *not* the psychological condition of believing that there is a God, then it follows that atheism is not the absence of the psychological condition of believing that God exists. . .[18]

With that clarification in place, Draper then undercuts any efforts to install negative atheism as the default sense of the word. "The 'a-' in 'atheism' must be understood as negation instead of absence, as 'not' instead of 'without.' Therefore, in philosophy at least, atheism should be construed as the proposition that God does not exist (or, more broadly, the proposition that there are no gods)."[19]

We find the same conventional usage affirmed in standard English dictionaries.[20] Theological dictionaries concur, as well.[21] Barker, on the other hand, customarily follows the negative, nonstandard sense of the term "atheism," meaning he prefers to treat "atheism" as "not theism" and "nontheism."[22] For him, this term-shift is not an accident. Several factors

---

17. Nielsen, "Comprehensive Definition of Atheism."

18. Draper, "Atheism and Agnosticism."

19. Draper, "Atheism and Agnosticism."

20. Simpson and Weinter, *Oxford English Dictionary*, s.v. "atheism"; *Cambridge Dictionary*, s.v. "atheism"; Little et al., *Oxford Universal Dictionary*, s.v. "atheism"; Webster, *Webster's New World Dictionary*, s.v. "atheism"; *American Heritage Dictionary of the English Language*, s.v. "atheism"; Webster, *Webster's Revised Unabridged Dictionary*, s.v. "atheism"; Ansley, *Columbia Encyclopedia*, s.v. "atheism"; *Collins English Dictionary*, s.v. "atheism"; Sinclair, *COBUILD Advanced English Dictionary*, s.v. "atheism"; Crystal, *Barnes and Noble Encyclopedia*, s.v. "atheism"; and *Encyclopædia Britannica*, s.v. "atheism."

21. Gentz, *Dictionary of the Bible and Religion*, s.v. "atheism"; and Buswell, "Atheism."

22. Barker, *godless*, 97, 99, 104; Dillahunty, "Does God Exist?," 25:48; God Who Speaks, "Is There a God Who Speaks?," 32:00, 34:15.

help explain why Barker and other New Atheists often favor the nonstandard definition of atheism.

WHY THE SHIFT IN TERMINOLOGY?

First, it shifts the burden of proof

Underneath the word studies and semantic arguments, there is a simple real-world benefit at work here: it shifts the burden of proof onto the theist. In his testimonial text, *godless*, Barker helps explain this shift by first emphasizing the negative sense of atheism.

> I am both an atheist and an agnostic. . . . Agnosticism addresses knowledge; atheism addresses belief. . . . The atheist says, "I don't have a belief that God exists." . . . Basic atheism is not a belief. . . . [it is an] "absence of theism." . . . *absence of belief* in a god or gods. . . . Atheism and nontheism are the same. . . . "Atheism" is a negatively constructed word—"not theism."[23]

Stipulating atheism this way, multiple times, he has set the stage for his next chapter, "Refuting God."[24] His argument strategy hinges critically on this negative definition, as he explains in terms of a debate.

> Let's not make the mistake of thinking it is a balanced controversy between two equally likely positions: "yes" for the theist, "no" for the atheist. The burden of proof is always on the shoulders of the affirmative, not the negative—innocent until proven guilty. . . . The proponent must make a case beyond a reasonable doubt. Everyone else is justified in withholding belief until evidence is produced and substantiated. . . . Atheism is the default position that remains when theistic claims are dismissed.[25]

In trying to explain his brand of atheism, Barker makes several mistakes. He is wrong to suggest that there is never a burden of proof for the negative. Sometimes there is a burden of proof, and sometimes there isn't, but when he appeals to a legal context for his frame of reference, saying, "innocent until proven guilty," he brings to mind a clear context where both sides have a burden of proof. In court cases, the disproportionate burden of proof rests on the plaintiff, but as the plaintiff's case mounts, the defense

---

23. Barker, *godless*, 96–9.

24. Barker, *godless*, 104–20.

25. Barker, *godless*, 104–5.

takes on its own (lesser) burden of proof in showing that the plaintiff's case is flawed, and the client is indeed innocent.

Moreover, negative *claims* carry a burden of proof. For example, "My client is innocent!" is a negative claim, and court cases include both a defense attorney and a prosecutor to make sure that despite the legal bias in favor of the defendant, the trial should not condemn innocent people and should have some realistic chance of convicting guilty parties. Even negative nonclaims can likewise carry a burden of proof, contextually, when there is some implied or required response, such as when a judge asks a defendant, "Do you have anything to say for yourself?" That defendant may say nothing, but his burden of proof remains over a host of implied claims, even if the defendant never claimed his innocence or guilt. Barker plainly overstates his case when he claims that the negative position never has a burden of proof.

Another mistake on Barker's part is failing to mention how his usage of the word "atheism" is nonstandard. He fails to use his turn signal, so to speak, when he veers from the normal and historic use of the term. He interacts with this definitional controversy only a little bit, but, without much digging, he settles on his own preferred sense of the term and proceeds to treat that sense as the default meaning.[26] His pragmatic reasons couldn't be clearer either. He is essentially "winning" the debate before it starts, by forcing the theist into an almost impossible scenario: prove "beyond a reasonable doubt" that all the objections and problems pitted against theism fail. No wonder he is so confident in his nonbelief; he doesn't have to do any work for it.

For the reasons stated above, the default sense of "atheism" is not a negative nonclaim but is a positive claim saying that, in reality, "there is no God." He can stipulate the term however he wants, and the English language permits nonstandard uses. But it's dishonest to do so without alerting one's audience. And in this case, it reflects a self-serving and entrenched confusion. Barker seems to honestly think that the term "atheism" has the root meaning (historically/etymologically) of "without theism." In this regard, he is simply wrong (see below).

But Barker also errs by misrepresenting the nature of formal debate.[27] In formal debate, whenever there is a straightforward prompt like "Does God Exist?" there are at least two declared positions: pro (affirmative) and con (negative). These two positions answer the debate prompt as "Yes, God

26. Barker, *godless*, 95–103.

27. For example, see the "Policy Debate," "Public Forum Debate," and "Lincoln-Douglas" debate styles as described in National Speech and Debate Association, *High School Unified Manual*, 23–31.

exists," and "No, God does not exist." When Barker accepts a debate invitation, agreeing to defend the con position, he is agreeing to defend the claim: "No, God does not exist."

In this way, both sides in formal debate have a burden of proof: one defending the "yes," the other defending the "no." Neither side is neutral, and neither side wins if the debate is a tie (i.e., equally effective/ineffective cases on both sides). Bear in mind, it does not matter whether Barker would *prefer* to defend nontheism, or whether he defines his own views consistently with negative atheism. It doesn't even matter whether he *holds* the position he's defending in the debate. If he has agreed to represent the con position in a formal debate about, "Does God Exist?" then he has accepted his share of the burden of proof and should defend the claim that God does not exist. If he is not content with debating the con position for this prompt, he should arrange for a different debate prompt, such as, "Does Dan Barker believe in God?"

For the sake of academic integrity and civil propriety, people should at least attempt to follow through on their agreements. If Barker does not want to debate the con position ("God does not exist"), then he shouldn't accept that debate invitation. Or he should negotiate for a different prompt or format which accommodates his nontheism.

Second, it's poorly deconstructed

Interpreting "atheism" as "without-theism" misrepresents its etymology, that is, how the word entered the English language; it's bad etymology. Etymology refers to the history of a word and takes into consideration word roots, languages of origin, and acquired usages over time. A good use of etymology can help us understand a word's origin, how it has been constructed from root words, and how its usage has changed over time until arriving at its present usage. Etymology is not the sole source in defining a word.[28] A word can take on entirely new significance, which could never have been predicated from its etymology. Nevertheless, etymology matters.

As mentioned, treating "atheism" as "without-theism" is just bad etymology. When Dan Barker says "'atheism' is merely the lack of theism" or "atheism and non-theism are the same," he reflects a common misunderstanding called the compositional fallacy.[29] Looking at the English term

28. Treating etymology as the defining feature in semantics is called the "etymological fallacy." James Barr explains that "the etymology of a word is not a statement about its meaning but about its history" (Barr, *Semantics of Biblical Language*, 109).

29. Patrick Hurley explains, "The fallacy of composition is committed when the

"atheism," one may think it's "a-theism," conjoining "a" (the alpha priva-
tive) and "theism" (God-belief), rendering "no God-belief" or "without
God-belief." But that's not how the term "atheism" arrived in the English
language. In the mid-to-late 1500s, the term was incorporated into English
translations somewhere around the early rise of the printing press.[30] The
term was called into service for the purpose of translating the Greek *atheos*
into an English equivalent. The word roots in Greek *a-theos* say nothing
about belief or knowledge but signify "no god" or "without God." The word
simply did not enter the English language by conjoining "a" and "theism."

To be fair, word roots do not necessarily dictate the meaning of a
word.[31] But in this case, the word stayed true to its roots. *Atheos* had roughly
three senses in Greek: (1) wicked, (2) without God/rejected by God, and (3)
one who rejects the gods worshiped by society.[32] In this way, early Christians
were often slandered with the term because they were deemed immoral and
unfavored by the Roman gods, perhaps because they openly rejected the
Roman gods.[33]

When the Greek *atheos* was imported into Latin, the spelling stayed
the same, and it was trimmed down to just that third sense: "atheist," that is,
"one who rejects the gods worshipped by society."[34] In English, interestingly,
all three senses from the Greek usage ("wicked," "without God," "rejects
God") are still operative today, equating roughly to (1) ungodly, (2) godless,
and (3) atheist.

The Greek sense of *atheos* remains in the foreground in some biblical-
theological circles so that the English "atheist" can signify the less-common
sense of "without God." For example, J. Oliver Buswell, in the *Baker's Dictionary of Theology*, says that "the term atheism is frequently employed to
designate a condition of being without the true God."[35] Yet even here, Bus-

---

conclusion of an argument depends on the erroneous transference of an attribute from
the parts of something onto the whole" (Hurley, *Logic*, 159).

30. Dictionaries vary in attesting to the first-usage date, ranging from 1517 to
1570. This brief history section is drawn largely from *Online Etymology Dictionary*, s.v.
"atheist."

31. See the "root fallacy" in Carson, *Exegetical Fallacies*, 28.

32. This summary is derived from *Thayer's Greek Lexicon*; *The King James Version
New Testament Greek Lexicon*; Zodhiates et al., *Lexical Aids to the New Testament*; and
Strong, *Strong's Concordance*, #112. See also Ephesians 2:12.

33. Martyr, 1 *Apol.* 4. Clement of Alexandria uses the positive/strong sense of the
word "atheism," perhaps as a retort akin to, "You call us atheists, but you are the atheists
for rejecting the only true God!" See *Strom.* 6.14–15; 7.1.

34. The base spelling of the word is the same between Latin and Greek, but differs
in parsing (Simpson, *Cassell's Latin Dictionary*, s.v. "ăthĕos").

35. Buswell, "Atheism," 70.

well never suggests the term ever meant "without theism" or "non-theism." Buswell clarifies this unusual sense of the word by alluding to an ancient setting: "the early Christians themselves were called atheists by the pagans," and then he returns to the convention, saying, "in its strictest definition, the term [atheism] designates the denial of the existence of any god of any kind."[36]

Third, it's confused with agnosticism

Barker's brand of atheism spells confusion in his understanding of agnosticism. He claims to be both atheist and agnostic, but it's not clear he has a critical understanding of either term. Over the last ten years or so, this confusion has proven rampant; Barker is not the only one to blur these two categories.[37] In Barker's words,

> People are invariably surprised to hear me say I am both an atheist and an agnostic, as if this somehow weakens my certainty. . . . Agnosticism addresses knowledge; atheism addresses belief. The agnostic says, "I don't have a knowledge that God exists. "The atheist says, "I don't have a belief that God exists." Some agnostics are atheistic and some are theistic. Agnosticism is the refusal to take as a fact any statement for which there is insufficient evidence.[38]

Barker then goes on to mention that Thomas Huxley first coined the term "agnostic" (*a-gnosis*) to describe his belief that God's existence cannot be known.[39] Agnosticism would eventually subdivide into a strong form (God's existence *cannot* be known) and a weak form (God's existence is not yet known but may be known eventually). Barker is right to acknowledge that agnosticism concerns "knowledge," but he is confused about both atheism and agnosticism, perhaps because he had not acknowledged that belief is a facet of *all* knowledge.

---

36. Buswell, "Atheism," 70.

37. Some have coined terms like "gnostic atheist," "agnostic atheist," "gnostic theist," "agnostic theist," "de-facto atheist," "de-facto theist," "pure agnostic," "implicit atheist,"and "explicit atheist." Often people have swirled in a jumble of factors to distinguish categories such as "proof," "certainty," "belief," "non-belief," "gnosticism," rendering new stipulated meanings for the words. See Ferrer, "Belief in No God, or No Belief in God."

38. Barker, *godless*, 96.

39. Barker, *godless*, 97.

The leading philosophical definition of "knowledge" is some sense of "true belief" (e.g., warranted true belief, justified true belief, etc.).[40] And rest assured, when Thomas Huxley refers to "knowledge" about supernature, he's referring to a formal, academically viable, sense of the term.[41] The "belief" noted within "true belief" refers to an attitude of assent, that is, a disposition of agreement, affirmation, or support. In this way, all knowledge entails belief. Agnosticism is about having no belief and no knowledge about God existing. Huxley himself freely mingled the notions of "knowledge" and "belief" in his definition of agnosticism.

1.   Agnosticism is of the essence of science, whether ancient or modern. It simply means that a man shall not say he knows or believes that which he has no scientific grounds for professing to know or believe.

2.   Consequently Agnosticism puts aside not only the greater part of popular theology, but also the greater part of anti-theology. On the whole, the "bosh" of heterodoxy is more offensive to me than that of orthodoxy, because heterodoxy professes to be guided by reason and science, and orthodoxy does not.[42]

Through a litany of debates, Barker has engaged voraciously in anti-theology, arguing against God's existence. In the eyes of Huxley, the definitive agnostic, Barker is "bosh" and disqualified from "agnosticism."

When we look past Barker's usage and go to the primary source, we find that agnosticism, properly understood, is easily distinguished from the classic sense of atheism, since agnosticism refers to psychological matters (belief, knowing), whereas atheism refers to metaphysical matters (God's nonexistence). To repeat Paul Draper: "atheism is not the absence of the psychological condition of *believing* that God exists . . . . atheism should be construed as the proposition that God does not exist (or, more broadly, the proposition that there are no gods)."[43]

Barker has been on the debate circuit for many years now. He's fairly intelligent, rhetorically savvy, and well-experienced in argumentation and

40. In epistemology, there is a great deal of debate over what exactly is meant by "knowledge." Yet most sides seem to agree that knowledge happens when there is a true claim met with some sort of warranted, justified, or formally impressed disposition of assent. Justified true belief (JTB theory) is widely affirmed, having roots in ancient Platonism. But this view has been famously challenged in Gettier, "Is Justified True Belief Knowledge?" Alvin Plantinga has offered an alternative model that has achieved some acclaim; see "warranted true belief" in Plantinga, *Warrant and Proper Function*.

41. Huxley, "Agnosticism: A Symposium," 5–6; and Huxley, "Agnosticism," 169–94.

42. Huxley, "Agnosticism," 5–6 (emphasis added).

43. Draper, "Atheism and Agnosticism."

debate. One thing he is not, however, is formally trained in philosophy. Barker is exposed when it comes to rigorous philosophical argumentation, even to the point of confusing atheism with agnosticism.[44]

In philosophical circles, a lot of work goes into the critical distinctions between metaphysics, epistemology, and linguistics. Yet in the internet era, it seems, populist models of learning predominate. Shallow, noncritical, and popular-level opinion abounds without a proportionate increase in rigorous formal education or systematic training. For atheists around world, the internet opens the door to more comradery and more information than ever before through chat rooms, social media, websites, comment threads, blogs, videos, and so forth. But there has not been a proportionate increase in access, time, or funding towards formal critical understanding. The mountain of data is growing faster than discernment can follow.

Barker is a veteran atheist, however, and his days of public debates and public advocacy predate the internet boom. He cannot blame any shallowness and amateur errors on the internet, since he had around ten years of public atheism before the internet came to fashion for the general public.[45] Yet, Barker has nonetheless proven confused (or misled) on the difference between (1) the classic and nonstandard uses of "atheism," between (2) knowledge and belief, and between (3) agnosticism and atheism. Without the formal philosophical training to support his busy debating schedule, it is no surprise to find him blurring categories in self-accommodating ways.[46]

Fourth, there's a philosophical case for negative atheism

Barker may be wrong to say, without qualification, that "a-theism simply means 'without-theism.'"[47] The *kind* of atheism he is explaining, however, does have a place in philosophy of religion. It's called negative atheism. Other titles for this view are "soft," "weak," and "implicit" atheism.[48] The

---

44. While Barker can often keep up with Christian apologists and theologians in a debate setting, he has shown a marked weakness when it comes to engaging and rebutting graduate-level philosophical explanations and arguments as seen in his debate with Richard Howe. See Barker and Howe, "Is There a God Who Speaks?"

45. On the shallowing effects of the internet and screen addiction, see Carr, *Shallows*.

46. Barker even admits that he only had one class on apologetics in seminary and then "promptly forgot" about what he learned (Barker, *godless*, 251).

47. God Who Speaks, "Is There a God Who Speaks?," 34:15.

48. Martin, *Atheism*, 26.

most authoritative statement of negative atheism comes from Antony Flew's 1950 paper, "Theology and Falsification."[49]

In that landmark article, Flew argues that, compared to theism, atheism is a more responsible starting-point for questioning God's existence. His method of argument revolves around an "invisible gardener." If we were to find a well-manicured garden in the middle of the woods, how is one to identify whether a gardener has been tending it? The believer trusts that a gardener is responsible, while the skeptic reserves judgment. When the gardener remains absent, the believer concludes that it must be an *invisible* gardener. Several attempts are made, indirectly, to identify this invisible gardener. The believer settles on a list of qualifications to reconcile his invisible-gardener belief with the fact that no empirical evidence can be found. The list ends up looking like a set of attributes typically ascribed to God. Flew's point is that the invisible gardener, by all accounts, is unfalsifiable, and so, indistinguishable from a nonexistent gardener.[50] From this perspective, atheism (no belief in a gardener) is the responsible default position. Flew later clarified his position in a 1972 paper, "The Presumption of Atheism."[51] In these two papers, plus about sixty-five years of hard labor in philosophy of religion and the added popularity of atheist-friendly philosophies like logical positivism, Flew helped shift almost the entire burden of proof onto theists in a way that all negative atheists can benefit from his work.[52]

---

49. Flew, "Theology and Falsification."

50. Additionally, Flew has been interpreted as arguing, in "Theology and Falsification," that theological language is void of content entirely for lack of falsification criteria. According to this interpretation, Flew's position is stronger than mere negative atheism, but extends into logical positivism and acognosticism (i.e., God's purported existence cannot be meaningfully or coherently asserted). See Peterson et al., *Philosophy of Religion*, 374.

51. Flew, "Presumption of Atheism."

52. Flew was a Logical Positivist, at least for a span, as typified by the early A. J. Ayer in *Language Truth and Logic*. Ayer argued that claims must be empirically verifiable or analytically (by-definition) true if they are to be linguistically meaningful. Theology, for Ayer, is not true, but nor is it even false. It is without meaning, and since its reference to God lacks analytic veracity and empirical testability, the notion cannot even be entertained as a proposition. It is like trying to argue, "I believe in 'ouch,'" or "I don't believe in 'um.'" These terms, "ouch" and "um," are emotive/gibberish terms that defy cognitive belief or disbelief. Truth and falsity do not apply to them, and, according to Ayer, nor do truth and falsity apply to any God-talk. The positivism of Ayer, Flew, and others was all the rage for a while, but today, few people are conscious advocates of logical positivism, even though its scope and influence is incredibly widespread. Ayer eventually repudiated logical positivism as its central tenet, the verification principle, is self-refuting (i.e., the verification principle is not itself empirically verifiable or true-by-definition). See Vargese, "Sir Alfred Ayer," 49.

But it's critically important to recognize that Antony Flew "always described himself as a 'negative atheist.'"[53] Flew was keenly aware that his negative atheism was not the normal use of the term "atheism." In Flew's *Dictionary of Philosophy*, he defines "atheism" in the positive, metaphysical, sense of the word:

> Atheism: the rejection of belief in God, whether on the grounds that it is meaningful but false to say that God exists, or as the logical positivists held, that it is meaningless and hence neither true nor false.[54]

Writing this dictionary entry fully seven years after his "Presumption of Atheism" paper, Flew was admitting that the classic, primary, and normal meaning of "atheism" is not the negative sense that he had come to favor. Rather, the default sense of the term "atheism" is positive atheism, "rejecting belief in God," or as Draper says, "the proposition that God does not exist."[55] Atheism is normally understood as a rejection of and not (merely) abstention from God-belief. Flew's work within the field of negative atheism is still an important contribution to philosophy of religion. And he helped establish a rational basis for negative atheists. He did not, however, redefine the default sense of "atheism," nor did he ever claim to do so.

If Barker were to do as Flew did and explain that he favors a non-standard sense of "atheism," namely, negative atheism, then he would be cleared of these charges and would do a great service for his audience. The English language is highly adaptable, and most of the argumentation above can be sidestepped if Barker were to clarify that he is stipulating a non-standard use of the term. He could attribute his use of the term to recent trends among atheists to deliberately redefine the word. Or Barker could explain his negative atheism, and then in debate settings clarify that even though he's defending the positive sense of "atheism," he is himself a negative atheist. People can stipulate word meanings however they like. We all can invent new words. We can use gibberish words if we want. And none of that need be dishonest. Every word in the English language was invented at some point. So, there is nothing intrinsically wrong with stipulating word meanings, inventing new words, or using words in nonstandard ways.

53. See "Professor Antony Flew."

54. Flew, *Dictionary of Philosophy*. Flew alludes to his negative atheism, via the presumption of atheism, when he says, in the same dictionary entry, "some atheists have maintained that the onus of proof is on the theist since atheism is prima facie the more reasonable position." He does not go so far, as Barker does, to say that the atheist has *no* burden of proof.

55. Draper, "Atheism and Agnosticism."

SO, WHAT'S THE BIG DEAL?

So, you may ask, "What is the big deal then?" In all honesty, this verbal dispute doesn't have to be a big deal. But it does expose some problems that could become a big deal if left unaddressed.

It's an obstacle to rational inquiry

At one level, redefining "atheism" obstructs careful rational inquiry into the topic of whether God exists. People can stipulate whatever meaning they want to a word, but they cannot change history on a whim. The conventional meaning of "atheism" is not simply a matter of recent popular invention. It also carries a historical and established significance so that veering from that usage stirs up confusion and ambiguity.

The cloud of confusion extends to all the audio, video, and written works that use "atheism" in its normal historic sense. If people are led to believe that "atheism" normally means what Barker says it means, then they are liable to misunderstand a wide range of debates, papers, books, interviews, reviews, and discussions that use the term conventionally. Confused onlookers will mistakenly think the entire burden of proof rests on the theist. Countless books and articles that argue in favor of atheism will seem like wasted energy defending a positive sense of "atheism" when, supposedly, they need only attack theism.

To illustrate the problem, imagine how a judge would score a presidential debate if he believed that one candidate is the default winner unless the opponent has a perfect or nearly perfect performance? Under that presumption, the judge will almost certainly rule the favored candidate as the winner—even if that candidate performs far worse than his opponent.

It's manipulative

Knowingly misrepresenting words risks manipulation. The fact at issue here is the acquired, historic, and conventional sense of the word "atheism," a sense which Barker obscures and defies when he defines "atheism" as if it did not come from the Greek, as if it was fabricated entirely from English roots. Now, again, I need to reiterate that I don't think this word shift is a big deal, or at least, it doesn't have to be. But it is still manipulative to use words in a misleading way to gain an advantage in argumentation.

This point becomes clearer when we remember that words convey meaning as part of sentences, within their respective context, as granted to them by conventional usage, inside of a language group. Words do not shift radically in their meaning just because one person, a group of people, or one dictionary stipulates a particular usage for that word. Even when a new usage of the word arises and gains popularity, that does not constitute a new convention sufficient to establish this term as the new standard (formal) definition. It would take a commanding shift in that word's popular usage, perhaps with an additional shift in its formal usage among relevant authorities (academics, scholars, professionals, governing officials, etc.), to signal a change that's wide enough, and formally established long enough, to change its lexical definition (the way it's explained in dictionaries, encyclopedias and lexicons). Now, I don't expect to hammer out all the complex problems in the philosophy of language here, but it's at least widely agreed upon that word meanings have at least some "stickiness" so that they don't just slip any which way the cultural wind blows.[56]

With atheism, the conventional sense of "atheism" remains positive atheism although, admittedly, there is a substantial and growing preference for the negative sense of the word. Even among those who favor the negative sense of the word, however, it's still dishonest to lie about the word's origins (i.e., "a + theism"); it's close-minded to suppress or ignore the mountains of evidence favoring its classical usage; and it's manipulative to then insert a nonstandard sense of the term as if it has always been the default sense of the word. That's not just a different sense of the word, that's manipulation. In this way, overzealous spokespeople risk a propagandist fallacy whenever they race ahead of convention to declare new meanings to words.

It undermines academic integrity

Another problem with this terminology is that this linguistic shift is grounds for questioning Barker's academic integrity. When Barker agrees to assume the con position in a debate, he should not defer to the non-position, settling into a covert, third option that is neither affirming nor denying the debate prompt. It is dishonest to adopt a different position from the outset than what was agreed upon within the debate. For many audiences who don't realize that Barker committed this sleight-of-hand, he may seem like the winner when instead, he has tricked them (see, "It's Manipulative" above).

56. For an introduction to philosophy of language, see Soames, *Philosophy of Language*.

It's imprecise and redundant

Barker's definition of "atheism" is indistinguishable from nontheism. He bluntly says that "atheism and non-theism are the same."[57] But, defining "atheism" identically with another word makes it redundant. And redundancy makes the term less precise than it could be. Instead of using the term in its default sense, where the argument can flow quickly across it without having to stop for explanation, the term now requires stopping and specifying that "atheist" is referring not to the default (positive) sense of the word, but a novel (negative) sense of "nontheist."

Bear in mind that the question of God's existence engages some of the most long-standing and carefully crafted arguments throughout the history of Western thought. With the kinds of precise arguments circling that epic question, imprecise and redundant terminology can be a heavy burden. It risks blunting the force of a good analytic argument. Trampling critically different words until they mean the same thing as each other is like trading your one and only Philips-head screwdriver to acquire another flathead. It's a bad trade since tactical variety would offer more explanatory options to suit one's needs. If nontheism already describes that state of "lacking theism," then the normal historic sense of the term "atheism" offers more utility and clarity than the redefinition can offer.

It can be true even if God exists

Perhaps the weirdest result with Barker's brand of atheism is that it doesn't say anything about whether God exists. Even if God exists, Barker's atheism could be true. That's a strange brand of atheism, aligning just fine with God's existence.

When Barker affirms atheism, he is not using "atheism" in the normal metaphysical sense, so he isn't making any claim beyond his own psychology. His atheism can be true so long as he is not a theist. This means that even if God exists, even if God came down to Los Angeles, California, dictated the Bible on live TV, ended the California drought with forty days of raining Cabernet (wine), and personally moonwalked across the set of *God's Not Dead III*—Barker's atheism would still be true so long as his atheism refers only to his lack of theism.

---

57. Barker, *godless*, 99.

It fosters intellectual laziness

The only way to reach the intellectual high ground is to earn it. When a popular definition comes along that serves our purposes and lightens our intellectual workload, then we can be biased in favor of that idea. We can all be self-serving like that (it's called "psychological egoism," in secular terms, or "total depravity" in spiritual terms). My point is that the "default atheism" view is self-serving for atheists. It can deceive atheists into thinking that they don't have to earn their academic high ground but can presume it while theists do all the work. Now, this point is a practical one and not an ideo-logical one. If we all agree that it's better to be intellectually rigorous than lazy, and we can agree that academic merit is hard work, then we can also agree that we should be careful about taking shortcuts. Barker's redefinition, unfortunately, has all the markings of a shortcut.

By defining "atheism" in a nonstandard way that ambiguates it with other, preestablished terms (i.e., nontheism, agnosticism, and theological skepticism), he may have already cut corners. This move clearly serves his own interests, creating a cloudier target for formal debate, as well as an easier debating stance for him since, he thinks, it absolves him of any burden of proof in the debate. And, from a critical standpoint, his debates have typically involved a chronic and deliberate evasion strategy where he shuns both the pro and con positions and ends up lost on the Island of Non. Barker is not dumb. He's well-read. He's intelligent. But he's not doing his acumen any favors by repeating the same spiel across his debate history and consistently defaulting on his case-for-atheism in almost all of them. In short, it's hard to imagine any given atheist will give his strongest and sharpest efforts when he also believes that he has no burden of proof, that he isn't making any claims about whether or not God exists, or that theists are saddled with all the evidential grunt-work.

Apologists can grant it, for the sake of argument, with nothing lost

Let us assume, however, that Barker's definition of atheism is well-intended, and this is only an accidental error on his part. I can give his intentions a charitable reading and assume he honestly believes that the better historical and evidential case supports his definition of the word "atheism." Even if the facts weighed against Barker, as I believe they do, people are still within their rights to use "atheism" in a secondary or nontraditional sense. Barker's negative atheism still entails a minority sense of the word "atheism," and people can use it that way without any impropriety.

I can even grant that there is a seismic shift of popular-level internet atheism, bringing with it a cornucopia of self-styled atheists stipulating and attempting to redefine "atheism" until the conventional sense of the term is lost within a generation. That's a possibility. And from all appearances, a rational case can be made that the default sense of this word is about to shift to "nontheism." Even if all that happened, however, a huge problem remains for Barker.

If Barker and the rest of the New Atheists (and any other modern atheists for that matter) were to collectively align on this refashioned sense of "atheism," the Christian apologist still has a ridiculously simple solution to bring the discussion back on track.

Apologists can ask the nontheist, "Is your nontheism reasonable?" If the atheist says, "No," then there's nothing to worry about. He's not claiming to be reasonable in his atheism, and so he has no *reasons* offered in his defense. If the atheist will not *claim* any intellectual credibility for his atheism, then apologists don't owe his atheism any intellectual respect. But if the atheist says, "Yes, it's reasonable," then he has made an affirmative claim and, to quote Barker, "the burden of proof is always on the shoulders of the affirmative."[58]

From that point on, the atheist would need to show that his definition of "atheism" is reasonable, and that means offering rationally compelling reasons for defining his "atheism" in that nonstandard way as well as for his choice to abstain from God-belief. From here, he can be pressed to explain why he finds positive atheism so unpersuasive that he favors negative atheism instead. His reasonable case for negative atheism, one would assume, includes consideration of the merits and demerits of positive atheism. If he finds positive atheism compelling, then he could be asked why he won't assert and defend positive atheism? If he finds positive atheism uncompelling, then that's rhetorical ammunition for theism—i.e., positive atheism hasn't paid its bills, positive atheism isn't convincing to the new breed of atheists, positive atheism and negative atheism can't get along, etc. When atheists are busy with friendly fire, so to speak, theists have fewer casualties.

WHAT CAN WE MAKE OF BARKER'S ATHEISM?

In the final evaluation, Barker's atheistic nontheism is supposed to offer a strategic advantage for him, so that he never has a burden of proof in defending his nonbelief. The tactic is easily sidestepped by asking him whether his nontheism is rational. He either admits that it's not rational—sacrificing

---

58. Barker, *godless*, 104.

his evidentially unburdened high ground—or he makes a claim that it's rational, acquiring his own burden of proof.

For Barker, this redefinition of "atheism," apparently, has been successful enough to where he still supports it after these many years of writing and speaking. Undoubtedly, he is a strong-willed person, so that may explain his predictable approach to debates. But he may have also seen the practical benefit, at least at a popular level, of redefining "atheism" to avoid any burden of proof. With this move, he can presume the rational high ground without having to earn it.

Reformed epistemologists may see a familiar strategy here.[59] Just as Christian philosopher Alvin Plantinga and his camp have argued for a *sensus divinitatis*, where God's existence is a "properly basic belief," Dan Barker has asserted a properly basic non-belief.[60] Atheists and skeptics are irrepressibly annoyed and generally unimpressed with Plantinga's "proper basicality," and theists, likewise, should be no more impressed with Barker's default atheism. It's fine to withhold one's belief about a claim, generally speaking. But, the question of God's existence is a little more pressing than most claims, so it seems unjustifiably biased to treat "God-belief" in league with trivial dismissals of "Santa-belief," "alien-belief," or "orbiting teapot-belief."[61] Not to mention, there is a substantial case supporting the notion of the *sensus divinitatis*, even before Plantinga ever put pen to paper.[62]

Barker is not an aberration here, unfortunately. There is a growing number of, typically popular-level, nontheists who are following the same

---

59. Reformed Epistemology, as developed by Alvin Plantinga, is known for granting God's existence as a "properly basic" fact. The concept of "God" is thereby treated with initial credibility according to the *sensus divinitatis* (a theory that human beings have an innate sense or knowledge of the reality of God). See Plantinga, *Warranted Christian Belief*. Other reformed epistemologists include William Alston and Nicholas Wolterstorff; see Bolos, "Reformed Epistemology."

60. One might be able to rebut Flew and Barker's presumption of atheism by considering the merit of God-belief as a "properly basic belief." Indeed, some studies suggest that God-belief is the developmental norm, and atheism is the deviation. On proper basicality, see Plantinga, *Warranted Christian Belief*, 175–80. On the subject of God-belief as the developmental norm, see Barrett, *Born Believers*.

61. William James would call God's existence a "live hypothesis" in that it is not responsibly treated with indifference, dismissal, or delay, even in the absence of conclusive evidence. See James, "Will to Believe." Also, a common strategy among New Atheists is to compare God to a trivial character like Santa Claus, the Tooth Fairy, or the Flying Spaghetti Monster. This trivialization is a strong clue that the person isn't considering a serious theistic proposal but thrashing at a strawman. See Atheists, Humanists, & Agnostics, "Does God Exist?," 27:05, cf. 43:30.

62. Rom 1:21. See relevant writings on the *sensus divinitatis* among Thomas Aquinas, Jonathan Edwards, John Calvin, Martin Luther, and others.

redefinition he uses, including the American Atheists Inc., Michael Martin, Simon Blackburn, Gordon Stein, George Smith, Matt Dillahunty, Randolph Richardson, and other prominent voices in contemporary atheism.[63] Christians and theistic apologists would do well to brace for this redefinitional wave. Barker is but one among many who, by all appearances, do not really care what the dictionaries, encyclopedias, and standard sources say. They are unphased by the fact that their forefathers in atheism were typically positive atheists, academically sharp, and often quite modest and respectful in the way they handled themselves in public. Modern atheists like Barker have had decades to submit to authoritative sources but, it seems, they have authority issues. Barker may have earned some modest respect as a semi-academic debater. But he leads a crowd of militant skeptics, vocal critics, and popular-level internet atheists, who have been weaned on memes, gifs, YouTube videos, social media shouting matches, and snarky websites. Top it all off with the fact that modern atheists have been armed with a definition of "atheism" where they can presume intellectual superiority over any theist they encounter without any significant intellectual work on their part. This recipe smells rotten.

CLOSING THOUGHTS

Barker, and those who follow in his footsteps, would do well to remember that abstaining from God-belief is nothing meritorious in itself. And neither does skepticism, agnosticism, or active questioning prove any special

---

63. American Atheists, "Atheism is One Thing"; Stein, *Anthology of Atheism and Rationalism*, 3; Smith, *Atheism: The Case Against God*, 7; Dillahunty, "Atheist Debates: You're Not an Atheist, You're an Agnostic"; Richardson, "Official Definitions of Atheism and Atheist"; Simon Blackburn is, perhaps, the most authoritative source I found for the negative sense as the default: "Atheism: Either the lack of belief that there exists a god, or the belief that there exists none. Sometimes thought itself to be more dogmatic than mere agnosticism, although atheists retort that everyone is an atheist about most gods, so they merely advance one step further" (Blackburn, "Atheism"). After Blackburn, Michael Martin might be the next most authoritative source in the bunch. He argues for the negative definition, after admitting that the dictionaries overwhelmingly contradict him: "If you look up 'atheism' in a dictionary, you will probably find it defined as the belief that there is no God. Certainly, many people understand atheism in this way. Yet many atheists do not, and this is not what the term means if one considers it from the point of view of its Greek roots. In Greek 'a' means 'without' or 'not' and 'theos' means 'god.' From this standpoint an atheist would simply be someone without a belief in God, not necessarily someone who believes that God does not exist. According to its Greek roots, then, atheism is a negative view, characterized by the absence of belief in God" (Martin, *Atheism*, 463).

intelligence. If Dan Barker wants to wear the mantle of intellectual respectability, he is going to have to earn it just like anyone else.

To be sure, many skeptics and atheists defy the stereotype of the "angry atheist" or the "pseudo-intellectual skeptic." But unfortunately, Barker is not one of them. He has all the snark and cynicism of the angry atheist. And his writing and debates so far, including his definition of "atheism," fit the profile of the pseudo-intellectual skeptic. Now, he's clearly an intelligent person, rhetorically sharp, well-versed in Christian apologetics tactics, and has loads of experience on the front lines of the worldview wars. But his brand of atheism is pretty typical of the New Atheists, weighing heavy on populism and light on academic rigor. Barker's brand of atheism is so common that it is probably here to stay. Christian apologists, professional and lay ministers, parents and students alike would all do well to prepare a ready response to Barker's "a-theism." Fortunately, his redefinitional game is easy to beat.

BIBLIOGRAPHY

"2014 Religious Landscape Study: Conducted June 4–September 30, 2014." *America's Changing Religious Landscape*. Washington, DC: Pew Research Center, 2015. http://www.pewforum.org/2015/05/12/americas-changing-religious-landscape/.

American Atheists. "Atheism Is One Thing: A Lack of Belief in Gods." https://www.atheists.org/activism/resources/about-atheism/.

American Heritage Dictionary of the English Language. 5th updated ed. Edited by the editors of the American Heritage Dictionaries. Boston: Houghton Mifflin Harcourt, 2015.

Ansley, Clark F. *Columbia Encyclopedia*. 6th ed. New York: Columbia University Press, 2001.

"Atheist." https://www.dictionary.com/browse/atheist?s=t.

"Atheist." https://www.etymonline.com/word/atheist.

Atheists, Humanists, & Agnostics. "Does God Exist?" *YouTube*, April 11, 2014. https://www.youtube.com/watch?v=oPio73maMRw&.

"Atheos." https://www.biblestudytools.com/lexicons/greek/kjv/atheos.html.

Audi, Robert, ed. *Cambridge Encyclopedia of Philosophy*. 2nd ed. Cambridge: Cambridge University Press, 2001.

Ayer, A. J. *Language Truth and Logic*. New York: Dover, 1952.

Barker, Dan. *godless: How an Evangelical Preacher Became One of America's Leading Atheists*. Berkeley: Ulysses, 2008.

Barnes and Noble Encyclopedia. Edited by David Crystal. Reprint, New York: Dorset, 1993.

Barr, James. *The Semantics of Biblical Language*. Oxford University Press, 1961.

Barrett, Justin. *Born Believers: The Science of Children's Religious Belief*. New York: Free Press, 2012.

Blackburn, Simon. *Oxford Dictionary of Philosophy*. 2nd rev. ed. Oxford: Oxford University Press, 2008.

Bolos, Anthony. "Reformed Epistemology." http://www.iep.utm.edu/ref-epis/#SH3c.

Borchert, Donald M., ed. *Encyclopedia of Philosophy*. 2nd ed. New York: McMillan Reference, 2006.

Bunnin, Nicholas, ed. *Blackwell Dictionary of Western Philosophy*. Malden: Wiley-Blackwell, 2004.

Buswell, J. Oliver. "Atheism." In *Baker's Dictionary of Theology*, edited by Everett F. Harrison, 70. Grand Rapids: Baker, 1960.

Cambridge Academic Content Dictionary. Edited by the editors of Cambridge University Press. Cambridge: Cambridge University Press, 2018.

Cambridge Dictionary. https://dictionary.cambridge.org.

Carr, Nicholas G. *The Shallows: What the Internet Is Doing to Our Brains*. New York: Norton, 2011.

Carrier, Richard. *Sense and Goodness Without God: A Defense of Metaphysical Naturalism*. Bloomington: AuthorHouse, 2005.

Carson, D. A. *Exegetical Fallacies*. 2nd ed. Grand Rapids: Baker, 1996.

Collins English Dictionary. Edited by the editors of Collins English Dictionary. New York: Harper-Collins, 2018. https://www.collinsdictionary.com/us/dictionary/english/atheism.

Craig, Edward, ed. *Routledge Encyclopedia of Philosophy*. London: Taylor & Francis, 1998.

Dillahunty, Matt. "Atheist Debates: You're Not an Atheist, You're Agnostic." *YouTube*, October 1, 2016. https://www.youtube.com/watch?v=BjY619aJ82Y.

————. "Does God Exist?" *YouTube*, November 26, 2015. https://www.youtube.com/watch?v=fUesg_IBL_A.

Draper, Paul. "Atheism and Agnosticism." https://plato.stanford.edu/entries/atheism-agnosticism/#toc.

Encyclopædia Britannica. Edited by the editors of Encyclopædia Britannica. Chicago: Britannica Group, 2000–2019. https://www.britannica.com/topic/atheism.

Ferm, Vergilius. "Atheism." In *Dictionary of Philosophy*. Edited by Dagobert D. Runes. New Jersey: Littlefield, Adams and Co. Philosophical Library, 1942.

Ferrer, John. "Belief in No God, or No Belief in God." https://crossexamined.org/defining-atheism-no-belief-in-god-or-belief-in-no-god/.

Flew, Antony. *Dictionary of Philosophy*. Rev. 2nd ed. New York: St. Martin's, 1979.

————. "The Presumption of Atheism." *Canadian Journal of Philosophy* 2 (1972) 29–46.

————. "Theology and Falsification." In *Reason and Responsibility: Readings in Some Basic Problems of Philosophy*, edited by Joel Feinberg, 48–49. Belmont: Dickenson, 1968.

Flew, Antony, and Paul Edwards. *God, Freedom, and Immortality*. Amherst: Prometheus, 1984.

Gentz, William H., ed. *The Dictionary of the Bible and Religion*. Nashville: Abingdon, 1986.

Gettier, Edmund L. "Is Justified True Belief Knowledge?" *Analysis* 23 (1963) 121–23.

The God Who Speaks. "Dan Barker Debates Richard Howe: Is There a God Who Speaks?" *YouTube*, October 18, 2017. https://www.youtube.com/watch?v=LD3-qK-2gu8&.

Haldeman-Julius, E. *The Meaning of Atheism*. Little Blue Book 1597. Girard, KS: Haldeman-Julius, 1931.

Honderich, Ted, ed. *Oxford Companion to Philosophy*. New ed. Oxford: Oxford University Press, 2005.

Hurley, Patrick J. *A Concise Introduction to Logic*. 10th ed. Belmont: Wadsworth, 2008.

Huxley, Thomas H. "Agnosticism." *The Nineteenth Century* 25 (1889) 169–94.

———. "Agnosticism: A Symposium." In *The Agnostic Annual*, edited by Charles Watts, 5–6. London: Watts, 1884.

James, William. "The Will to Believe." In *The Will to Believe and Other Essays in Popular Philosophy*, edited by William James, 1–31. New York: Longman, Green, & Co., 1912.

The King James Version New Testament Greek Lexicon. https://www.biblestudytools.com/lexicons/greek/kjv.

Little, William, et al., eds. *Oxford Universal Dictionary on Historical Principles*. 3rd rev. ed. Oxford: Oxford University Press, 1955.

Loftus, John. *The Outsider Test of Faith*. Amherst: Prometheus, 2013.

Martin, Michael. *Atheism: A Philosophical Justification*. Philadelphia: Temple University Press, 1990.

Martyr, Justin. *First Apology*. In *Ante-Nicene Fathers*, translated by Marcus Dods and George Reith, edited by Alexander Roberts, et al., 1:159–87. Rev. ed. Buffalo: Christian Literature, 1885. http://www.newadvent.org/fathers/0126.htm.

McCormick, Matt. "Atheism." https://www.iep.utm.edu/atheism/.

National Speech and Debate Association. *High School Unified Manual: Chapter Rules and Tournament Operations, 2017–2018*. West Des Moines: National Forensic League, 2018.

Newport, Frank. "2017 Update on Americans and Religion." *Gallup*, December 22, 2017. http://news.gallup.com/poll/224642/2017-update-americans-religion.aspx.

Nielsen, Kai E. "Comprehensive Definition of Atheism." https://www.britannica.com/topic/atheism/Comprehensive-definition-of-atheism.

———. "Definition of Atheism." http://www.evilbible.com/definition-of-atheism/.

Peterson, Michael, et al. *Philosophy of Religion: Selected Readings*. 2nd ed. New York: Oxford University Press, 2001.

Plantinga, Alvin. *Warrant and Proper Function*. New York: Oxford University Press, 1993.

———. *Warranted Christian Belief*. New York: Oxford University Press, 2000.

"Professor Antony Flew." *The Telegraph*, April 13, 2010. https://www.telegraph.co.uk/news/obituaries/culture-obituaries/books-obituaries/7586929/Professor-Antony-Flew.html.

Ra, Aron. "You're Either Theist or A-theist; There Is No Agnostic Third Option." *Patheos* 3 (2013). https://www.patheos.com/blogs/reasonadvocates/2013/10/03/youre-either-theist-or-a-theist-there-is-no-agnostic-3rd-option/.

Random House Unabridged Dictionary. New York: Random House-Penguin, 2020. https://www.dictionary.com.

Richardson, Randolph. "Definitions of 'Atheism' and 'Atheist.'" https://www.defineatheism.com/.

Simpson, D. P., ed. *Cassell's Latin Dictionary*. New York: Wiley, 1968.

Simpson, J. A., and E. S. C. Weinter, eds. *Oxford English Dictionary*. 2nd ed. New York: Oxford University Press, 1989.

Sinclair, John, ed. "Atheism." *COBUILD Advanced English Dictionary*. New York: Harper-Collins, 2018. https://www.collinsdictionary.com/dictionary/english/atheism.

Smart, J. J. C. "Atheism and Agnosticism." https://stanford.library.sydney.edu.au/archives/sum2004/entries/atheism-agnosticism/.

Smith, George H. *Atheism: The Case Against God*. Amherst: Prometheus, 1989.

———. *Why Atheism?* Amherst: Prometheus, 2000.

Soames, Scott. *Philosophy of Language*. Princeton Foundations of Contemporary Philosophy. Reprint, Princeton: Princeton University Press, 2012.

Stein, Gordon, ed. *An Anthology of Atheism and Rationalism*. Amherst: Prometheus, 1980.

———. *The New Encyclopedia of Unbelief*. Amherst: Prometheus, 2007.

Strong, James. *The New Strong's Exhaustive Concordance of the Bible*. Rev. ed. Nashville: Nelson, 2003.

Vargese, Roy A. "Sir Alfred Ayer." In *Great Thinkers on Great Questions*, edited by Roy A. Vargese, 49. Rockport: OneWorld, 1998.

Vitz, Paul. *Faith of the Fatherless*. San Francisco: Ignatius, 2013.

Webster, Noah, ed. *Webster's New World Dictionary*. Encyclopedic ed. Cleveland: New World, 1960.

———. *Webster's Revised Unabridged Dictionary*. Springfield: Merriam, 1913.

White, James E. *Rise of the Nones: Understanding and Reaching the Religiously Unaffiliated*. Grand Rapids: Baker, 2014.

Wolf, Gary. "The Church of the Non-Believers." *Wired Magazine*, November 1, 2006. https://www.wired.com/2006/11/atheism/.

Zodhiates, Spiros, et al., eds. *Lexical Aids to the New Testament in Keyword Study Bible, New International Version*. Chattanooga: AMG, 1996.

2

Are Faith and Reason Compatible?

—B. Kyle Keltz

Like the lonely heart who keeps waiting for the phone to ring, I kept trusting that God would someday come through. He never did. The only proposed answer was *faith*, and I gradually grew to dislike the smell of that word. I finally realized that faith is a cop-out, a defeat—an admission that the truths of religion are unknowable through evidence and reason.

—Dan Barker[1]

Of all the concepts associated with Christianity, faith is probably the one that is most abused by atheist proselytizers. Often it is claimed that "faith" is "believing something without evidence or despite evidence to the contrary," and faith and reason are incompatible. For example, in *Atheism: The Case Against God*, George Smith says, "Faith is belief without, or in spite of, reason."[2] In *The God Delusion*, Richard Dawkins says, "It is in the nature of faith that one is capable, like Jung, of holding a belief without adequate reason to do so."[3] Dan Barker agrees in *godless* when he says that "religious faith is not adjustable. It remains strong in spite of a lack of evidence, or in

1. Barker, *godless*, 39.
2. Smith, *Atheism*, 98.
3. Dawkins, *God Delusion*, 74.

spite of contrary evidence."[4] Yet Smith, Dawkins, and Barker are abusing the definition of "faith" because in each one of these cases, "faith" is defined without any mention of how Christians define "faith." These comments are misleading because they can lead people to think they represent the only definition of "faith" or that they are referring to what Christians believe.

In light of this problem, in this chapter I will explain a major Christian position regarding the relation between faith and reason. First, I will discuss Dan Barker's understanding of faith as per his statements in his book *godless*. Next, I will explain the classical Christian position regarding faith and reason as presented by Thomas Aquinas. After this, I will contrast Barker's understanding of faith with Aquinas's understanding. I will conclude that Barker is defining "faith" as he experienced it during his days as a Christian evangelist and not as it is understood by Christian theologians. I will emphasize that Barker is free to reject what he is defining as "faith," but this is not a rejection of faith as understood in the classical Christian tradition.

DAN BARKER ON FAITH AND REASON

Barker did not devote an entire chapter to his understanding of faith as he did with many other topics in *godless*. However, he says enough to give a good idea of what he thinks faith is. He mainly talks about faith in chapter 5, "Why I am an Atheist."

Barker mentions what he thinks of faith while discussing the Christian idea that faith is a virtue. He says,

> Faith would be unnecessary, they remind us, if God's existence were proved to be a blunt fact of reality. . . . But this is a huge cop out. If the only way you can accept an assertion is by faith, then you are admitting that the assertion can't be taken on its own merits. If something is true, we don't invoke faith. Instead, we use reason to prove it. With faith, you don't have to put any work into proving your case or overcoming objections. You can "just believe."[5]

Here Barker is describing faith as the act of believing a proposition without any evidence. This is in the context of a hypothetical fideistic argument in which a Christian is claiming that God's existence should be taken only on faith. So, Barker objects by saying that truth should be sought through

4. Barker, *godless*, 102.
5. Barker, *godless*, 101.

reason, and if reason cannot be used to justify a belief, then there is no good reason to hold to it.

Next, Barker mentions, "Faith is actually agnosticism. Faith is what you use when you don't have knowledge. When someone says, 'The meeting is at 7:30, I believe,' they are expressing some doubt. When you tack 'I believe' onto a comment, does that make it stronger?"[6] Here again Barker is describing faith as the act of believing a proposition without any evidence. Earlier in *godless*, Barker defines "agnosticism" as "the refusal to take as a fact any statement for which there is insufficient evidence."[7] So when he says that faith is agnosticism, he means that faith is the act of believing a proposition without sufficient evidence.

After these statements, Barker emphasizes that the acceptance of faith, as he defines it, could justify someone to believe anything. He says,

> If faith is valid, then anything goes. Muslims believe in Allah by faith, so they must be right. The Hindus are right. The Greeks and Romans were right. More people claim to have seen or been healed by Elvis Presley than ever claimed to have seen the resurrected Jesus. With faith, *everybody* is right.[8]

If it is okay to believe something without any evidence, this means that it is okay to believe in anything and suggests that all religions are right, although most religions make opposing claims regarding the nature of reality and the purpose of humanity. Barker mentions that even atheism could be taken on faith according to this definition.[9]

Barker goes on to expand his definition of "faith" in chapter 5. He objects to the claim that atheists also act on faith and answers by saying that atheists usually act on the expectations they have gained from experience. For example, when an atheist flips on a light switch, he is not doing so because he believes without reason that a bulb will light, but on the basis that there is a high probability a bulb will light. This is where Barker mentions that "religious faith is not adjustable" and says that faith "remains strong in spite of a lack of evidence, or in spite of contrary evidence." So, Barker is expanding his definition of "faith" to include not only the act of believing a proposition without evidence, but also the act of believing a proposition although it is contradicted by the only evidence available. This is confirmed

6. Barker, *godless*, 101.

7. Barker, *godless*, 96.

8. Barker, *godless*, 101.

9. Barker, *godless*, 101.

again at the end of the chapter when Barker says, "religious faith . . . makes a leap from possibility to fact. Or, often, from impossibility to fact."[10]

A CLASSICAL UNDERSTANDING OF FAITH AND REASON

In the history of Christianity and Christian philosophy, there have been several views on the relation between faith and reason.[11] Some Christians, such as Søren Kierkegaard, Karl Barth, and Cornelius Van Til, have argued in various ways that Christian beliefs cannot be proved by or believed on the basis of reason. Other Christians, like Alvin Plantinga, have argued that Christian beliefs are no different from other beliefs people hold (e.g., the existence of an external world, the reality of the past, and the existence of other minds besides their own) that are rational to believe, yet are unprovable. This position that emphasizes faith over reason is called *fideism* (from the Latin *fides*, meaning "trust, confidence, or faith"). In religious epistemology (i.e., the study of religious knowledge), there is a position on how beliefs ought to be justified called *evidentialism*. Evidentialism is the position that it is only rational to hold any given belief if there is sufficient evidence to warrant holding such a belief. Many Christians throughout the history of Christianity (e.g., René Descartes, Gottfried Leibnez, and Stuart Hackett) have more or less granted a type of evidentialism and argued that God's existence and many of God's attributes can be demonstrated solely using reason. In contrast to fideism, evidentialism emphasizes reason over faith.

However, although there has been much debate over the relation between faith and reason in modern and contemporary times, faith and reason have been classically understood in Christianity as compatible with one another.[12] While fideism places emphasis on faith, and evidentialism places emphasis on reason, there is a middle-ground position that entails faith and reason both have their specific roles in Christian thought and overlap in relation to Christian beliefs. The medieval philosopher/theologian Thomas Aquinas was one such Christian who held this middle view.

10. Barker, *godless*, 103.

11. Norman Geisler provides a good overview and critique of major Christian positions on faith and reason in Geisler, *Christian Apologetics*, 3–136. For an explanation of and debate over three contemporary Christian views on faith and reason, see Wilkins, *Faith and Reason*.

12. As Richard Howe explains in his chapter, the "classical" in "classical Christianity" denotes the traditional beliefs of Christianity, which were influenced by classical Greek philosophy and were held for the "bulk" of Church history.

Faith

Aquinas talks at length about faith in his mature work, the *Summa Theolo-giae*. In it, he defines "faith" in agreement with the author of Hebrews: "Faith is the substance of things hoped for, the evidence of things that appear not [Heb. 11:1]."[13] Aquinas says this definition contains all of the pertinent aspects of his view regarding the nature of faith.[14]

The Act of Faith

To understand Aquinas's definition of the term "faith," it is good to note his distinction between the act of faith and the object of faith. Aquinas says, "the act of faith is to believe, as stated above, which is an act of the intellect determinate to one object of the will's command."[15] In giving this definition, he refers to an earlier discussion of the act of faith in the *Summa Theologiae*.[16] In this earlier discussion, he goes into detail regarding the definition of "belief" and several important aspects of belief.

First, he defines "belief" and gives the definition he adopted from Augustine's *On the Predestination of the Saints*: "to believe is to think with assent."[17] Explaining what he means by the term "think" in this definition, he says, "'to think' is more strictly taken for that consideration of the intellect, which is accompanied by some kind of inquiry, and which precedes the intellect's arrival at the stage of perfection that comes with the certitude of sight."[18] What he is saying is that belief involves thinking in which the mind is considering a proposition, but is not yet sure of its truth because it has not experienced a demonstration of the proposition's truth. In this way, belief involves thinking that is to be distinguished from philosophical and scientific reasoning and opinion.[19]

---

13. Aquinas, *Summa Theologiae* (*ST*) II-II, q. 4, a. 1. See also Aquinas, *Quaestiones disputatae de veritate* (*De Veritate*), q. 14, a. 2. All English quotes from the *Summa Theologiae* are from Aquinas, *Summa Theologica*. All quotes from *De Veritate* are from Aquinas, *Questions I–IX*.

14. Aquinas, *ST* II-II, q. 4, a. 1. See also Aquinas, *De Veritate*, q. 14, a. 2.

15. Aquinas, *ST* II-II, q. 4, a. 1. See also Aquinas, *De Veritate*, q. 14, a. 2.

16. Aquinas, *ST* II-II, q. 2, a. 1.

17. Aquinas, *ST* II-II, q. 2, a. 1. See also Aquinas, *De Veritate*, q. 14, a. 1; and Aquinas, *Super Epistolam B. Pauli ad Hebraeos lectura* (*In Heb.*), c. 11, 11–1.

18. Aquinas, *ST* II-II, q. 2, a. 1. See also Aquinas, *De Veritate*, q. 14, a. 1.

19. Stump, *Aquinas*, 363. By "scientific reasoning," I am referring not to reasoning using the modern notion of science, but Aquinas's understanding of "science," which is a field of study that has its basis either in self-evident principles or takes its principles

Aquinas explains this further when he says,

> For among the acts belonging to the intellect, some have a firm assent without any such kind of thinking, as when a man considers the things that he knows by science, or understands, for this consideration is already formed. But some acts of the intellect have unformed thought devoid of a firm assent, whether they incline to neither side, as in one who "doubts"; or incline to one side rather than the other, but on account of some slight motive, as in one who "suspects"; or incline to one side yet with fear of the other, as in one who "opines."[20]

Here Aquinas is giving examples of several different types of intellectual acts that are associated with reasoning, opinion, and belief. The first type of thinking involves an assent to a proposition based on the firsthand experience of the truth of the proposition. Aquinas's example is something a person might consider that the person already knows or understands through some type of legitimate field of study.

An example of this first type of thinking could be getting asked the question, "Is it true that four times four equals sixteen?" For most adults, there is no need to consider this question because the product of four times four is known to be sixteen. The truth of the proposition "$4 \times 4 = 16$" is known and understood through the methods and concepts of mathematics. This means that there is no room for the will to assent to the truth of this proposition because its truth is a matter of fact.

The second type of thinking Aquinas mentions does not involve scientific reasoning. This is when the truth of a proposition has not been experienced firsthand, so its truth value is uncertain. This entails that the will must intervene if assent is to be given to the proposition. In this case, Aquinas mentions that there are three types of situations: those involving doubt, suspicion, and opinion.

Aquinas explains that doubting occurs when a person fails to assent to either possibility when considering a proposition. If a person is inclined to a particular side of the consideration for some small reason, then that person suspects. Opining is when a person inclines to a particular side of the consideration for some reason yet is weary of the other side.

Aquinas is saying that belief is closest to suspecting the truth of a proposition. To this effect, he adds,

---

from a more foundational field of study.

20. Aquinas, *ST* II-II, q. 2, a. 1. See also Aquinas, *De Veritate*, q. 14, a. 1.

But this act "to believe," cleaves firmly to one side, in which respect belief has something in common with science and understanding; yet its knowledge does not attain the perfection of clear sight, wherein it agrees with doubt, suspicion and opinion. Hence it is proper to the believer to think with assent: so that the act of believing is distinguished from all the other acts of the intellect, which are about the true or the false.[21]

Belief differs from philosophical and scientific reasoning because the truth of a proposition that is believed is not experienced and is not certain. Additionally, belief differs from opinion because the will has assented to the truth of a proposition that is believed. This means that the person is not inclined to the opposing side of the consideration due to the assent given. Belief is closest to suspicion but is different because the assent given is due to more than merely a "slight motive." This entails that sufficient evidence is necessary for assenting to a proposition in belief.

Aquinas is saying that the act of faith is belief, which is when the will commands the intellect to assent to the truth of a proposition based on some type of consideration. The object of faith cannot be something known with certainty or through firsthand experience. Belief is not based on certainty, yet it differs from opinion because the will assents to the truth of a belief without any inclination to the opposing consideration.

The Object of Faith

Returning to Aquinas's discussion of his definition of "faith," he explains the object of faith after establishing that the act of faith is belief. He says, "Now it has been already stated that the object of faith is the First Truth, as unseen, and whatever we hold on account thereof."[22] Here Aquinas is saying that the object of faith, regarding theology, is God.

In an earlier discussion in the *Summa Theologiae*, Aquinas establishes several things regarding the object of faith.[23] He determines that the object of faith must be God: unseen, not fully known, yet partly known through propositions. In discussing that the object of faith is God, Aquinas says, "Now the object of the theological virtues is God Himself, Who is the last

21. Aquinas, *ST* II-II, q. 2, a. 1. See also Aquinas, *De Veritate*, q. 14, a. 1.

22. Aquinas, *ST* II-II, q. 4, a. 1. See also Aquinas, *De Veritate*, q. 14, a. 8; and *In Heb.* c. 11, 11–1.

23. Aquinas, *ST* II-II, q. 1, a. 1–5.

end of all, as surpassing the knowledge of our reason."[24] Because all theological truths are about God, it follows that God is the object of faith.

As the object of faith, God cannot be fully known or seen. Aquinas
explains, "Now those things are said to be seen which, of themselves, move
the intellect or the senses to knowledge of them. Wherefore it is evident that
neither faith nor opinion can be of things seen either by the senses or by
the intellect."[25] Anything that is seen or fully known with certainty cannot
be an object of faith because the truth of a proposition that is experienced
with the senses or reached as the conclusion of a logical demonstration is
certain. The intellect has assented to its truth on the basis of its self-evidence
or demonstrated veracity.

Knowing something with certainty leaves no role for the will to play
because the will does not need to move the intellect to assent to the truth
of a proposition that is known with certainty. To believe a proposition is to
assent to its truth on the basis of some consideration when its truth is not
certain. Thus, something that is seen or fully known through logical demonstration cannot be an object of faith. However, God is partly known through
propositions based in reasoning and in God's revelation to humanity. God's
authority as Creator and Sustainer of the universe provides the basis for
assenting to the truths of faith.

Returning to Aquinas's preferred definition of "faith" as "the substance
of things hoped for, the evidence of things that appear not [Heb. 11:1]," it
is now evident why he thinks that this is a sufficient definition. Aquinas
explains that "the substance of things hoped for" is a reference to the object
of faith, which is God.[26] God as the object of faith is "hoped for" because
the believer does not yet have full knowledge of God, which can only be obtained through the beatific vision in heaven.[27] The "evidence of things that
appear not" refers to the act of faith. Assent is given by the intellect on command of the will based on the available evidence in considering the truth of
Scripture. This is belief because the truths of faith are not certain in that they
are beyond the reach of natural theology. They cannot be demonstrated or
experienced through the senses, and their truth must be assented to on the
authority of their source, which is God.

24. Aquinas, *ST* I-II, q. 62, a. 2. See also Aquinas, *De Veritate*, q. 14, a. 8.

25. Aquinas, *ST* II-II, q. 1, a. 4. See also Aquinas, *De Veritate*, q. 14, a. 9 and Aquinas, *In Heb.* c. 11, 11–1.

26. Aquinas, *ST* II-II, q. 1, a. 4.

27. See Aquinas's discussions of the ultimate end of humanity and the beatific vision
at *ST* I-II, q. 1–5 and Aquinas, *Summa contra Gentiles* (*SCG*) III, c. 2–40. All quotes
from the *SCG* are from Aquinas, *Summa Contra Gentiles*.

Reason

Aquinas also talks at length about reason in the *Summa Theologiae*.[28] His discussion regarding reason is mainly found in his treatise on man.[29] This is where Aquinas describes the hylomorphic understanding of human nature that he adopted from Aristotle.

The Act of Reason

As with faith, Aquinas maintains the distinction between the acts of reason and the objects of reason. The acts of reason, in the classical sense, are every way in which the human intellect is capable of attaining knowledge. These are what are known as the *three acts of the mind.*

In writing the *Summa Theologiae*, Aquinas was targeting an audience with a classical understanding of the three acts of the mind.[30] The three acts of the mind or intellect are *simple apprehension* (i.e., understanding), *judgment*, and *reasoning*. Aquinas mentions these in his discussion regarding the different modes of understanding.[31] He says,

> The human intellect must of necessity understand by composition and division. For since the intellect passes from potentiality to act, it has a likeness to things which are generated, which do not attain to perfection all at once but acquire it by degrees: so likewise the human intellect does not acquire perfect knowledge by the first act of apprehension; but it first apprehends something about its object, such as its quiddity, and this is its first and proper object; and then it understands the properties, accidents, and the various relations of the essence. Thus it necessarily compares one thing with another by composition or division; and from one composition and division it proceeds to another, which is the process of reasoning.[32]

Here Aquinas is talking about all of the processes by which the intellect comes to understand or to know something, all of the ways that knowledge can be attained through reason.

---

28. Aquinas, *ST* I, q. 84–88.
29. Aquinas, *ST* I, q. 75–102.
30. Davies, *Thomas Aquinas's Summa Theologiae*, 12.
31. Aquinas, *ST* I, q. 85.
32. Aquinas, *ST* I, q. 85.

Aquinas's philosophy of mind entails that the intellect is a power (i.e., ability) of the human soul.[33] In this way, his philosophy concerning the soul is distinct from Cartesian dualism, which views the soul and the mind as identical. The intellect, according to Aquinas, is composed of two distinct powers: the passive intellect and the active intellect.[34]

The active intellect is the power that abstracts the universal nature of things from their particular instances and deposits these natures in the passive intellect, which results in understanding. Aquinas gives a helpful illustration of this in the *Summa contra Gentiles* where he explains, "Now, the possible intellect, since it is a passive power in some sense, has its proper corresponding agent, namely, the agent intellect which is related to the possible intellect as light is to sight."[35] Sight is a passive ability because the eyes do not actively cause things to be seen. Instead, light illuminates objects, which makes it possible for them to be detected by sight. In the same way, the active intellect is the power that makes understanding possible by illuminating the natures of things and causes understanding by placing these natures in the passive intellect.

The interactions between the active and passive intellects are what constitute the three acts of the mind. As Aquinas explains, "apprehension" is what occurs when the intellect "first apprehends something about its object." Apprehension occurs when the active intellect abstracts the essence or nature from an object. This is the first act of the mind: simple apprehension or understanding.

An example of understanding is when a person looks at an apple. Light rays bounce off the apple and illuminate the eyes of the person viewing the apple. The light is turned into signals that are sent to the brain. The active intellect abstracts the essence of the apple from the signals and places it in the passive intellect. The knower then contains the form of an apple and understands apple-ness.

Next Aquinas mentions that the intellect "understands the properties, accidents, and the various relations of the essence" of the understood object. This is when the intellect compares the many different things (such as properties) apprehended about the object. This is the second act of the mind: judgment.

33. Aquinas, *ST* I, q. 79, a. 1; Aquinas, *Quaestiones disputatae de anima* (*De Anima*), a. 12; Aquinas, *De Veritate*, q. 10, a. 1; and Aquinas, *Quaestiones disputatae de spiritualibus creaturis* (*De spirit. creat.*), a. 11. For a great introductory text on the philosophy of mind and a defense of Aquinas's position, see Madden, *Mind, Matter, and Nature*.

34. Aquinas, *ST* I, q. 79, a. 2–3; Aquinas, *De Anima*, a. 4; Aquinas, *SCG* II, c. 77; and Aquinas, *De spirit. creat.*, a. 9.

35. Aquinas, *SCG* III, c. 45.

A judgment is more complex than a proposition known through simple apprehension. Returning to the example of the apple, instead of a simple concept such as "apple" or "red," a judgment consists of a more complex concept such as "This apple is red." The active intellect has already abstracted the concepts of "apple," "red," "fruit," "tasty," etc. However, in judging it combines the concepts according to their relations.

So, the active intellect works on the collection of the apprehended concepts just as it did the apple. It abstracts the relations just as it did the essence of the apple and the apple's various properties. First, the active intellect abstracted "apple" and "red." It then abstracted the relation between the two concepts and placed this relational concept in the passive intellect. The mind then knows, "This apple is red."

Finally, Aquinas mentions that the intellect proceeds from one composition and division to another, "which is the process of reasoning." What he means is that, similar to the process of judgment, the intellect combines several concepts to reach a more complex concept in the process of reasoning. The difference between judgment and reasoning is that in judging, the intellect combines two or more simple concepts, and in reasoning, the intellect combines two or more judgments. This is the third act of the mind: reasoning.

So, the conclusions of reasoning are more complex than judgments. Returning to the apple illustration, instead of a judgment that combines simple concepts such as "this apple is red," or "an edible object with seeds is fruit," the intellect can reason to the conclusion that "this apple is fruit because it has seeds."

The active intellect has already abstracted the relations between the apple and its properties and between the definition of fruit and its components. In reasoning, the active intellect abstracts the relation between the two judgments and then places this conclusion in the passive intellect. The mind then knows, "This red apple is fruit."

The Object of Reason

Keeping the definition of the object of faith in mind, the objects of reason are all the things that the intellect can know through the three acts of the mind. It is important to remember that the act of faith is something that involves the will. The will is involved because it must command the intellect to assent to the truth of a proposition that is not certain. Thus, anything that is an object of reason is certain because it has been apprehended, judged, or concluded through reason.

This is why Aquinas emphasizes that the object of faith cannot be seen or known through reason. He says, "Now those things are said to be seen which, of themselves, move the intellect or the senses to knowledge of them. Wherefore it is evident that neither faith nor opinion can be of things seen either by the senses or by the intellect."[36] If the truth of a proposition is apprehended by the intellect through the senses, then the will does not need to command the intellect to assent to the truth of the proposition. The object of the senses itself is what moves the intellect to assent to the truth of the proposition. Likewise, if the truth of a proposition is known through judgment or reasoning, then the will does not need to command the intellect. Thus, only those truths that can be discovered through the senses and reasoning are the proper objects of reason. So, knowledge gained through reason cannot involve the will as with opinion or belief.

Here it will be good to distinguish a couple aspects of the Thomistic understanding of epistemology from other contemporary theories of epistemology. It is important to note that Aquinas's understanding of knowledge is different from the contemporary understanding. The most widely held definition of "knowledge" today is that knowledge is "justified true belief." William Lane Craig and J. P. Moreland explain,

> Ever since the time of Plato, philosophers have tried to offer an adequate definition of propositional knowledge (hereafter, simply called knowledge). In his dialogue *Theaetetus*, Plato offered (though he did not completely endorse) what is known as the standard definition of (propositional) knowledge. The standard way of stating this definition is to say that knowledge is justified true belief.[37]

According to this definition, for a proposition to count as knowledge, it must be true, believed by the knower, and the knower must be justified in holding this belief.

Aquinas's definition of "knowledge" is different. His understanding is that knowledge occurs when the knower and the known are one.[38] This was seen in the above discussion regarding the passive and active intellects. The

---

36. Aquinas, *ST* II-II, q. 1, a. 4. See also Aquinas, *De Veritate*, q. 14, a. 9 and Aquinas, *In Heb.*, c. 11, 11-1.

37. Moreland and Craig, *Philosophical Foundations for a Christian Worldview*, 73.

38. There is not enough space to expound on Aquinas's epistemology. But he certainly did not agree that knowledge is justified true belief. It should already be apparent that he did not agree with the belief requirement for knowledge. Aquinas says that belief is when the will commands the intellect to assent to the truth of a proposition. If belief, as defined by Aquinas, were a requirement for knowledge, then none of the objects of reason could be objects of knowledge.

active intellect abstracts the form of things and places them in the passive intellect, resulting in knowledge. The intellect takes on the form of an external thing and results in the human knowing the thing. Aquinas explains that

> intelligent beings are distinguished from non-intelligent beings in that the latter possess only their own form; whereas the intelligent being is naturally adapted to have also the form of some other thing; for the idea of the thing known is in the knower . . . Knowledge is according to the mode of the one who knows; for the thing known is in the knower according to the mode of the knower.[39]

Although Aquinas mentions certainty when discussing knowledge, his definition of "knowledge" as the knower and the known becoming one does not necessarily entail that experiential cognition and reasoning are infallible. Aquinas knew that people often err. In his work *Quaestiones disputate de veritate*, he discusses why people are often wrong:

> In its relation to a human intellect, however, an inequality of thing with intellect, caused in some way by the thing, is occasionally found; for a thing makes itself known in the soul by its exterior appearance, since our cognition takes its beginning from sense, whose direct object is sensible qualities. For this reason it is said in *The Soul*: "Accidents greatly contribute to our knowledge of the quiddity." Consequently, when there are manifested in any object sensible qualities indicating a nature which does not actually underlie them, that thing is said to be false.[40]

In other words, because knowledge must come through the senses, it is not always guaranteed that the thing known in the intellect will be an exact similitude of the thing sensed. Sometimes people make mistakes in their reasoning, and sometimes people see what is not there. Being wrong or partially incorrect makes it so that the thing as it is in reality is not in the knower. Thus, for Aquinas, someone who is wrong or partially incorrect is someone without knowledge or only partial knowledge.

The Relation between Faith and Reason

As mentioned above, the object of faith is God partly known through Scripture and the principles of theology. An object of reason is anything that can be known by means of the unaided intellect. So basically, what is in view

---

39. Aquinas, *ST* I, q. 14, a. 1. See also Aquinas, *De Veritate*, q. 1, a. 3.
40. Aquinas, *De Veritate*, q. 1, a. 10.

here is all of the propositions that can be known about God through Scripture (objects of faith) and all of the propositions that can be known through the use of human reasoning (objects of reason).

Aquinas's view of the relation between the objects of faith and reason is a middle ground between the extremes of evidentialism and fideism. Thomism entails three types of truths: truths that are solely the object of faith, truths that can both be the object of faith and reason, and truths that are solely the object of reason. Aquinas talks about this division of truths at the beginning of his *Summa contra Gentiles*. He says, "One kind of divine truth the investigation of the reason is competent to reach, whereas the other surpasses every effort of the reason. I am speaking of a 'twofold truth of divine things,' not on the part of God Himself, Who is truth one and simple, but from the point of view of our knowledge, which is variously related to the knowledge of divine things."[41] Here Aquinas discusses truths that can either be solely the object of faith or both the object of faith and reason.

It is easy to determine which truths Aquinas believed can only be the objects of faith and which can be both the objects of faith and reason. He discusses this in the *Summa contra Gentiles*. He explains,

> This, then, is the manner of procedure we intend to follow. We shall first seek to make known that truth which faith professes and reason investigates. This we shall do by bringing forward both demonstrative and probable arguments, some of which were drawn from the books of the philosophers and of the saints, through which truth is strengthened and its adversary overcome.
>
> Then, in order to follow a development from the more manifest to the less manifest, we shall proceed to make known that truth which surpasses reason, answering the objections of its adversaries and setting forth the truth of faith by probable arguments and by authorities, to the best of our ability.[42]

Following this procedure, Aquinas sets out all of the truths that can be known by both faith and reason in the first three books of the *Summa contra Gentiles*. The first book, *God*, covers topics including God's existence and many of his attributes such as his eternality, simplicity, perfection, goodness, immutability, etc. The second book, *Creation*, covers topics including God's omnipotence, God's free-will choice to create, God's reason for creating, the existence and nature of the human soul, etc. The third book, *Providence*, covers topics relevant to the problem of evil, humanity's purpose,

---

41. Aquinas, *SCG* I, c. 9. See also Aquinas, *ST* I, q. 1, a. 1.
42. Aquinas, *SCG* I, c. 9.

God's sustaining activity, natural law, etc. Finally, Aquinas covers the truths that are solely considered as the objects of faith in the fourth book. In book 4, *Salvation*, he covers topics including the Trinity, the incarnation of Christ, the virgin birth, baptism, resurrection of the saints, etc.

Again, it is important to note that Aquinas believes that something cannot be the object of faith and reason simultaneously. It was shown above that Aquinas's definition of the act of faith includes an act of the will, which is necessary because the truth of an object of faith is not known through demonstration. If the truth of an object of faith is demonstrated with reason, then that proposition is no longer an object of faith, but an object of reason.

This distinction entails that all of the truths contained in Scripture can be taken on faith. Some can be demonstrated with reason, while others cannot. However, there is nothing wrong with someone, a layperson for example, to take truths such as God's existence on faith. Aquinas explains,

> Hence it was necessary for the salvation of man that certain truths which exceed human reason should be made known to him by divine revelation. Even as regards those truths about God which human reason could have discovered, it was necessary that man should be taught by a divine revelation; because the truth about God such as reason could discover, would only be known by a few, and that after a long time, and with the admixture of many errors. Whereas man's whole salvation, which is in God, depends upon the knowledge of this truth. Therefore, in order that the salvation of men might be brought about more fitly and more surely, it was necessary that they should be taught divine truths by divine revelation.[43]

Aquinas is saying that divine revelation is necessary for at least two reasons. One is that divine revelation contains all the knowledge necessary for salvation, and much of this knowledge is beyond the reach of unaided reason. So, without it, humanity would remain lost. A second reason is that if revelation contained only truths that cannot be reached with reason, then this would make it necessary for all people to learn and fully understand natural theology. However, instead God saw fit to reveal even the truths that can be reached with unaided reason because not everyone has the means, time, ability, or motivation to learn natural theology.

Some have taken Aquinas's words regarding the distinction between the objects of faith and reason to mean that only the intellectual elite can have knowledge of God's existence, attributes, etc., and everyone else has to

43. Aquinas, *ST* I, q. 1, a. 1. See also Aquinas, *SCG* I, c. 4.

take this on faith (entailing that they lack knowledge).[44] It is true that Aquinas is saying that only a few have the opportunity to study and understand the truths of natural theology. But it is not true that Aquinas believes that the objects of faith are not knowledge. This is evident when Aquinas says,

> Knowledge can have two meanings: sight or assent. When it refers to sight, it is distinguished from faith. . . . But, in so far as there is certainty of assent, faith is knowledge, and as such can be called certain knowledge and sight.[45]

Here we see Aquinas referring to assent as knowledge. This means that beliefs, for Aquinas, can count as knowledge. It is important to remember that Aquinas understands knowledge to be when the knower and the known become one. So, as long as someone knows the truth, he has knowledge. Thus, the objects of faith can be knowledge.

Summary of Aquinas on Faith and Reason

To summarize Aquinas's position on the relation between the objects of faith and reason, Aquinas makes a distinction between the acts of faith and reason and the objects of faith and reason. The act of faith, in theology, is the will commanding the intellect to assent to the truth of a proposition based on the authority of God. The act of reason is any combination of the three acts of the mind: apprehension, judgment, and reasoning. In theology, the object of faith is God. The object of reason is anything that is known through the three acts of the mind apart from a special revelation from God.

These distinctions helped Aquinas explain the relation between the objects of faith and reason. There are truths that are only known through reason, such as the number of planets in the solar system, the atomic mass of oxygen, and the lifecycles of butterflies. There are truths that are known through both faith and reason, such as the existence of God, the existence of the soul, and the resurrection of Jesus. Finally, there are truths of faith that are known only on the authority of God, such as God's triunity, Jesus's death on the cross atoned for the sins of humanity, and the resurrection and judgment of the dead at the end of days.

---

44. For example, Alvin Plantinga mistakes Aquinas's discussion to mean that truths taken on faith are not knowledge. See Plantinga, "Reason and Belief in God," 44.

45. Aquinas, *De Veritate*, q. 14, a. 2, ad. 15.

BARKER'S TESTIMONY IN LIGHT OF THE CLASSICAL RELATION BETWEEN FAITH AND REASON

It is strange that Barker has talked and written so much without mentioning the classical view of faith and reason, especially since it has been a major Christian view for centuries. In his book *godless*, he gives the impression that Christianity is based on faith, which he says is believing in God without evidence or with evidence to the contrary. Given that he was a pastor for so long prior to becoming an atheist, his readers might get the impression that this is how all Christians think of faith. Such a representation can only be based in ignorance or deceit. In being generous to Barker, I do not want to say that it is because he is being deceitful. Instead, I think this is because he is unaware of Aquinas's classical view (and possibly all other historical and contemporary Christian views on faith and reason).

I think he is unaware of Aquinas's view based on his testimony in *godless*. This seems to be the case based on his discussion of how he approached his religious studies at Azusa Pacific College. It seems that Barker was not very motivated to learn about Christianity in-depth. For example, he recalls,

> I was in college, and getting decent grades, but I wasn't sure why I was there, when there was so little time left to live on this late, great planet. I was dismissive of ordination or degrees. I figured I didn't need a piece of paper bestowed by humans to tell me what I already knew: that God personally called me to the ministry of the Gospel. After four full-time years, I fell nine elective units short of graduation and never went back to finish. (In 1988, Azusa Pacific University allowed me to transfer some creative writing units from the University of Wisconsin and mailed me my degree in religion.)[46]

From these words, it seems that Barker was not as much concerned with learning about Christianity as he was eager to leave college to preach. Elsewhere, he specifically explains how he approached the one apologetics class he took:

> In my four years of religious study at Azusa Pacific College, I took many bible classes—an entire course about the book of Romans, another very useful class about Hebrew wisdom literature, and so on—but I was offered only one course in Christian apologetics. It was called "Christian Evidences" and I found it to be the least useful of all my studies. Not that it was a bad class, but it seemed so unnecessary. It provided an answer to a question

46. Barker, *godless*, 19–20.

nobody was asking. Since I preferred evangelism to academics, I found the information mildly interesting and somewhat confirming (though my faith did not need such confirmation), and mainly irrelevant. The class did not delve deeply into the ancient documents. We recited the roster of early historians and read some of the church fathers, and then promptly forgot them all.[47]

With this admission of his attitude toward his studies, there is a high probability that Barker is not being deceitful when he misrepresents the Christian view of faith, and he simply has never heard of it (or maybe he forgot).[48]

This would make sense, too, given the definition of "faith" that Barker presents throughout *godless*. As mentioned, he repeatedly expresses his opinion that faith is believing in something without evidence or believing in something although there exists evidence to the contrary. It seems like this is more a definition of "faith" as he experienced it rather than a definition of "faith" that he learned from his teachers. Barker squandered his chance to gain a deep understanding of Christianity, encountered some objections to Christianity, and then, for some reason, put much more effort into learning about atheism than he ever did Christianity.

Aquinas's understanding of faith shows how Barker was able to give up Christianity so easily, intellectually speaking. Barker took all the truths of Christianity on faith. He never considered arguments for God's existence or the historical evidences for the life and death of Jesus Christ. Instead, he assented to the truth of these beliefs on the authority of his pastors and teachers. Once he found some considerations that shed doubt on his faith, he turned to those he trusted for answers, but he found that the people whose authority he had accepted did not have the answers he was seeking. Without any authority, Barker's faith was shattered.

All of this shows that Barker is rejecting a view of faith and reason that is foreign to Christianity. Although Barker was a pastor educated at Azusa Pacific College, he fails to realize (or refuses to mention) that there have been many more views of faith and reason held by Christians throughout the history of the church. While Barker is free to reject any view of faith and reason that he wants to reject, his readers need to realize that he is tacitly misrepresenting Christian views of faith and reason.

47. Barker, *godless*, 251.

48. I was surprised that he admitted to not caring about his religious studies in *godless*. The book's title makes it sound like the reader should be surprised or shocked that an "evangelical preacher" could become "one of America's leading atheists." However, I find nothing surprising or shocking with someone who knows nothing of apologetics (i.e., the study of why Christians believe Christianity is true) becoming an atheist.

CONCLUSION

Atheist proselytizers, including Dan Barker, continue to abuse Christian views of faith and reason. They often define "faith" as "believing something without any evidence or with evidence to the contrary." However, such a definition is not how Christians have historically understood faith and its relation to reason. While some Christians have emphasized faith over reason (fideists), many Christians have viewed faith and reason as compatible.

Thomas Aquinas explains in his writings a classical Christian view of the relation between faith and reason. He distinguishes between the acts of faith (assenting to the truth of an uncertain proposition based on some consideration) and reason (simple apprehension, judgment, reasoning) and the objects of faith (God) and reason (all things known through the acts of the mind). Aquinas explains that there are three types of truths: those known through faith alone, those known through faith or reason, and those known through reason alone.

Aquinas's position is a middle ground between fideism and evidentialism. It emphasizes that some truths can only be known through faith. Yet it allows for many truths of Christianity to be known through human reasoning. Knowledge of God can be attained by rigorous philosophy, and it can also be attained by laypeople through faith.

Dan Barker once took all of the truths of Christianity on faith based on the authority of his pastors and teachers. However, once he realized that no one he knew had the answers for which he was searching, he lost the basis for believing in Christianity. Instead of searching for answers, he intellectually embraced atheism instead. Now, he describes faith as he understood it in his ignorance and portrays the Christian view of faith and reason as the same as his under-informed view. Barker rejects faith—but not the faith of classical Christianity.

BIBLIOGRAPHY

Aquinas, Thomas. *Questions I–IX*. Vol. 1, *Truth*. Translated by Robert W. Mulligan. Eugene: Wipf & Stock, 2008.

———. *Summa Contra Gentiles*. Translated by Anton C. Pegis et al. Notre Dame: University of Notre Dame Press, 1975.

———. *Summa Theologica*. First complete American ed. Translated by Fathers of the English Dominican Province. New York: Benziger, 1947.

Barker, Dan. *godless: How an Evangelical Preacher Became One of America's Leading Atheists*. Berkeley: Ulysses, 2008.

Davies, Brian. *Thomas Aquinas's Summa Theologiae: A Guide and Commentary*. New York: Oxford University Press, 2014.

Dawkins, Richard. *The God Delusion*. New York: Mariner, 2008.

Geisler, Norman L. *Christian Apologetics*. 2nd ed. Grand Rapids: Baker Academic, 2013.

Madden, James D. *Mind, Matter, and Nature: A Thomistic Proposal for the Philosophy of Mind*. Washington, DC: The Catholic University of America Press, 2013.

Moreland, J. P., and William Lane Craig. *Philosophical Foundations for a Christian Worldview*. Downers Grove: InterVarsity, 2003.

Plantinga, Alvin. "Reason and Belief in God." In *Faith and Rationality: Reason and Belief in God*, edited by Alvin Plantinga and Nicholas Wolterstorff, 16–93. Notre Dame: University of Notre Dame Press, 1983.

Smith, George H. *Atheism: The Case against God*. New York: Prometheus, 1989.

Stump, Eleonore. *Aquinas*. New York: Routledge, 2003.

Wilkins, Steve, ed. *Faith and Reason: Three Views*. Downers Grove: InterVarsity, 2014.

3

Categorical Kalamities

An Exercise in Understanding an Argument

—Jason B. McCracken

The clause "Everything that begins to exist" sounds artificial. . . . To "exist" (as an object) means to occupy space and time. Things that exist are measurable. . . . To say that God does not exist within space-time is to say that God does not exist.

—Dan Barker[1]

In godless: How an *Evangelical Preacher Became One of America's Leading Atheists*, Dan Barker critiques various philosophical arguments for the existence of God. Many of these critiques, however, betray Barker's lack of understanding concerning the arguments and the vast literature that engages them. Philosophical arguments are built upon categorizing concepts in specific ways in order to make claims about those concepts that support a conclusion. When one rejects the conclusion of an argument without properly understanding the classification, he makes a category mistake. For instance, a visitor to Oxford makes a category mistake when, after having been shown residence halls, libraries, chapels, playing fields, administrative

---

1. Barker, *godless*, 130, 138.

offices, employees, etc., he now asks to see the "University."[2] The visitor places "University" into the wrong conceptual category, thinking it to be another physical location or group of people, when the concept refers to the way these various objects are organized into one federation. Category mistakes are potentially damaging to the uninformed reader because if the logic of the critique is valid, one appears rational in rejecting the conclusion. The problem is that the critique targets the wrong concept, one that the proponent does not use to support his conclusion. These misunderstandings should be cleared up because they cheat everyone from a proper engagement with the argument.

My aim in this chapter is to clear up Barker's misunderstandings in his most sustained case, against the Kalam Cosmological Argument (henceforth called the Kalam), in chapter 8 of his book, so that readers can have a clearer engagement with that argument.[3] The Kalam is an attempt to move the audience from a belief in the beginning of the universe to the existence of God as its Creator. Here is Barker's presentation of the argument:

1. Everything that begins to exist has a cause.

2. The universe began to exist.

3. Therefore, the universe has a cause.[4]

The argument as stated is technically considered the Kalam, but through further conceptual analysis, one can see numerous characteristics the cause of the universe must possess. For example, William Lane Craig and James D. Sinclair add these two additional propositions:

4. If the universe has a cause, then an uncaused, personal Creator of the universe exists, who sans the universe is beginningless, changeless, immaterial, timeless, spaceless, and enormously powerful.

5. Therefore, an uncaused, personal Creator of the universe exists, who sans the universe is beginningless, changeless, immaterial, timeless, spaceless, and enormously powerful.[5]

---

2. This is the textbook example, raised by Ryle, *Concept of Mind*, 16. Ryle coined the term "category mistake" in this work, which is a critique of Descartes's mind-body dualism.

3. A comprehensive defense of the Kalam against all critiques offered by detractors is beyond the scope of this chapter, or perhaps any single book. An excellent resource is Craig and Sinclair, "*Kalam* Cosmological Argument."

4. Barker, *godless*, 131.

5. Craig and Sinclair, "*Kalam* Cosmological Argument," 194. Barker's engagement with the Kalam is from Craig's earlier presentation in Craig, *Reasonable Faith*, which was updated in 2008. Craig and Sinclair, "*Kalam* Cosmological Argument," includes

These characteristics, theists argue, fit a core of the traditional concept of God. In chapter 8 of *godless*, Barker critiques various aspects of this argument, but his major concerns result from category mistakes. Through these misunderstandings, Barker rejects a God that the theist does not believe exists either, while giving Barker (and his readers) the impression that he is rationally rejecting the traditional view of God. Let us now trace the Kalam, meeting Barker's category mistakes along the way.

"EVERYTHING THAT BEGINS TO EXIST HAS A CAUSE"

The first premise of the Kalam implicitly divides reality into two categories, which (following Barker) we can call: (1) BE, or things that begin to exist, and (2) NBE, or things that *do not* begin to exist. It may be helpful to see the relationship between various terms we will be talking about in this chapter mapped out visually, so we will begin that here. This premise conceptually divides reality, or the set of all things, this way:

Barker is suspicious of this division of reality. He believes the theist is artificially imposing a strange language on her audience to beg the question in favor of (1) the universe having a cause and, more importantly, (2) God's existence.[6] He argues that the theist uses NBE as a synonym for God. If

---

scientific additions from Sinclair, but in all three, the basic reasoning is the same.

6. Barker also sees this language as an attempt to get around earlier failed cosmological arguments that used the premise "everything that exists is caused." He connects this supposedly earlier form of the premise with the "unmoved first mover," which was Aristotle's terminology. I am not sure where he thinks Aristotle, or any other historic philosopher for that matter, uses the supposedly earlier premise. Aristotle spoke of things that are in motion (i.e., things that change) needing a cause for their motion, but "everything that is in motion" is a different concept than "everything that exists" because some thing(s) could be changeless. Aristotle's discussion of the unmoved mover is found in *Physics, VIII* and *Metaphysics, XII*, older English translations of which can be found online at http://classics.mit.edu/Aristotle/physics.8.viii.html and http://classics.mit.edu/Aristotle/metaphysics.12.xii.html, with numerous newer translations in print as well. This historical inaccuracy on Barker's part unfairly casts theists in a negative light (suggesting that theists have moved the goal post after a failed argument to try to save an irrational belief) before even hearing the argument Barker wants his reader to engage with. Even if Barker's historical claim were true, his critique would be guilty of committing the genetic fallacy. An argument must be assessed on its own logical merit, not on how the proponent came to form the current argument.

NBE were a synonym for God, then the theist's argument would be equivalent to:

1'. Everything except God has a cause.

2'. The universe is not God.

3. Therefore, the universe has a cause.[7]

The Kalam is supposedly an attempt to answer the question of whether the universe has a cause or not. To state, without further support, that all things that are not God have a cause would clearly beg this question. If this first premise is true, then, by definition, the universe, which is obviously not God for the theist, would need a cause.[8] Further still, when the Kalam proponent later claims that the cause of the universe must be uncaused, God is the only candidate available. Therefore, the theist would also beg the question of God's existence in favor of theism. Barker likens this move to a one-candidate election where the winner is rigged by the number of candidates placed before the electorate.

To avoid begging these questions, Barker states, one's argument needs to have the feature of accommodation. He explains that "the question of accommodation is not whether the set *does not* contain more or less than one item; it's whether it *cannot* contain other than one."[9] An incumbent dictator rigs the election because only one person could have become the elected president, not because there will only be one president. This effectively makes the incumbent dictator and the future president synonyms. If there are two or more candidates placed on the ballot, then, even though there would only be one president, the feature of accommodation is present because the "set of presidents" could have contained other than the person who ended up as president. For the Kalam to avoid rigging the question of God's existence, NBE cannot come into the argument as a synonym for God. If NBE is not a synonym for God, then Barker's critique fails.

Here we meet Barker's first category mistake: the theist does not use NBE as a synonym for God.[10] Barker implies that the theist conceives of reality like this:

7. Barker, *godless*, 132.

8. A pantheist would say that God is the universe, but pantheists do not typically argue for the Kalam.

9. Barker, *godless*, 132 (emphasis in original).

10. Barker pushes this critique of theists but later in the chapter states that Craig may not be guilty of using NBE as a synonym of God. Barker writes: "But perhaps there could be something outside the natural universe that would be accommodated by NBE, besides God. (Craig seems to allow this ontological possibility when he 'infers'

This incorrectly places NBE and God on the same logical level. Numerous members of NBE are littered throughout the history of human thought. Various conceptions of gods may be the first beginningless options that come to mind, but they are not the only candidates. Plato taught an eternal world of forms and many scientists have asserted the eternal nature of the energy of our spatio-temporal universe, for example. This background is implicit within the first premise of the Kalam. This updates our categorization:

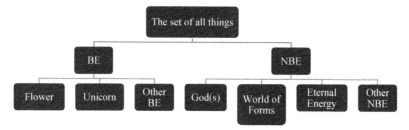

NBE is at the second logical level here, while God is at the third level alongside other members of NBE. God is clearly not a synonym for NBE in this schema. According to Barker's reasoning above, NBE is accommodating, and the theist does not beg the question of God's existence. Barker is unwarranted, then, in asserting that the theist's premise is equivalent to "everything except God has a cause," and his critique fails.

Barker also mistakenly assumes that the first premise of the Kalam asserts a claim about the objective existence of NBE. It does not. The theist's use of the phrase "everything that begins to exist" necessitates no position on the existence of any member of BE or NBE. From the figure above, both flowers and unicorns are members of BE. Most people agree that flowers exist, while unicorns do not. We are talking about *objective*, or mind-independent, existence here. Unicorns exist as concepts but do not exist outside of human minds. But, within their make-believe worlds, unicorns are (traditionally) not eternal beings. One's membership in BE is a separate question from its objective existence. The same goes with members of NBE. So, we see that the BE/NBE division is a valid conceptual distinction to

that the external cause of the universe is an 'agent causation,' implying that it might be otherwise" (Barker, *godless*, 133).

make concerning reality. In doing so, these initial categories do not beg the question either in favor of, or against, theism.

The first premise goes beyond mere phrases, however, to make a specific claim about reality. But, when it does so, it talks about BE, not NBE. The theist takes for granted that some BE do exist, and most detractors, including Barker, readily agree. The further claim of this first premise is that all BE have a cause for their existence. One could disagree with this claim, and some do, but Barker does not in the chapter we are concerned with. That discussion is for another day. Our next task is to clarify the second premise of the Kalam.

"THE UNIVERSE BEGAN TO EXIST"

While the first premise makes a general claim about things that begin to exist, this second premise claims that a specific thing, termed the "universe," is a member of BE.[11] This would update our previous conceptualization to:

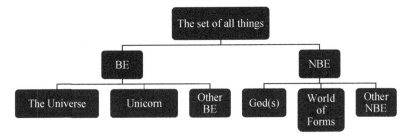

The universe is at the third logical level, underneath the larger category of BE, which is itself one member (along with NBE) of the top logical level, "the set of all things" or reality. Barker argues that the implication of the universe existing within a larger category, alongside other possible things, begs the question in favor of supernaturalism over naturalism. If there is something outside of the natural universe, by definition, it would have to be supernatural. Barker also asserts that this contradicts the way scientists and philosophers normally define "universe." He writes that "'the 'universe' to philosophers (or 'the cosmos,' to cosmologists), is the set of all things."[12]

This understanding of "universe" is Barker's second category mistake. Part of Barker's error mirrors the last section. He fails to distinguish a conceptualization from a claim about objective existence. Our categorizations

11. With this claim, "eternal energy" would need to be removed from underneath NBE in our classification since energy is included in the idea of the natural universe.

12. Barker, godless, 140.

above, remember, do not necessitate the objective existence of each item listed. Noting that there are conceptions of things that would be external to our universe does not mean one is assuming those conceptions objectively exist. To conceptually divide reality into the natural and the supernatural does not mean the supernatural exists. One divides reality conceptually in this way to purposefully avoid begging the question of objective existence either for or against supernaturalism.

Looking closer at the term 'universe,' one can see it is Barker's definition that begs the question in favor of *naturalism*.[13] This may be missed if we look at the direct definition he gives, which we already noted as "the set of all things." This definition could classify reality in the following way:

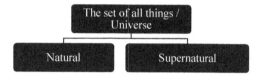

This classification would allow for the existence of the supernatural within the universe. But this is not what Barker means. Barker has in mind the physical, or natural, world alone, just like most people would, when speaking of the universe. One's definition must accurately portray one's usage. Adding this element to his stated definition, the "natural universe," for Barker, becomes identical to the set of all things, which he places at the top logical level.

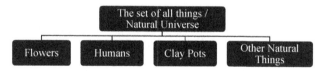

For Barker, the natural universe and the set of all things are synonyms. This should raise a red flag, given the previous critique where Barker (wrongly) faulted theists for using NBE as a synonym for God. This keeps the set of all things (i.e., reality) from having the feature of accommodation because only natural objects can be members of it. This is not a question of accommodation being met by the fact that there would be multiple natural objects. The truth of naturalism is rigged because the set of all things can (by Barker's definition) only accommodate natural objects. It would be impossible for any other kind of object to exist. But whether any other kind of

13. Here "naturalism" (used in a simplified way) means something like "the claim that only natural things objectively exist." Thus, reality would be exhausted by physical material and contain nothing supernatural in it.

object can exist is the very question being asked. Barker's definition, not any argument, rules out any nonnatural kind of object. Thus, his definition of "universe" would be guilty of begging the question in favor of naturalism.

We need to separate Barker's use of "universe" to refer to the natural world from his naturalistic addition. An initial thought is to define "universe" as something like "the set of all *natural* things." I am not sure this fully captures the intent of the Kalam, however. There may still be a danger of thinking the theist commits the fallacy of composition, as Barker also claims. The fallacy of composition arises when one infers that something is true of the whole from the fact that it is true of parts of that whole. For instance, inferring that water is not wet because neither hydrogen nor oxygen are wet on their own commits a fallacy of composition. Barker claims the Kalam infers a truth of the whole (i.e., the universe began to exist) from truths about parts of that whole (i.e., items within the universe begin to exist). Therefore, the theist is guilty of the fallacy of composition.

The problem for Barker is that the Kalam does not make this kind of inference.[14] Craig and others do not argue that the universe must have had a beginning because all natural things (such as flowers, bees, humans, etc.) have beginnings. Theists offer numerous scientific and philosophical arguments that argue for the beginning of matter itself. When one says that the universe began to exist, one is more specifically referring to the matter that everything in the natural universe is comprised of. To say the universe began to exist is to say that spatio-temporal matter itself began to exist.

This meaning of "universe" avoids begging the question in favor of, or against, supernaturalism, categorizing reality in the following way:

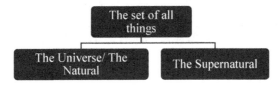

Here "universe" is a synonym for the matter of the natural world, rather than "the set of all things." The supernatural remains a conceptual category, without assuming any supernatural thing objectively exists. Or, if we want to return to the BE/NBE division:

---

14. Not all part-to-whole inferences are invalid. For example, if a brick wall is made up of individual red bricks, then the whole wall will necessarily be red.

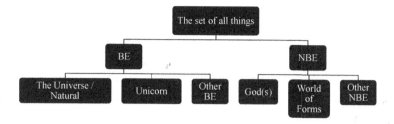

Let us take stock of where we are at. In the first premise, the Kalam conceptually divides reality into BE and NBE but only asserts that members of BE have a cause for their existence, saying nothing about NBE objectively existing. In the second premise, the Kalam claims that the material universe is a member of BE, saying nothing about the supernatural objectively existing. Theists support this second premise with multiple scientific and philosophical arguments, which could be critiqued, but Barker does not do it here. If these premises are true, then it logically follows that the universe has a cause for its existence. The next question becomes what this cause is like, if we can know anything about it.

WHAT WE CAN KNOW ABOUT THE CAUSE OF THE UNIVERSE

Theists assert that there are numerous things we can know about the cause of the universe. Three of these characteristics are important for our purposes: that the cause of the universe is supernatural, a member of NBE, and personal. These are not assumptions (like we have seen Barker claim, concerning the first two features) but conclusions of supported reasoning from theists. First, the cause of the universe is supernatural. With the truth of the first two premises, we have now reached the conclusion that the matter of the universe has a cause. That cause cannot itself be material because self-causation is impossible. To be self-causing, an object would have to exist prior to its own existence, which is nonsense. The cause must exist outside of the material universe, then. Since the material universe is synonymous with what we call the "natural," this cause must be outside of nature. That which exists outside of nature, by definition, is supernatural.

Second, the cause of the universe is a member of NBE. The cause of the universe must be uncaused because an infinite regress of causes is impossible. One could claim that the direct cause of the universe was itself caused by something else and that such a cause was itself caused by something further still, but the point is that the causal chain must terminate somewhere, which it can only do in an uncaused cause. This ultimate cause, no matter how many intermediate causes exist between it and the beginning of the universe, is what the Kalam is after.[15] If the cause is uncaused, it must also be beginningless, or a member of NBE. If things that begin to exist have a cause (as the first premise claims), then it is also true to say that things which are uncaused are beginningless. This is what is known as contraposition.[16] So, contra Barker, theists do not beg the objective existence of the supernatural or NBE through the first premise but logically conclude these two features as a result of the Kalam.

Third, the cause of the universe is personal. Here is where Barker commits a third category mistake. If Barker's critique were correct and the cause of the universe could be impersonal, then one would be rational to reject the theistic conclusion of the Kalam. Unfortunately, for Barker's case, he understands "personal" and "complexity" to be intricately linked, even synonyms of a sort. He writes that the argument for a personal cause rests on the idea that "a creator must be at least as complex as the thing it created."[17] Since the natural universe contains free personal agents (such as humans), the cause of the universe must be at least as intellectually complex as those personal agents. An impersonal cause is not complex enough. Barker then counters this principle with various examples of less complex causes resulting in more complex effects, such as humans building IBM's Deep Blue computer, which beat the world champion Garry Kasparov in a game of chess. In doing so, Barker believes he has refuted the theist's claim.

The problem for Barker is that the proponent of the Kalam does not use this principle in support of the Kalam. In the work Barker mainly engages with, Craig uses the principle that only an eternal cause (as the cause of the universe is) that is personal could have a temporal effect (as the universe is). A personal agent that is eternal can have a temporal effect. For example, a man who was sitting from eternity (an eternal cause) could choose to stand up (a temporal effect). But why could something eternal and impersonal not cause a *temporal* effect, as well? To help see the answer, Craig invites us to think about water freezing. To simplify matters,

15. Ockham's Razor leads us to not posit causes beyond necessity, so until further evidence arises, necessitating prior caused causes of our universe, one should favor an immediate first cause of the universe, but either way the point remains.

16. Contraposition is the logically valid conversion of a proposition to its contrapositive. In other words, it is logically valid to convert a phrase "all (A) is (B)" into the statement "all (not-B) is (not-A)." For instance, since it is true that "all (cats) are (mammals)," it is also true that "all (non-mammals) are (not cats)." In the Kalam, we can convert "all (things that begin to exist, or BE) are (caused things)" into the statement "all (uncaused things) are (things that do not begin to exist, or NBE)."

17. Barker, *godless*, 134.

let us say the cause of water freezing is a temperature of thirty-two degrees Fahrenheit. This temperature is an impersonal cause. If the temperature has always been thirty-two degrees Fahrenheit, then any water present would also have always been frozen. The effect, frozen water, would be as eternal as the cause.[18] All impersonal causes that are eternal will have eternal effects. Since the universe is not eternal, it cannot be the effect of an impersonal, eternal cause. Only a personal agent can be the cause of the universe. Barker ignores this reasoning completely.[19]

In writings since Barker's *godless*, Craig offers two more lines of support, within the Kalam, for the cause of the universe being personal.[20] One, following Richard Swinburne, Craig notes there are two types of causal explanation: scientific (i.e., laws and initial conditions) and personal (agents and their volitions). The first state of the universe could not have a scientific explanation because there would be no laws and no initial conditions for the laws to work on, since such features would themselves constitute a state of the universe. We would then have a state of the universe prior to the first state of the universe, which is nonsense. This leaves only a personal explanation for the universe, which does not run into the same kind of self-defeating incoherence. Two, the personhood of the cause is suggested by the other characteristics that can be separately argued for, such as the cause being immaterial, beginningless, uncaused, timeless, and spaceless. Unembodied minds and abstract objects are the only two candidates that fit this group of characteristics. Abstract objects do not have causal power. That leaves only an unembodied, personal mind as the remaining candidate, and it does not run into similar incoherencies.

It may now help to introduce another visual that takes our discussion into account. This one will include the idea of objective existence. So,

18. If the temperature has not always been thirty-two degrees Fahrenheit, but reached this temperature at some point, then the effect (frozen water) would have begun to exist at some point. Of course, this would now mean that the cause is not eternal. If the cause is not eternal, then this is no longer analogical to the cause of the universe, which is eternal.

19. Instead, Barker addresses what Craig offers as additional "powerful scientific confirmation from the observed fine-tuning of the universe, which bespeaks intelligent design" (Craig, *Reasonable Faith*, 118). Craig delves deeper into the fine-tuning of the universe in Craig, "Teleological Argument and the Anthropic Principle," 127–53. In *The Blackwell Companion*, the fine-tuning of the universe gets its own chapter, written by Robin Collins. Unfortunately, Barker's critique completely misunderstands Craig's argument there as well. Craig's fine-tuning argument concerns the cause having specific purposes in mind and the ability to accomplish those purposes. Only personal agents are capable of such a thing. But even if the fine-tuning argument is unsound, one must deal with the arguments offered in the Kalam.

20. Craig and Sinclair, "*Kalam* Cosmological Argument," 192–93.

instead of "the set of all things," which leaves open the question of objective existence, we can talk about the "set of all things that objectively exist." If our discussion is sound so far, then we would have:

Because of the Kalam, one is warranted to believe that the supernatural objectively exists, that NBE has at least one objectively existing member, and that the cause of the universe is personal. We focused on just these three features, because those are what Barker's critiques touch upon, and to include the other characteristics (uncaused, beginningless, changeless, immaterial, timeless, spaceless, and enormously powerful) would make the visual too cumbersome.

What I want to note is that once these characteristics are compiled, we discover that it describes the core of the traditional view of God. This list (rather than NBE as Barker thinks) is the synonym for God in proponents' eyes. No other candidate seems viable. The Kalam eliminates caused candidates, impersonal candidates (such as Plato's Forms or eternal energy), candidates that are BE, candidates that change prior to the universe, material candidates (such as the Mormon view of God), temporal candidates, spatial candidates, and weak candidates from being the cause of the universe. The only plausible candidate left appears to be the God of traditional theism. So, we could update our latest classification to the following:

Barker seemingly has two kinds of defenses against the Kalam's conclusion here. One, he could suggest other candidates that also make it through the same eliminations or, two, show that the theist's God is logically contradictory in some way. Barker takes the second approach. He thinks that the Kalam itself provides us with a reason to reject the traditional God as the cause of the universe. To see this, we must return to the philosophical reasoning offered in support of premise (2). The argument Barker addresses is usually called the "argument from the impossibility of an actual infinite." The theist argues that an actual infinite cannot exist. She then contends that the temporal history of a beginningless universe would be an actual infinite. Since this could not be the case, the temporal history of our universe must have a beginning. One could go into further detail, of course, but Barker assumes the argument is sound for the sake of his critique, so we need not.

The problem, as Barker sees it, is that the theist who asserts this is shooting herself in the foot. The theists, at least most who argue for the Kalam's soundness, consider God to be infinite. Barker writes that "if an actual infinity cannot be a part of reality, then God, if he is actually infinite, cannot exist."[21] The support for a non-infinite universe would appear to be an argument against an infinite God as well. Either God does not exist, or if he does, he could not be beginningless. At best this would move God from being a member of NBE to a member of BE:

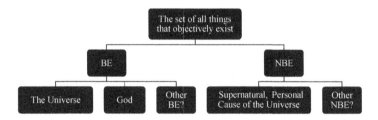

If God were a member of BE, then two things would follow that proponents of the Kalam would not want to affirm. One, if the cause of the universe is a member of NBE (as the Kalam later posits), then God could not be the cause of the universe since he is a member of BE. Two, according to the first premise of the Kalam, God, as a member of BE, would need a cause of his existence, and, therefore, would not be the sovereign being his followers believe him to be.

Barker's reasoning is logically valid, but it misses the mark because of a fourth category mistake. For theists, "a system is said to be infinite if a part of that system can be put into a one-to-one correspondence with the whole."[22] The set of whole numbers is an actual infinite because part of that system (for instance, the set of even numbers) can be put into a one-to-one correspondence with the whole. The zero from the set of whole numbers, which we can call $W(0)$, corresponds to the zero from the set of even numbers, which we can call $E(0)$. Going further, $W(1)$ corresponds to $E(2)$, $W(2)$

21. Barker, *godless*, 135.

22. Craig and Sinclair, "*Kalam* Cosmological Argument," 103–4. They use Richard Dedekind's definition from Dedekind, *Essays*, 63.

corresponds to E(4), ... W(1,000,000) corresponds to E(2,000,000), and so on, without end. A finite set cannot do this; one is going to run out of numbers to pair up. The set of whole numbers from zero to four, for example, does not have a one-to-one correspondence with its subset that contains the odd numbers between zero and four. Here we would have X(0) correspond with Y(1), and X(1) would correspond with Y(3), but nothing would correspond with X(2) or X(3) or X(4). This set is not an actual infinite. Another way to look at it is that the mathematical actual infinite involves an infinite number of discrete segments or parts. This is like the individual numbers one would say while starting to count to infinity. One would move from one discrete segment (one) to the next (two, three, four, and so on). When talking about the temporal history of the universe being beginningless, we would be talking about an infinite number of discrete segments, one moment followed by another, stretching back eternally. An "actual infinite" is a technical mathematical term. According to the Kalam, such an actual infinite cannot exist.

On the other hand, when calling God infinite, the theist does not mean God contains an infinite number of discrete parts. There are more ways for something to be infinite than the actual infinity considered by the Kalam. I will not try to adjudicate between the competing formulations of what divine infinity exactly means. For our purposes, the main point is that God's infinity is a quality rather than a quantity. "Divine infinity" is a term referring to certain superlative characteristics, being unlimited in power and knowledge, or something close to this. Barker thinks (or acts as though) there is only one kind of infinity. Therefore, he places an infinite God in the wrong category. The reasoning within the Kalam only applies to the impossibility of a mathematical infinity existing in objective reality. Since God's infinity is not a mathematical infinity, the reasoning of the Kalam does not disprove God's objective existence or lead to God necessarily having a beginning.

Barker directly addresses this point in his book, wondering why the Kalam only applies to mathematical infinities within the physical universe. He writes that if theists are saying "the transcendent, timeless domain of the creator is an entirely different kind of 'infinity' that is not subject to the same laws, then they are begging the question."[23] This still treats infinities as one identical concept applied to different domains, however. The difference is not about a supernatural domain versus a natural one. The real issue is that there are two different kinds of infinity: a mathematical infinity and divine infinity. A mathematical infinity objectively existing is said to be

23. Barker, *godless*, 136.

impossible because it involves infinite discrete segments, not because it is not supernatural.

Barker also points out a possible dilemma for the theist. Either God is an actual infinite (which the Kalam argues cannot exist), or God began to exist. We have seen that the theist does not think God is an actual infinite, but why would the alternative involve God beginning to exist? Barker talks about the "series of antecedent causal events [that] must exist in the mind of a time-transcendent creator, if such a being exists."[24] This concerns God's decision to create the universe. God's free choice to create a temporal universe is followed by God's act of creating that universe. By "followed by," we mean that the act of creation *logically* follows the decision to create; the decision process is timeless.[25] Both members of this causal series occur in the "same" timeless "moment." Barker claims this non-temporal logical series would show that God began to exist with that initial decision to create.

This conclusion does not follow. There is nothing incoherent in a beginningless, timeless being having a decision to create something and, in the same timeless moment, creating that object. This is what is required of a timeless existence, if it is possible, and Barker assumes such an existence is logically possible for the sake of his critique. Now, if the timeless being changed his mind about the decision, then he could be said to be temporal, but theists do not believe this accurately describes God. Proponents of the Kalam usually believe God existed changelessly and, from eternity, freely willed to create a temporal universe. God's decision to create only logically precedes God's act of creation. This series has a beginning point, but this does not mean that the one thinking this logical series began to exist at any point.

Craig's analogy of the eternally standing man that wants to, and accomplishes, sitting down may help us again.[26] Imagine that this man has always freely willed to sit, never having changed his mind on the matter. This decision to sit is logically, but not temporally, followed by the man sitting. Yet, when the man sits, a change has occurred. We might say that he

---

24. Barker, *godless*, 137.

25. Barker is uncertain what it would mean for God to be outside of time, but he does grant the possibility that our human imagination is just too weak to grasp this concept. Barker could, of course, fall back to this belief if this current critique fails. I do not think he is correct in that assessment, but to spend time in support of the coherence of a timeless God would take us too long here.

26. Even if such a thing were illogical for some reason (that a man, by definition, is temporal or some other factor), this does not damage the analogical point being made. Barker is assuming that a timeless being can exist. Assuming this kind of man to be logical, we are interested in what we might learn about the relationship between an eternal being and the logic of its decision making.

has become a temporal being, but he was timeless "prior" to that. The man does not only begin to exist once he sits down, he existed logically prior to sitting. "Before" he sat, he made the choice to change his position from sitting to standing. We can say there is a logical "beginning" to the decision process, located in the man's free agency to want to sit and terminating in his execution of the desired action. Therefore, we have a man who is temporally beginningless, yet whose decision process has a logical beginning. In the same way, God's decision process to create the universe could have a logical beginning, located in God's free agency to create a temporal world, without making God a member of BE. Therefore, Barker's latest critique fails. The philosophical support for the second premise, in arguing against the existence of actual infinites, does not argue against the existence of an infinite God.

CONCLUSION

Barker summarizes his objections at the end of his chapter by asking three groups of questions and saying that without good answers to these questions, one ought to reject the Kalam Cosmological Argument. Here are his questions:

1. Is God the only object accommodated by the set of things that do not begin to exist? If yes, then why is the cosmological argument not begging the question? If no, then what are the other candidates for the cause of the universe and how have they been eliminated?

2. Does the logic of Kalam apply only to temporal antecedents in the real world? If yes, this assumes the existence of nontemporal antecedents in the real world, so why is this not begging the question? If no, then why doesn't the impossibility of an actual infinity disprove the existence of an actually infinite God?

3. Is the universe (cosmos) a member of itself? If not, then how can its "beginning" be compared with other beginnings?[27]

Let me now respond to these questions for my summary. One, we have seen that NBE accommodates for more than just God in the phrasing of its first premise. Therefore, the Kalam does not beg the question. In fact, the existence of at least one NBE (the cause of the universe) is a conclusion that results from the truth of the Kalam. From this conclusion, we also see why other (specific and general) candidates for the cause of the universe

27. Barker, *godless*, 143–44.

have been eliminated. Two, we saw that the theist does not partake in special pleading for an infinite God to avoid the Kalam's argument against the existence of actual infinites. There are more ways for a being to be infinite than the actual infinity considered by the Kalam; God is said to be infinite qualitatively, not quantitatively. Three, the Kalam does not treat the universe as a "member of itself" and commit the fallacy of composition, begging supernaturalism along the way. The objective existence of the supernatural is a conclusion of the Kalam, which also provides multiple supports for the beginning of the material universe. Barker's questions arise out of an analysis full of category mistakes, resulting in the rejection of a straw God. Hopefully, I have cleared up Barker's misunderstandings to allow the reader a chance to more accurately engage the Kalam and the God it shows to exist.

BIBLIOGRAPHY

Barker, Dan. *godless: How an Evangelical Preacher Became one of America's Leading Atheists*. Berkeley: Ulysses, 2008.

Craig, William Lane. *Reasonable Faith: Christian Truth and Apologetics*. Wheaton: Crossway, 2008.

———. "The Teleological Argument and the Anthropic Principle." In *The Logic of Rational Theism*, edited by William Lane Craig and Mark S. McLeod, 127–53. Lewiston: Edwin Mellen, 1990.

Craig, William Lane, and James D. Sinclair. "The *Kalam* Cosmological Argument." In *The Blackwell Companion to Natural Theology*, edited by William Lane Craig and J. P. Moreland, 101–201. Malden: Blackwell, 2009.

Dedekind, Richard, ed. *Essays on the Theory of Numbers*. Translated by W. W. Beman. New York: Dover, 1963.

Ryle, Gilbert. *Concept of Mind*. New York: Barnes and Noble, 1949.

4

A Thomistic Argument
for God's Existence

—Richard G. Howe

The old cosmological argument claimed that since everything has a cause, there must be a first cause, an "unmoved first mover." Today no theistic philosophers defend that primitive line because if *everything* needs a cause, so does God.

—Dan Barker[1]

Atheist Dan Barker is a well-known figure in the debate circuit. I had the opportunity to debate him in 1997 at the University of Florida. It was my first public, semi-formal debate on the question of God's existence. Since that debate, my interests and studies in Thomistic philosophy have given me deep appreciation of how Thomas Aquinas defends the existence of God. Over the years, I began to notice that such classical arguments (as they are sometimes collectively called) are rarely employed by Evangelicals in their debates with atheists.[2] Because of the dearth of such arguments, it is perhaps

---

1. Barker, *godless*, 130.

2. The qualifier "classical" is meant to highlight two things. First, more technically, it is a reference to the fact that this understanding of God follows the contours of the metaphysical categories of Plato, Aristotle, and certain others from the Classical Era. These categories are philosophical. As such, they are complemented by additional

no mystery that many atheists show little, if any, acquaintance with these arguments. This is certainly true of Dan Barker.

I had the opportunity to debate Dan Barker on the existence of God at Southern Evangelical Seminary's 2017 National Conference on Christian Apologetics. In my preparation for the debate, I pored over not only recordings of other debates in which Dan Barker had participated, but also his definitive book *godless: How an Evangelical Preacher Became One of America's Leading Atheists*. One thing one should notice (particularly in the book) is Barker's not-too-uncommon reference to philosophy. He characterizes his arguments for unbelief as philosophical.[3] He accuses Dinesh D'Souza of having a weaker understanding of philosophy than D'Souza's own "shallow" knowledge of the Bible,[4] suggesting to me that Barker considers himself knowledgeable enough of and having sufficient understanding of philosophy to judge another person on such matters.

These factors (my growing affinity with Aquinas's argument together with Barker's pretense in his book of sufficient philosophical knowledge and understanding) motivated me to take a different tact in my 2017 debate with Barker than I had taken in the 1997 debate. In the earlier debate, I utilized the theistic arguments with which I was more familiar, particularly the Kalam Cosmological Argument, on which I had written my master's thesis several years earlier. In my 2017 debate, I decided to use one of Aquinas's arguments. I wanted to expose the fact that Barker has neither a knowledge of nor understanding of philosophy relevant to the question of God's existence. Indeed, Barker seems to be almost entirely unaware of the standard classical arguments.[5] While he does discuss Anselm's ontological argument in his book, it was evident during our debate that he completely missed the argument I gave that night in as much as he characterized my argument (in one of the few times he actually tried to respond to my argument in any of his rebuttals) as the ontological argument. As I hope the reader will see in this chapter, my argument here (which is the one I gave that night) is not at all the ontological argument but is, instead, one of the

---

categories arising from revealed truth (Special Revelation). Second, "classical" is more or less a synonym for "traditional" meaning that this picture of what God is like is one that has come down to us from the bulk of church history.

3. Barker, *godless*, xiv.

4. Barker, *godless*, 82.

5. Despite the fact that Barker tried to write a book on the existence of God, his index lists nothing about Plato, Aristotle, Plotinus, Pseudo-Dionysius, Avicenna, Maimonides, Thomas Aquinas, John Duns Scotus, René Descartes, or Gottfried Leibniz—some of the most important voices throughout history who have contributed to this discussion.

most sophisticated metaphysical cosmological arguments I have ever encountered. It is an argument from Aquinas based upon his metaphysical doctrine of the distinction between essence and existence.

UNDERSTANDING AQUINAS ON EXISTENCE AND THE ESSENCE/EXISTENCE DISTINCTION

Aquinas's doctrine of existence, together with his doctrine of the distinction of essence and existence, serve as the most radical break he has with Aristotle. I mention Aquinas's accounting of these doctrines vis-à-vis Aristotle mainly because of the great extent to which the philosophy of Aquinas otherwise tracks the philosophy of Aristotle. These doctrines of existence and the distinction of essence and existence (but not necessarily these doctrines alone) constitute a metaphysical innovation whose significance is virtually inestimable. They are what enable Aquinas to turn the pagan philosophy of Aristotle into the Christian philosophy that Thomism is, particularly regarding the existence and attributes of God and the doctrine of creation.[6]

It should be noted that Aquinas's accounting of these doctrines is not without its antecedent inspirations. Indeed, both the discussion of existence and the discussion of the distinction between essence and existence (including whether there is any distinction and, if so, what might be the nature of that distinction) were topics of philosophical interest to some going back to *Liber de Causis* (*The Book of Causes*), an anonymous work at one time wrongly attributed to Aristotle, the contents of which is largely taken from Proclus's (412–85) *Elements of Theology*; to the works of Pseudo-Dionysius (late 400s–early 500s), especially his *On the Divine Names*, which is referenced frequently by Aquinas in his discussion of God's attributes; and to certain Islamic philosophers including al-Farabi (872–950) and Avicenna (980–1037). Aquinas readily acknowledges such influences, adopting, modifying, or inverting their ideas as seems to him most appropriate to advance his own views.

Much ink has been spilled in exploring these influences and the influences of others, looking both at the doctrines as they are found in these various sources and looking at the degree of influence these had on Aquinas's views (both by example and counterexample). It is not my purpose here to explore these influences in any appreciable degree nor to referee specific controversies surrounding such exploration. I shall proceed with the tacit acknowledgement that there are these influences, thus avoiding

---

6. I will not be dealing with the doctrine of creation in this chapter beyond my comment in footnote 13.

the charge of overstating (in some people's estimation) Aquinas's originality regarding his own views about these matters. At the same time, however, I am (so far) of the opinion that the crux of Aquinas's accounting of existence and the essence/existence distinction does constitute an innovation whose philosophical significance and subsequent influence is profound. To my knowledge, none of these predecessors pressed their own accounting of existence and/or the essence/existence distinction into the service of their overall philosophy to the extent that Aquinas did for his.

Aquinas lays out his understanding of existence and the essence/existence distinction in works such as *De ente et essentia* (*De Ente*), *Quaestiones disputatae de veritate* (*De Veritate*), *Quaestiones disputatae de potentia* (*De Potentia*), and the *Summa Theologiae* (*ST*).[7] I should first like to state very directly what the essence/existence distinction is. I shall then, by way of re-hearsing a few basics in Aristotle's metaphysics that Aquinas takes up as his own (with some slight modifications in certain places), set the philosophical background. Afterwards, I will explore more in-depth the essence/existence distinction and then visit specifically Aquinas's notion of existence. All of this is to the end of showing how these philosophical notions figure into Aquinas's argument for God's existence and attributes.

THE ESSENCE/EXISTENCE DISTINCTION STATED

The essence/existence distinction maintains that there is a real distinction in a created thing between its essence and its existence. A thing's essence is *what* it is. Its existence is *that* it is. To illustrate, consider yourself as a human being: your essence is what makes you a human; your existence is what makes you a being. That essence and existence are distinct in sensible objects (i.e., objects that are evident to the senses) is evident from the fact that one can understand the essence of a thing without knowing whether it exists. Aquinas argues in *De Ente*, "Now, every essence . . . can be understood without knowing anything about its being. I can know, for instance, what a man or a phoenix is and still be ignorant whether it has being in reality. From this it is clear that being is other than essence . . . unless perhaps there is a reality who quiddity [i.e., essence] is its being."[8] The fact that we

7. Unless otherwise noted, all English translations herein are from these sources: Aquinas, *On Being and Essence*; Aquinas, *Truth*; Aquinas, *On the Power of God*; Aquinas, *St. Thomas Aquinas Summa Theologica*.

8. Aquinas, *De Ente*, c. 4. Elsewhere Aquinas argues, "Everything that is in the genus of substance is composite with a real composition, because whatever is in the category of substance is subsistent in its own existence, and its own act of existing must be distinct from the thing itself; otherwise it could not be distinct in existence from the

can know that something exists without knowing what it is, and that we can know what something is without knowing that it exists, suggests that, at some level, there is a distinction between essence and existence. Such a cognitive distinction does not alone establish that the distinction is real and not merely intellectual. But given how Aquinas understands existence itself is sufficient to show that, given this (at least) cognitive distinction, the distinction is real.

PHILOSOPHICAL BACKGROUND

Act and Potency

The Metaphysics of Act and Potency

Aquinas adopts Aristotle's metaphysical categories of act and potency. These categories provide the basis for how Aristotle (and later Aquinas) accounts for change in a sensible object. Definitionally, "act" (or actuality) is "to be real" whereas "potency" (or potentiality) is "the power or capacity to be actual or real." Potencies can be thought of, roughly, as a capacity in a substance or thing. As such, a potency cannot exist on its own, but can only "exist" as a potency that a thing possesses. But here, the term "exists" can be misleading. Potency occupies a sort of middle ground between existing in full reality and not existing at all.

Aristotle utilized act and potency as a means (in principle) of countering the arguments of Parmenides who denied the reality of change and multiplicity.[9] Parmenides did so by arguing that there are only two ways that things can differ: either by their being or by their non-being (an excluded middle). He argued that things cannot differ by their being since "being" is the one thing in respect to which they are the same; which is to say, their both being "beings" is the very way in which they are alike. But they also cannot differ by their non-being since to differ by non-being is just not to differ at all. Thus, Parmenides concluded, things cannot differ at all, and, thus, all things are the same thing, and there is no change.

---

other things with which it agrees in the formal character of its quiddity; for such agreement is required in all things that are directly in a category. Consequently, everything that is directly in the category of substance is composed at least of the act of being and the subject of being" (Aquinas, *De Veritate*, q. 27, a. 1, ad. 8).

9. I am taking a fairly standard interpretation of Parmenides arising from Aristotle in his *Metaph.* III, 4, 1001^{a}32ff that I will here neither defend nor challenge. I am indebted to Frederick Copleston for this understanding of Aristotle vis-à-vis Parmenides. See his *History of Philosophy*, 311.

Aristotle countered that there is a *tertium quid*—a third alternative between being and non-being—viz., that of potentiality or potency.[10] He comments, "So it is possible that a thing may be capable of being and not be, and capable of not being and yet be. . . . For of non-existent things some exist potentially; but they do not exist because they do not exist in complete reality."[11]

Aquinas employs the same notions of act and potency as Aristotle. "By non-existence we understand not simply those things which do not exist, but those which are potential, and not actual."[12] Elsewhere Aquinas says, "Observe that some things can exist though they do not exist, while other things do exist. That which can be is said to exist in potency; that which already exists is said to be in act."[13]

To illustrate act and potency, consider a person who is actually sitting but not actually standing.[14] Such a person, though sitting, nevertheless has

10. This was not the only way that two things could differ.

11. Aristotle, *Metaph.* Θ (IX), 3, $1047^a20, 35-1047^b1$.

12. Aquinas, *ST* I, q. 5, a. 2.

13. Aquinas, *On the Principles of Nature*, 61. He also argues, "Now, from the foregoing it is evident that in created intellectual substances there is composition of act and potentiality. For in whatever thing we find two, one of which is the complement of the other, the proportion of one of them to the other is as the proportion of potentiality to act; for nothing is completed except by its proper act" (Aquinas, *Summa contra Gentiles*, II, c. 53).

In addition to this metaphysical accounting of potency, there is also a logical accounting which refers to those situations where the predicate of a proposition is not opposed to the subject. In this case, Aquinas could say that before God created the world, there was the potential for the world to be, without at the same time committing himself to saying that there was a metaphysical potency that existed before the world existed. He says, "Before the world existed it was possible for the world to be, not, indeed, according to a passive power which is matter, but according to the active power of God; and also, according as a thing is called absolutely possible, not in relation to any power, but from the sole habitude of the terms which are not repugnant to each other; in which sense possible is opposed to impossible, as appears from the Philosopher (*Metaphysics* v, text. 17)" (Aquinas, *ST* I, q. 46, a. 1, ad. 1).

14. Here I am interested in merely illustrating the act/potency distinction without regard to the distinction between a subject's proper accidents and its accidents and without regard to the distinction between active potency and passive potencies. Proper accidents (sometimes called "properties") are those attributes of a thing that arise necessarily out of the nature of a thing but do not enter into the definition of that thing. For example, while rationality is the specific difference within the genus "animal" that defines the species "human," a human's risibility arises from the aspects of the human nature though risibility is not part of the definition of "human." Accidents are those attributes of a thing that do not arise necessarily from the nature of that thing. Thus, it is accidental to a human to live in a certain city. Active potencies are the capacities for a thing to act. A sitting human has the capacity to stand. Passive potencies are capacities for a thing to be acted upon. A pale human has the capacity to be made tan by the sun's rays.

the potential or power or capacity (different English words for the same metaphysical reality) to stand. Upon standing, the person actualizes his potential to stand, his standing becomes actual, and his sitting now becomes potential. In all these instances, the potency to stand while sitting and the potency to sit while standing must be actualized, if they are to be actualized at all, by something that is already in act, viz., the same subject in some other respect. Philosopher Bernard J. Wuellner summarizes, "Howsoever anything acts, it does so inasmuch as it is in act; howsoever anything receives, it does so inasmuch as it is in potency."[15]

To focus in on the fact that such a potential is something real in the person, compare the sitting and standing of the person to a rock. While a man who is actually sitting has the potential to stand, or who is actually standing has the potential to sit, a rock lacks the potency to stand or sit. Note, then, the difference between the nonexisting of the standing in a sitting man and the nonexisting of the standing in the rock. While both are nonexisting, there remains a modicum of reality to the nonexisting of the standing in the sitting man. It "exists" as a potential in the man in a way in which its nonexisting does not in any way exist in the rock.

The Significance of Aquinas's Employment of Act and Potency

One should notice already that such parsing out of things in the categories of act and potency gives rise to a robust accounting of causality.[16] The ability for a potential to be actualized, which is to say, the ability for the standing or sitting to be caused, must be either from the nature of the thing possessing the potency or from something outside the nature of the thing. So far, this is just like Aristotle. Aquinas will argue that sensible things are not able to ultimately account for the actualization of all of their own potentialities. The act/potency of sensible things stands in stark contrast to God's nature of being pure actuality. But act/potency cannot get one beyond the multiple, impersonal gods of Aristotle. It will take Aquinas's accounting of existence and the essence/existence distinction to take us all the way to the God of classical theism.

---

15. Wuellner, *Summary of Scholastic Principles*, 5.

16. Of course, the categories of act and potency are not the only ones relevant to a classical notion of causality. Factoring in the relationship to substance and accidents shows how the classical notion of causality is immune to the Humean critiques of cause. See Knasas, *Being and Some Twentieth-Century Thomists*, 214–21.

Form and Matter

The Metaphysics of Form and Matter

Not surprisingly, Aquinas follows Aristotle in the notions of Form and Matter. "Because the definition telling what a thing is signifies that by which a thing is located in its genus or species, philosophers have substituted the term 'quiddity' for the term 'essence.' The Philosopher [i.e., Aristotle] frequently calls this 'what something was to be' [quod quid erat esse; τὸ τί ἦν εἶναι]; that is to say, that which makes a thing to be what it is. It is also called 'form.'"[17]

The Form of a sensible object is what makes it be the kind of thing that it is. Not surprisingly, the Form is the "formal" cause of a thing. The formal cause does not cause a thing to exist (at least, not for Aquinas), but, more narrowly, it makes a thing to exist *in a certain way*, as, for example, a human or a horse.

Matter is that metaphysical aspect of a sensible object by which the Form is individuated to be this man or this horse. Utilizing the act/potency categories, Form actualizes Matter; Matter is in potency to Form. Matter and Form together constitute the essence of the sensible object. Such a Matter/Form combination (which characterizes all sensible objects) is called hylomorphism—from ὕλη (*hule*), Matter, and μορφή (*morphe*), Form.[18]

The Significance of Aquinas's Employment of Form and Matter

The significance of Aquinas's employment of Form and Matter is that Thomas will argue that sensible things, being composed of Form and Matter, are not ultimately able to account for their own existence and thus will need a First Efficient Cause as their cause. Further, he will unpack the metaphysical attributes of God demonstrating that the particular aspects of the nature of God stand in stark contrast to the Form and Matter aspects of sensible things.

17. Aquinas, *De Ente*, c. 1. Other specific terms can be noted. The "whatness" of a thing with respect to Matter is called Form; with respect to Operations is called Nature; with respect to Accidents is called Substance; with respect to Mind is called Quiddity; and with respect to Existence is called Essence.

18. Aquinas again, "Form and matter are found in composite substances, as for example the soul and body in man" (Aquinas, *De Ente*, c. 2). Further, he says, "It is evident, therefore, that essence embraces both matter and form" (Aquinas, *De Ente*, c. 2).

HISTORICAL BACKGROUND

Aristotle on Existence and the Essence/Existence Distinction

Aristotle's highest category in his metaphysics is Form. To be is to be a Form. This is to say that Aristotle does not have a philosophical category of existence. As such, there can be no philosophical distinction in Aristotle's philosophy between essence and existence. He says, "For 'one man' and 'man' are the same thing, and so are 'existing man' and 'man' and the doubling of the words in 'one man' and 'one existing man' does not express anything different."[19] Charles Kahn observes, "The upshot is that, although we can recognize at least three different kinds of existential questions discussed by Aristotle, Aristotle himself neither distinguishes these questions from one another nor brings them together under any common head or topic which might be set in contrast to other themes in his general discussion of Being."[20] Joseph Owens remarks, "From the viewpoint of the much later distinction between essence and the act of existing, this treatment must mean that Aristotle is leaving the act of existence entirely outside the scope of his philosophy. The act of existing must be wholly escaping his *scientific* consideration. All necessary and definite connections between things can be reduced to essence."[21]

Aristotle is not alone here, for there does not seem to be a distinctive philosophical discussion of existence as such in any Ancient Greek philosophy, and, thus, no notion of an essence/existence distinction among the Ancient Greeks. Charles Kahn again, in his aptly titled article, "Why Existence Does Not Emerge as a Distinct Concept in Greek Philosophy," says,

> In the extended discussion of the concept (or concepts) of Being in Greek philosophy from Parmenides to Aristotle, the theme of existence does not figure as a distinct topic for philosophical reflection. . . . I must make clear that my thesis about the non-emergence of existence as a distinct topic is not intended as a denial of the obvious fact that the Greek philosophers occasionally *discuss* questions of existence. My thesis is rather that the concept of existence is never "thematized": it itself does not become a subject for philosophical reflection.[22]

19. Aristotle, *Metaph.* Γ (4), 2, 1003^{b}26–27.

20. Kahn, "Why Existence Does Not Emerge as a Distinct Concept in Greek Philosophy," 10.

21. Owens, *Doctrine of Being in the Aristotelian Metaphysics*, 309 (emphasis in original).

22. Kahn, "Why Existence Does Not Emerge as a Distinct Concept in Greek

Regarding the further point of the influence of Christianity upon Greek thought, Kahn observes, "My general view of the historical development is that existence in the modern sense becomes a central concept in philosophy only in the period when Greek ontology is radically revised in the light of a metaphysics of creation: that is to say, under the influence of Biblical religion."[23]

Existence and the Essence/Existence Distinction after Aquinas

Various opinions on the nature of the essence/existence distinction, or, indeed, whether the distinction was real, arose right after Aquinas's death.[24] What is more, controversy over the place of existence in Aquinas's philosophy in light of the essence/existence distinction erupted right after Aquinas's death, as well. By the sixteenth century, Dominic Bañez, in his commentary on Aquinas's *Summa Theologiae*,[25] defended the notion (against his contemporaries) that in the philosophy of Thomas Aquinas, existence is the primary metaphysical notion.[26]

AQUINAS'S NOTION OF EXISTENCE

The full import of the essence/existence distinction is easily missed until Aquinas's notion of existence is unpacked. Once one appreciates what Aquinas says about existence, then, when coupled with the real distinction between essence and existence, one can begin to see its profound implications for the existence and attributes of the God of classical Christianity.

Philosophy," 7, 9 (emphasis in original).

23. Kahn, "Why Existence Does Not Emerge as a Distinct Concept in Greek Philosophy," 7.

24. For a treatment of the views from "lesser known" philosophers (in contrast to Duns Scotus's more prominent view in which he regarded the distinction as only formal), see Wippel, "Relationship Between Essence and Existence in Late Thirteenth-Century Thought."

25. Bañez, *Primacy of Existence in Thomas Aquinas*.

26. There has been a small controversy over whether Bañez was consistently faithful to Aquinas's view of the primacy of existence or, perhaps more accurately, whether he was faithful to Aquinas's view of *actus essendi*. Joseph Owens maintains that Bañez is not (see Owens, *Elementary Christian Metaphysics*, 104n11). He quotes Bañez's formula, "being is really distinct from essence as thing from thing," as rendering *esse* no longer an act but a substance. This take on Bañez is also picked up by Armand A. Maurer in Maurer, *Medieval Philosophy*, 353–54. For a discussion of this and a defense of Bañez, see Llamzon, "Specification of *Esse*," and especially Llamzon, "Suppositional and Accidental *Esse*."

As I seek to unpack Aquinas's accounting of existence, for the sake of clarity, I should like to introduce some vocabulary. The infinitive of the Latin verb to be, *sum* (I am), is *esse*, and is often translated into English as "being" or "existence." This can be misleading for the English reader since the English "being" can be both a noun and a verb. Further, "existence" is always a noun. What will be important in due course is the emphasis upon the infinitive sense of *esse*. A literal translation of "to be," however, tends to be awkward and probably no less misleading than the more common English renderings.

While it was not uncommon in the Middle Ages for philosophers to use the term *esse* as a synonym for "essence," Aquinas explicitly distinguished the two, describing the latter as that which receives *esse*. In Aquinas's metaphysical schema, Form and Matter in sensible things together constitute an essence. Essence and *esse* together constitute a being (*ens*, the participle of the Latin verb "to be"). As Matter is in potency to Form, the combination of Form and Matter (i.e., an essence) is in potency to existence (*esse*). Form actualizes Matter; existence (*esse*) actualizes essence. Owens summarizes, "When existence is considered in relation to the thing it makes exist, it may be regarded as actualizing the thing and, accordingly, it appears as the actuality that gives the thing existence."[27] Aquinas puts it thusly, "Wherefore it is clear that being as we understand it here is the actuality of all acts, and therefore the perfection of all perfections."[28]

But what is Aquinas getting at here? There are at least two aspects of Aquinas's accounting of existence that are crucial to understand, viz., that the existing of a created thing is constantly being caused and, second, that existence as such, i.e., existence *per se*, contains all perfections.[29]

As for the first (that the existing of a created thing is constantly being caused), consider this illustration, despite the fact that, when pressed too far, the illustration gets the point more wrong than right. If you saw a giant glass ball in front of you, you might ask, "How did it come to be?" If someone answered that the giant glass ball was manufactured in a nearby factory and moved here as a promotional gimmick for a local retail service, you

27. Owens, *Interpretation of Existence*, 51.

28. Aquinas, *De Potentia*, q. 7, a. 2, ad. 9.

29. For a very helpful treatment of this Thomistic accounting of existence at a relatively non-technical level, see Owens, *Interpretation of Existence*. For a technical treatment, particularly in light of other accountings of existence, see Gilson, *Being and Some Philosophers*. For a treatment of this specific accounting of existence in light of other accountings among Thomistic philosophers, see Knasas, *Being and Some Twentieth-Century Thomists*. For a short, but insightful, treatment of Aquinas's notion of existence in contrast to contemporary analytic notions, see Kerr, *Aquinas's Way to God*, 66–90.

would likely be satisfied with that answer. What is more, your satisfaction would have nothing to do with knowing much more about the factory that made the glass ball beyond the fact that it manufactured it. Indeed, while it might be interesting for other reasons, whether the factory still exists would, for the most part, be irrelevant to your satisfaction with the explanation of the glass ball in front of you.

Contrast this encounter with the glass ball with a different kind of encounter. Suppose, as you were looking at the glass ball, you were hearing music. In this case, you would *not* ask, "Where did the music came from?" or "How did the music come to be?" Rather, you would ask, "What *is causing the music to be right now*?" This is so because, unlike the glass ball (as far as my illustration goes), you realize that music is music only as it is being caused to be music at every instance that it is music. As soon as the cause of the music stops causing the music, the music goes out of existence. Music as music must constantly be caused to be music if it is to be music at all.

In a parallel way, this is how Aquinas regards existence in creatures. As that which actualizes an essence, that essence exists only as it is being caused to exist at every moment of its existence, which is to say, that essence exists only as it is being continuously actualized. As soon as the cause of the existence of the essence stops causing the existence of the essence, the essence goes out of existence.

As for the second (that existence contains all perfections), bear in mind here that the notion of "perfection" is not a moral one. While moral perfection can be parsed out within this category, here "perfection" is a broader notion.[30] For the most part, to perfect something is to actualize it.

---

30. That moral perfection (but not the moral virtues as attributed to God) can be (indeed, must be) parsed out in the category of the actualization of potencies is the essence of Natural Law Theory. For a very helpful summary of this, especially regarding God's relationship to the matter, see Feser, "Does Morality Depend on God?" See also Howe, "Does Morality Need God in Order to Be Objective?," where I summarize Feser's article and nest the discussion in a summary of Natural Law Theory. For more in-depth discussions, see Budziszewski, *Written on the Heart*; Charles, *Retrieving the Natural Law*; Clark, "Calvin on the *Lex Naturalis*"; Covington et al., *Natural Law and Evangelical Political Thought*; Fagothey, *Right and Reason*; Grabill, *Rediscovering the Natural Law in Reformed Theological Ethics*; McNeill, "Natural Law in the Teaching of the Reformers"; VanDrunen, *Divine Covenants and Moral Order: A Biblical Theology of Natural Law*; and VanDrunen, "Medieval Natural Law and the Reformation: A Comparison of Aquinas and Calvin." Much of the above is against the backdrop of Aristotle and Aquinas. For them, see Aristotle's *Nicomachean Ethics* and Aquinas's *ST* I-II, q. 1–114, especially his *Treatise on Law* (q. 90–144, sometimes published separately). Finally, it should be noted (without at this point much supporting argument) that the reason the actualization of a potential is a perfection, or, more to the point, is an actualization of a thing's good, is because, in Aquinas's thinking, the terms "being" and "good" are convertible. For a discussion of this, see Aertsen, "Convertibility of Being and Good in St. Thomas

Aristotle used these terms interchangeably (ἐνεργάζομαι, ἐνεργέια: actualize, actuality; ἐντελέχεια: perfection).[31] That "perfection" is an apt word to use in this context is argued by Owens.

> An alternate word for actuality in this respect is "perfection" (*entelecheia*). It was used by Aristotle along with actuality to designate the formal elements in things. These perfected the material element in the sense of filling its potentiality and completing the thing. Since existence is required to complete the thing and all the formal elements and activities, it may be aptly called the perfection of all perfections.[32]

These notions of current causality (i.e., existence as an act) and existence as possessing all perfections are crucial to understanding the whole of Aquinas's metaphysics.[33] Their cash value (if you will) is how they philosophically deliver both the existence of God and also all of the classical attributes of God (sans those attributes contained exclusively in revealed truth like, for example, the Trinity). It is to these two considerations that I would like to turn my attention.

EXISTENCE AND THE ESSENCE/EXISTENCE DISTINCTION AS AN ARGUMENT FOR GOD'S EXISTENCE

Aquinas sets forth some of the basics of his accounting of existence and essence in his *De ente et essentia*.[34] Whether he is there pressing these elements into the service of an argument for the existence of God is somewhat (perhaps mildly) disputed.[35] In q. 3 of his *Summa Theologiae*, Aquinas dis-

Aquinas"; and Aertsen, "Good as Transcendental and the Transcendence of the Good."

31. It is interesting to note that the word ἐντελέχεια arises from the root words ἐν (in) + τέλος (end, goal) and ἔχειν (to have). See Sachs, "Aristotle: Motion and Its Place in Nature."

32. Owens, *Interpretation of Existence*, 52–53.

33. This is not to say that there are no other essential elements of Aquinas's philosophy. Along with Aquinas's accounting of existence, one must also have a proper application of Aquinas's notion of the analogy of being. For a varied discussion of this admittedly difficult topic, see Clarke, "Analogy and the Meaningfulness of Language about God"; Klubertanz, *St. Thomas Aquinas on Analogy*; Mascall, *Existence and Analogy*; Mondin, *Principle of Analogy in Protestant and Catholic Theology*; Owens, "Analogy as a Thomistic Approach to Being"; and Rocca, *Speaking the Incomprehensible God*.

34. See footnote 7 of this chapter.

35. In this translation of *De Ente*, Maurer puts Joseph Owens in the camp of those who affirm that Aquinas uses this as an argument for God's existence and Étienne

cusses the essence/existence distinction as a means of demonstrating God's simplicity. Having already in the previous question demonstrated God's existence with his famous "Five Ways," it seems clear to some that here in q. 3 in the *Summa* he is not using the essence/existence distinction as an argument for God's existence.[36] But Owens argues that not only is Aquinas making an argument for God's existence here in *De ente et essentia*, but that he makes this same argument in other places as well.[37]

With this, let us look directly at the argument. Consider yourself as a human being. Whatever is true of you is true of you either because of your essence or not. In other words, whatever properties, conditions, states, etc. that obtain with you must arise either because of the kind of thing you are (i.e., because of your essence) or because of something besides your essence. Aquinas argues, "**Whatever belongs to a thing is either caused by the principles of its nature . . . or comes to it from an extrinsic principle . . .**"[38]

For example, the reason you as a human being have rationality is because you are a human. It is part of your essence as a human to have rationality. You have rationality by virtue of being human. Rationality is caused by your essence. These are four ways of saying the same thing. Again, the reason you have risibility (to use Aquinas's own example) is because you are

---

Gilson in the camp of those who deny that Aquinas uses this as an argument for God's existence. Most contemporary Thomists with whom I am familiar now affirm that this is indeed an argument for God's existence. For sources on this, see Kerr, *Aquinas's Way to God*.

36. In reality, it is slightly more complicated than I am making it sound here. Owens argues powerfully that all of Aquinas's "Five Ways" in q. 2 are employing Aquinas's notion of *esse*. See Owens, "Aquinas and the Five Ways."

37. See Owens, "Aquinas and the Five Ways," 17–18, n32. It is important to note that even Aquinas himself, in certain places, attributes the argument to others (e.g., Avicenna). For example, in *De Potentia*, Aquinas says, "Now there is a being that is its own being: and this follows from the fact that there must needs be a being that is pure act and wherein there is not composition. Hence from that one being all other beings that are not their own being, but have being by participation, must needs proceed. This is the argument of Avicenna" (q. 3, a. 5).

38. Aquinas, *De Ente*, c. 4. Note that one can distinguish those principles that arise from the very essence, which is to say, the definition, of the thing (like rationality for a human) and those aspects of a thing that, while not themselves part of the definition of the thing, nevertheless are necessary aspects (proper accidents) that arise by those principles that are part of the definition. Thus, as my example perhaps oversimplifies, the principles of rationality (which enable one to grasp incongruity), together with the capacity to make vocal sounds, give rise to the necessary aspect (proper accident) of the ability to laugh. I owe John Knasas for this helpful observation. See Knasas, *Being and Some Twentieth-Century Thomists*, 215–16, n12.

a human. It is part of your essence as a human to have risibility. You have risibility by virtue of being human. Risibility is caused by your essence.[39]

But consider something else that is true of you. Is the reason you are reading this chapter because you are a human? Is it part of your essence as a human to be reading this chapter? Are you reading this chapter by virtue of being a human? Is reading this chapter caused by your essence? The answer is clearly "no" since, if you were reading this chapter by virtue of being a human, then all others who are not reading this chapter would not be human. You can also think about it this way: sometimes both Aristotle and Aquinas understand Form as that which constitutes the definition of a thing. But one should be careful not to think of "definition" here as merely being a modern logical notion. Instead it is a metaphysical notion. In Aristotle and Aquinas, a thing is defined precisely because of its occupation within its species.[40] Thinking of it this way, it is easy to say that "reading this chapter" is not part of the definition of human.

Given that you are reading this chapter, one must ask how this can be the case. Why are you able to be reading this chapter even though it is not part of your essence to be reading this chapter? The answer, of course is quite simple. You are reading this chapter because you caused yourself to be reading this chapter. Let us, then, press the matter. Instead of your rationality, risibility, or reading this chapter, consider your existence. Is the reason you exist because you are a human? Is it part of your essence to exist? Do you exist by virtue of being human? Is your existence caused by your essence? Here the answer is, again, clearly "no"; and it should be easy to see why. As Aquinas points out, "Now being itself cannot be caused by the form . . . of a thing (by 'caused' I mean by an efficient cause), because that thing would then be its own cause and it would bring itself into being, which is impossible."[41]

We all learned in Apologetics 101 that nothing can be the cause of its own existence, the atheist philosopher Quentin Smith notwithstanding.[42] But if you cannot be the cause of your own existence, then your existence must be caused by something else. Aquinas summarizes, "It follows that

39. Strictly speaking, Aquinas would say that risibility arises from the principles within the essences. My wording is shorthand for Aquinas's wording and makes the same point.

40. "A species is defined by giving its genus (*genos*) and its differentia (*diaphora*): the genus is the kind under which the species falls, and the differentia tells what characterizes the species within that genus. As an example, *human* might be defined as *animal* (the genus) *having the capacity to reason* (the differentia)" (Smith, "Aristotle's Logic").

41. Aquinas, *De Ente*, c. 4.

42. See Smith, "Reason the Universe Exists Is that It Caused Itself to Exist."

everything whose being is distinct from its nature must have being from another."[43] But what about that thing's existence? It either exists by virtue of its essence, or it is caused to exist by something else. Now, can this go on to infinity? Aquinas again, "There must be a reality that is the cause of being for all other things, because it is pure being. If this were not so, we would go on to infinity in causes, for everything that is not pure being has a cause of its being, as has been said."[44]

This specter of the infinite regress arises within three of Aquinas's "Five Ways."[45] The question can be asked, "Why can there not be an infinite regress?" One thing that needs to be noted here is that Aquinas's argument in these three of his Five Ways goes in the opposite direction than how he is often taken. Usually, Aquinas is taken to mean that since there cannot be an infinite regress (for whatever reasons), then there must be a first cause. In other words, it is common for the critic to take Aquinas to be arguing a Kalam Cosmological Argument. From this point, the critic of Aquinas's arguments would go on to challenge the assertion that there cannot be such an infinite regress, mistakenly thinking that the impossibility of an infinite regress is a necessary condition for the truth of Aquinas's conclusions.

I submit, however, that he is actually arguing the reverse, viz., that since there must be a first cause, then there cannot be an infinite regress. This interpretation that Aquinas is not making the Kalam type of argument here is supported by the fact that in the *Summa Theologiae* q. 46, he explicitly rejects that philosophy can disprove the possibility of such an infinite regress.[46]

Taking this interpretation of the Five Ways requires the discussion to focus, not on whether there could be an infinite regress of the Kalam type, but why it is that the necessity of a first cause precludes the possibility of an infinite regress. What one finds upon a closer examination not very much further along into the *Summa Theologiae* is that, for Aquinas, there are in

43. Aquinas, *De Ente*, c. 4.

44. Aquinas, *De Ente*, c. 4.

45. In the First Way, he says, "If that by which it is put in motion be itself put in motion, then this also must needs be put in motion by another, and that by another again. But *this cannot go on to infinity*, because then there would be no first mover." The Second Way says, "Now in efficient causes, *it is not possible to go on to infinity*, because in all efficient causes following in order, the first is the cause of the intermediate cause. The Third Way says, "But every necessary thing either has its necessity caused by another, or not. Now *it is impossible to go on to infinity* in necessary things which have their necessity caused by another, as has been already proved in regard to efficient causes" (Aquinas, *ST* I, q. 2, a .3, emphasis added).

46. For a discussion of this, see Howe, "Two Notions of the Infinite in Thomas Aquinas' *Summa Theologiae* I, Questions 2 and 46."

fact two different types of infinites—an infinite *per se* and an infinite *per accidens*. Aquinas discusses the differences in q. 46 of the *Summa*. There he says, "In efficient causes it is impossible to proceed to infinity per se—thus, there cannot be an infinite number of causes that are per se required for a certain effect . . . But it is not impossible to proceed to infinity accidentally as regards efficient causes."[47]

Aquinas illustrates the difference by contrasting the causal sequence of father to son with the causal sequences of a hand moving a stick that is moving a stone. With the former, a man can father a son who can then grow up to father a son and so on infinitely (according to Aquinas); or, if you need to think of it in the opposite order, a son was fathered by his father who was, in turn, fathered by his father, and so on. The reason he thinks that such a causal sequence can be infinite (or, at least, this infinite cannot be philosophically demonstrated to be impossible) is because the causal connections are only accidental. When the son goes on to father a son, his own father is causally uninvolved. His own father could go out of existence, and yet the son could go on to father his own son. Thus, the father, while being a cause of the son, is not a cause of the son's causing his own son. To say it another way, the father, while being a cause of the son, is not a cause of the son's being a father. Aquinas says, "It is accidental to this particular man as generator to be generated by another man; for he generates as a man, and not as the son of another man."[48]

But contrast this with the nature of the causal sequence of a hand moving a stick that is moving a stone. It is not only the case that the hand is moving the stick and that the stick is moving the stone, but more than that: the hand is the cause of the stick *being a cause of the moving of the stone*. In contrast to the father/son illustration, the father is not the cause of the son's being a cause of his own son. However, the hand is not only the cause of the stick's moving, but it is also the cause of the stick being a mover of the stone. The father is the cause of the son, but he is not the cause of the son's being a father. The hand not only causes the stick to move, but it also causes the stick to be a mover of the stone. Here, then, the hand/stick/stone causal relationship is *per se*, and the father/son/son causal relationship is *per accidens*.[49]

---

47. Aquinas, *ST* I, q. 46, a. 2, ad. 7.

48. Aquinas, *ST* I, q. 46, a. 2, ad. 7.

49. To say it another way: in a *per accidens* infinite, the cause of an effect is only accidentally related to the effect being itself a cause of a further effect whereas in an infinite *per se* the cause of the effect is what causes the effect itself to be a cause. When the cause of w is the cause of w's causing x, and x is the cause of y's causing z, then there must be a first cause; otherwise, z would not be caused. Since there must be a first cause, this

The imagery of a series of interlocking turning gears might be helpful. That a gear is turning requires that either turning is part of its essence as a gear, or it is being turned by a gear for which turning is part of its essence as a gear. There could not be an infinite series of gears without a "first" gear doing the turning. Or consider looking into facing mirrors where you see a seemingly endless "regression" of images of your face. There could not be an infinite number of reflections; otherwise, there would be no face that is being reflected.

Where, then, does this leave us? Returning back to our original argument about a thing's existence being caused by something outside itself: it follows that whatever is being caused to exist must be currently being caused to exist by something that is uncaused. Aquinas puts it this way: "Now since God is very being by His own essence, created being must be His proper effect . . . Now God causes this effect in things not only when they first begin to be, but as long as they are preserved in being."[50] Again, he argues, "As the production of a thing into existence depends on the will of God, so likewise it depends on His will that things should be preserved; for He does not preserve them otherwise than by ever giving them existence; hence if He took away His action from them, all things would be reduced to nothing."[51] For anything whose existence is not its essence, it must be being caused to exist by something whose existence is its essence, which is to say a thing that exists because its very essence is existence. Anything that exists for which existence is not its essence must be being caused by that for which there is no essence/existence distinction. It is substantial existence itself—*ipsum esse subsistens*. As Aquinas summarizes, "God is supremely being, inasmuch as His being is not determined by any nature to which it is adjoined; since He is being itself, subsistent, absolutely undetermined."[52] "To God alone does it belong to be His own subsistent being. . . . for no creature is its own existence, forasmuch as its existence is participated."[53]

---

series cannot be an infinite. However, when the cause of *w* is not the cause of *w*'s causing *x*, and *x* is not the cause of *y*'s causing *z*, then this series can be infinite (in Aquinas's understanding) since the infinity of the series is only accidental to *z*'s being caused.

50. Aquinas, *ST* I, q. 8, a. 1.

51. Aquinas, *ST* I, q. 9, a. 2.

52. Aquinas, *ST* I, q. 11, a. 4.

53. Aquinas, *ST* I, q. 12, a. 4.

EXISTENCE AND THE ESSENCE/EXISTENCE DISTINCTION AS AN ARGUMENT FOR GOD'S ATTRIBUTES

To round out the topic at hand, I want to say a few things about how Aquinas's accounting of existence entails the classical attributes of God. Since *esse* is the actualization of all actualities and the perfection of all perfections, Aquinas would insist that *esse* as such is unlimited and contains all perfections. All the perfections that are exemplified by creatures are made actual by *esse*. The *esse* of a thing is limited when conjoined with Form or with Form and Matter, which is to say, an essence. But since there has to be something whose essence does not *have* existence but, rather, whose essence *is* existence, then that thing's perfections are unlimited since they are not limited by the *esse* of the thing being conjoined with a Form or essence that is other than its existence.

Perhaps an illustration will help—what I call the balloon illustration (which I borrowed from the philosopher Max Herrera). When one blows up a balloon, the air expands to fill the balloon up to the extent of and according to the shape of the balloon. By parallel, the *esse* (the act of existing) of a creature "fills up" the Form or essence of the creature to the extent of and according to the "shape" of the Form or essence of that creature. Thus, a horse contains all the perfections of *esse* (existence) up to the extent of and according to the limitations of the essence of horse. A human contains all the perfections of existence and up to the extent of and according to the limitations of the essence of human. Since in God there is no essence/existence distinction, then all the perfections of existence are in God because God's being is not conjoined with (and, thus, not limited by) Form. He is his own form or his own being. As Aquinas points out, "God is absolute form, or rather absolute being."[54] He argues that a being whose essence is *esse* possesses all perfections in superabundance. As he says it, "All perfections existing in creatures divided and multiplied, pre-exist in God unitedly."[55]

For Aquinas, once one understands what existence is and what it means to say that in God there is no essence/existence distinction, then all the classical attributes of God—simplicity, perfection, goodness, infinity, immutability, eternity, unity, omniscience, life, love, justice, omnipotence, and more—cascade seamlessly. As a word of warning to my fellow Evangelicals, it would seem on this account that these classical attributes are tethered

---

54. Aquinas, *ST* I, q. 3, a. 2; and I, q. 3, a. 7.
55. Aquinas, *ST* I, q. 13, a. 5.

together such that, if one of them is rejected, there is nothing to forestall the others disappearing as well.[56]

Marrying the metaphysics of Aristotle with the innovations of *esse* and the essence/existence distinction, Aquinas was able to demonstrate the existence and attributes of a God that Aristotle's philosophy could never foresee. Aquinas concludes, "It is evident, then . . . that it holds its being from the first being, which is being in all its purity; and this is the first cause, God."[57] As he aphoristically goes on to say, "All men know this to be God."[58]

Some suggest that this is how God identified himself to Moses in Exodus 3. "'Indeed, when I come to the children of Israel and say to them, "The God of your fathers has sent me to you," and they say to me, "What is His name?" what shall I say to them?' And God said to Moses, 'I AM WHO I AM.' And He said, 'Thus you shall say to the children of Israel, "I AM has sent me to you."'"[59] If we are right in making this connection, then Gaven Kerr's comment in his *Aquinas's Way to God* is spot on: "So it seems that without any deep metaphysical insight nor with any explicit prior determination as such, the author of the biblical text has managed to offer an expression of God that just happens to be in accord with some of the most profound metaphysical reasoning about the nature of God and His relation to the world in the history of Western thought."[60]

56. For a defense of these classical attributes of God, see Geisler et al., *Battle for God*; and Dolezal, *All That Is in God*.

57. Aquinas, *De Ente*, c. 4.

58. Aquinas, *ST* I, q. 2, a. 3. Étienne Gilson deftly summarizes the situation: "Thomism was not the upshot of a better understanding of Aristotle. It did not come out of Aristotelianism by way of evolution, but of revolution. Thomas uses the language of Aristotle everywhere to make the Philosopher say that there is only one God, the pure Act of Being, Creator of the world, infinite and omnipotent, a providence for all that which is, intimately present to every one of his creatures, especially to men, every one of whom is endowed with a personally immortal soul naturally able to survive the death of its body. The best way to make Aristotle say so many things he never said was not to show that, had he understood himself better than he did, he would have said them. For indeed Aristotle seems to have understood himself pretty well. He has said what he had to say, given the meaning which he himself attributed to the principles of his own philosophy. Even the dialectical acumen of Saint Thomas Aquinas could not have extracted from the principles of Aristotle more than what they could possibly yield. The true reason why his conclusions were different from those of Aristotle was that his own principles themselves were different. . . . In order to metamorphose the doctrine of Aristotle, Thomas has ascribed a new meaning to the principles of Aristotle. As a philosophy, Thomism is essentially a metaphysics. It is a revolution in the history of the metaphysical interpretation of the first principle, which is 'being'" (Gilson, *History of Christian Philosophy in the Middle Ages*, 365).

59. Exod 3:13–14, NKJV.

60. Kerr, *Aquinas's Way to God*, 169.

CONCLUSION

In my attempt that night to expose Barker as being ignorant of the main philosophical issues regarding the case for the existence of the God of classical theism, I know some in the audience were disappointed. Some of them were as unacquainted with the argument I gave as Barker was. But I suspect that none of them are writing books touting their own philosophical prowess or traveling the country defending a point of view about a profoundly philosophical issue while being woefully ignorant of the relevant literature on the subject. Dan Barker is seemingly almost completely unaware of how the conversation about the existence and nature of God has been going on for over 2,300 years in Western civilization. I do not mean to suggest that if Barker were more informed of the classical philosophical case for the existence of God, he would become a theist. But I do maintain that, having become so informed and remaining an atheist, his atheism would have quite a bit more integrity.

BIBLIOGRAPHY

Aertsen, Jan A. "The Convertibility of Being and Good in St. Thomas Aquinas." *New Scholasticism* 59 (1985) 449–70.

———. "Good as Transcendental and the Transcendence of the Good." In *Being and Goodness: The Concept of the Good in Metaphysics and Philosophical Theology*, edited by Scott MacDonald, 56–73. Ithaca: Cornell University Press, 1991.

Aquinas, Thomas. *On Being and Essence*. Translated by Armand Maurer. Toronto: The Pontifical Institute of Medieval Studies, 1968.

———. *On the Power of God*. Translated by the English Dominican Fathers. Reprint, Eugene: Wipf & Stock, 2004.

———. *On the Principles of Nature*. In *The Pocket Aquinas*, edited by Vernon J. Bourke, 61–76. New York: Washington Square, 1960.

———. *St. Thomas Aquinas Summa Theologica*. 5 vols. Translated by the Fathers of the English Dominican Province. Westminster: Christian Classics, 1981.

———. *Summa Contra Gentiles, Book Two: Creation*. Translated by James F. Anderson. Reprint, Notre Dame: University of Notre Dame Press, 2012.

———. *Truth*. 3 vols. Translated by Robert W. Mulligan et al. Indianapolis: Hackett, 1994.

Aristotle. *Metaphysics*. In *The Basic Works of Aristotle*, edited by Richard McKeon and translated by W. D. Ross, 689–934. New York: Random House, 1941.

Bañez, Dominic. *The Primacy of Existence in Thomas Aquinas: A Commentary in Thomistic Metaphysics*. Translated by Benjamin S. Llamzon. Chicago: Regnery, 1966.

Barker, Dan. *godless: How an Evangelical Preacher Became One of America's Leading Atheists*. Berkeley: Ulysses, 2008.

Budziszewski, J. *Written on the Heart: The Case for Natural Law.* Downers Grove: InterVarsity, 1997.

Charles, Daryl J. *Retrieving the Natural Law: A Return to Moral First Things.* Grand Rapids: Eerdmans, 2008.

Clark, R. S. "Calvin on the *Lex Naturalis.*" *Stulos Theological Journal* 6 (1998) 1–22.

Clarke, W. Norris. "Analogy and the Meaningfulness of Language about God: A Reply to Kai Nielsen." *Thomist* 40 (1976) 61–95.

Copleston, Frederick. *A History of Philosophy Vol. I: Greece and Rome.* Garden City: Image, 1985.

Covington, Jesse, et al. *Natural Law and Evangelical Political Thought.* Lanham: Lexington, 2013.

Dolezal, James E. *All That Is in God: Evangelical Theology and the Challenge of Classical Christian Theism.* Grand Rapids: Reformation Heritage, 2017.

Fagothey, Austin. *Right and Reason: Ethics in Theory and Practice Based on the Teachings of Aristotle and St. Thomas Aquinas.* 2nd ed. Charlotte: Tan, 1959.

Feser, Edward. "Does Morality Depend on God? (Updated)." http://edwardfeser. blogspot.com/2011/07/does-morality-depend-on-god.html.

Geisler, Norman L., et al. *The Battle for God: Responding to the Challenge of Neotheism.* Grand Rapids: Kregel, 2001.

Gilson, Étienne. *Being and Some Philosophers.* Toronto: Pontifical Institute of Mediaeval Studies, 1952.

———. *History of Christian Philosophy in the Middle Ages.* New York: Random House, 1955.

Grabill, Stephen J. *Rediscovering the Natural Law in Reformed Theological Ethics.* Grand Rapids: Eerdmans, 2006.

Howe, Richard G. "Does Morality Need God in Order to Be Objective? The 'Yes and No' Answer of Thomism." http://richardghowe.com/index_htm_files/Morality.pdf.

———. "Two Notions of the Infinite in Thomas Aquinas' *Summa Theologiae* I, Questions 2 and 46." *Christian Apologetics Journal* 8 (2009) 71–86.

Kahn, Charles H. "Why Existence Does Not Emerge as a Distinct Concept in Greek Philosophy." In *Philosophies of Existence: Ancient and Medieval,* edited by Parviz Morewedge, 7–17. New York: Fordham University Press, 1982.

Kerr, Gaven. *Aquinas's Way to God: The Proof in* De Ente et Essentia. New York: Oxford University Press, 2015.

Klubertanz, George P. *St. Thomas Aquinas on Analogy.* Chicago: Loyola University Press, 1960.

Knasas, John F. X. *Being and Some Twentieth-Century Thomists.* New York: Fordham University Press, 2003.

Llamzon, Benjamin S. "The Specification of *Esse*: A Study of Bañez." *The Modern Schoolman* 41 (1964) 123–43.

———. "Suppositional and Accidental *Esse*: A Study in Bañez." *The New Scholasticism* 39 (1965) 170–88.

Mascall, E. L. *Existence and Analogy: A Sequel to "He Who Is."* Reprint, Hamden, CT: Archon, 1967.

Maurer Armand A. *Medieval Philosophy.* A History of Philosophy 2. New York: Random House, 1962.

McNeill, John T. "Natural Law in the Teaching of the Reformers." *The Journal of Religion* 26 (1946) 168–82.

Mondin, Battista. *The Principle of Analogy in Protestant and Catholic Theology*. The Hague: Nijhoff, 1968.

Owens, Joseph. "Analogy as a Thomistic Approach to Being." *Medieval Studies* 24 (1962) 303–22.

———. "Aquinas and the Five Ways." *Monist* 58 (1974) 16–35.

———. *The Doctrine of Being in the Aristotelian Metaphysics: A Study in the Greek Background of Mediaeval Thought*. 3rd ed. Toronto: The Pontifical Institute of Mediaeval Studies, 1978.

———. *An Elementary Christian Metaphysics*. Houston: Center for Thomistic Studies, 1963.

———. *An Interpretation of Existence*. Houston: Center for Thomistic Studies, 1968.

Rocca, Gregory P. *Speaking the Incomprehensible God*. Washington: The Catholic University of America Press, 2004.

Sachs, Joe. "Aristotle: Motion and Its Place in Nature." https://www.iep.utm.edu/aris-mot/#H2.

Smith, Quentin. "The Reason the Universe Exists Is that It Caused Itself to Exist." *Philosophy* 74 (1999) 579–86.

Smith, Robin. "Aristotle's Logic." https://plato.stanford.edu/archives/sum2019/entries/aristotle-logic/.

VanDrunen, David. *Divine Covenants and Moral Order: A Biblical Theology of Natural Law*. Grand Rapids: Eerdmans, 2014.

———. "Medieval Natural Law and the Reformation: A Comparison of Aquinas and Calvin." *American Catholic Philosophical Quarterly* 80 (2006) 77–98.

Wippel, John F. "The Relationship Between Essence and Existence in Late Thirteenth-Century Thought: Giles of Rome, Henry of Ghent, Godfrey of Fontaines, and James of Viterbo." In *Philosophies of Existence: Ancient and Medieval*, edited by Parviz Morewedge, 131–64. New York: Fordham University Press, 1982.

Wuellner, Bernard J. *Summary of Scholastic Principles*. Chicago: Loyola University Press, 1956.

5

Are God's Attributes Incoherent and Incompatible?

—B. Kyle Keltz

Looking back, I can see that most of the religion courses (with a couple notable exceptions) were simply glorified Sunday school classes and I don't remember that we delved very deeply into the evidences or arguments for or against Christianity. It wouldn't have mattered anyway, since I wanted to be out in the streets preaching the gospel, not stuck in a classroom chewing over pointless history and philosophy.

—Dan Barker[1]

As I concluded in my chapter on faith and reason, Dan Barker argues against a caricature of the Christian view of faith and reason. It seems that his shallow knowledge of Christianity does not end at the relation between faith and reason, however. As the above quote shows, Barker admits that he thought philosophy is pointless. Nowhere is this more obvious than in his chapter on God's attributes in his book *godless* ("Omni-Aqueous").[2] Here Barker shows that he does not know of, or does not understand, the attributes of God as they have been understood in classical Christianity. In that

1. Barker, *godless*, 17.
2. Barker, *godless*, 121–29.

chapter, he argues that God's omniscience, omnipotence, omnibenevolence, and omnipresence are incoherent and incompatible attributes. At almost every point in his arguments, he shows dreadful ignorance of God's attributes as understood throughout any period in Christian history.

In this chapter, I will respond to Barker's objections to God's attributes. First, I will explain Barker's objections. After this, similar to my chapter on faith and reason, I will discuss each attribute, focusing on how each is explained in Thomas Aquinas's writings. Next, I will return to Barker's objections and show how they fail to cause problems for God's attributes as they have been understood in Christianity for centuries. I will conclude that, similar to his discussion regarding faith, Barker either is not aware of the Christian understanding of God's attributes or is intentionally misleading his readers.

DAN BARKER ON GOD'S ATTRIBUTES

As mentioned, Barker spends an entire chapter objecting to God's attributes in his book *godless*. Barker objects to the attributes of omniscience, omnipotence, and omnipresence. He argues that each attribute is incoherent and also that several of the attributes are incompatible with each other.

Barker on Omniscience

Barker first touches on the attribute of God's omniscience. His understanding of omniscience is that it is the belief that God is all-knowing. Barker explains, "According to Christianity, God is omniscient—'all-knowing.' Although this doctrine is fundamental, it is rarely defined or examined. It is simply a given."[3] He argues that omniscience, as an attribute of God, is an incoherent concept. This is mainly because, he says, an infinite being would need to have infinite knowledge of itself. Barker argues,

> To "know" is to contain a true image or idea within a mind. A being that knows *everything* must also know itself. Therefore, the mind of an omniscient being must contain an image of itself within itself. It would also have to contain an image of the image of itself, and an image of that image, and so on. It would have to know that it contains those images, and also contain an image of itself knowing that it contains not only those images but the

3. Barker, *godless*, 121.

image of knowing that it contains the knowledge of such images—well, you see where this is going.[4]

Barker uses an analogy involving a perfect map. He asks the reader to imagine a map that is so accurate it even shows blades of grass, shingles on roofs, etc. To show such minute details, the map must be extremely large. It should be at least a few square miles in size and be placed outside somewhere in the desert. However, Barker says that the perfect map must also contain a map of itself (otherwise it would be missing some details and would not be perfect), and the map on the map of the map must also contain a map, ad infinitum. Barker says the problem gets even worse if we imagine that there is a supercomputer trying to maintain a four-dimensional map of the universe. Similar to the two-dimensional map, the four-dimensional map would need to contain a map of itself. The same problem would arise, and the supercomputer would quickly use all its energy trying to map itself.

Barker argues that the same problem arises for God:

> In order for God to know everything, he has to know not only about all the unknown galaxies and extrasolar planetary systems and where all the undiscovered diamond mines and my missing socks are located, he also has to know everything about *himself*. He has to know what he is going to think next. He has to anticipate that he is going to need to know what he is going to think next, and after that into the infinite future. Like the computer virus, an omniscient God gets caught in an infinite loop keeping track of itself and cannot have a single thought.[5]

Since God must have an internal representation of himself, as Barker argues, then God could not do anything else at any moment because God would be infinitely contemplating himself. With this argument against omniscience in mind, Barker concludes,

> It doesn't matter what method God uses to store and retrieve data in his super mind, he has to have *some* kind of internal representation. If theists argue that the intelligence of God is something altogether different from human or computer intelligence, then they are admitting that the idea of omniscience is meaningless. If "all-knowing" does not compare with "knowing," then the phrase lacks relevance to human understanding

---

4. Barker, *godless*, 122 (emphasis in original).

5. Barker, *godless*, 123 (emphasis in original).

and we may as well say that "God is mmpfghrmpf" instead of "God is omniscient."[6]

Thus, for Barker, God cannot be omniscient because this would make it so that God would be contemplating himself infinitely at each moment. Also, if God does not know everything in the way that humans and computers do, then "omniscience" is meaningless.

Barker on Omnipotence

Regarding God's omnipotence, Barker first discusses the definition of "power." He says that "power" is a word that either refers to ability or authority.[7] Since "omnipotence" is derived from the word "potent," he says that it most likely refers to "power." Regarding "power," Barker says, "Power is the ability to do a certain amount of work in a certain amount of time. Power (or energy) is a physical force, at least."[8] With this definition of "power" in mind, he concludes, "An omnipotent God must be able to counteract the greatest possible force that could exist in the universe."[9] Barker says that God must be infinitely powerful to be able to possibly counteract a black hole created by the universe collapsing on itself.

Barker not only defines what he thinks omnipotence is, but also discusses implications he thinks omnipotence has for what God is like. He says,

> The universe (or more properly the cosmos) encompasses all the mass/energy available anywhere. If God possesses energy that not only created but also interacts with the material world, then by definition, he is part of the natural universe or the universe is part of him, which is the same thing. Whatever God's source of energy might be, it exists *somewhere*, adding to the size of the cosmos.[10]

Since the universe is defined as "all the mass/energy available anywhere," God must be in the universe if God has power. Otherwise, God would have power outside of the universe, which would contradict Barker's definition of "universe." Thus, Barker concludes, God must be in the universe if God has any power.

However, Barker argues that this creates problems. He notes,

6. Barker, *godless*, 123 (emphasis in original).

7. Barker, *godless*, 124.

8. Barker, *godless*, 124.

9. Barker, *godless*, 124.

10. Barker, *godless*, 124 (emphasis in original).

> An omnipotent God would make the cosmos infinitely massive,
> a fact contradicted by the expansion of the universe (or, if God is
> outside our own pocket universe, by the uniformity of such ex-
> pansion), or by the fact that we are not all instantly compressed
> by the gravity of infinite matter or incinerated with heat by be-
> ing in the presence of such a grotesquely massive black hole out
> there.[11]

Since omnipotence entails that God is physically infinite, this means that
the universe would include infinite mass. Yet, since the universe is expanding, there cannot be an infinite amount of mass in or outside the universe.
Thus, Barker concludes, God cannot be omnipotent.

Next, Barker makes an argument against God being omnipotent and
immaterial. Confusingly, Barker mentions, "Some argue that it is provincial
for us locals to picture God as a huge physical being with infinite mass."[12]
This is confusing because Barker is supposed to be arguing against Christianity, and there have been no orthodox Christians who have said that God
is infinite mass in the history of Christianity. However, it seems that Barker
is referring to the Christian concept that God is infinite, immaterial, and
transcendent. Right after mentioning that "some" people say God is infinite
mass, Barker argues,

> But if "omnipotence" is meaningful, it has to indicate something
> to us humans who do not transcend nature. By definition a
> "spirit" is nonphysical, so a "spiritual god" should have no pow-
> er—no real power—at all. . . . If God is "directing" nature from
> outside, he is still required to do so in a way that causes ordinary
> matter to react. There needs to be an energy/mass nexus, or con-
> nection, for any work to be done. (Of course, claiming that god
> is "energy" is to deny that he is "spirit.") If "all-powerful" does
> not relate to "powerful," as we humans understand the word,
> then the phrase is incoherent. We may as well say that "God is
> rrrghphrrth" instead of "God is omnipotent."[13]

In other words, God cannot be spirit because spiritual things are non-phys-
ical. If power can only come from something physical, as Barker believes,
God cannot have power and also be immaterial.

---

11. Barker, *godless*, 124.

12. Barker, *godless*, 125.

13. Barker, *godless*, 125.

Barker on Omnipresence

Finally, Barker objects to God's omnipresence. He says,

> Omnipresence is also a problem. To be "present" means for mat-
> ter and/or energy to occupy space-time at some spatial coordi-
> nates at a particular point in time. Technology extends our sense
> with machines, allowing viewers, for example, to be "present" at
> a televised event, but even this requires a physical connection:
> camera, microphone, sense, receiver, speaker. God is not "pres-
> ent" at every location in the universe, not in any ordinary sense.
> To say that God is present in a "spiritual" sense is meaningless
> until "spirit" is defined. Since spirit is normally described as
> something "immaterial" or "transcendent" (which merely iden-
> tify what it is *not*, not what it *is*), this means that being present
> spiritually is not to be present at all. We may as well say that
> "God is sshhffhgtyrh" rather than "God is omnipresent."[14]

Here Barker defines "present" as a physical term similar to "power." Thus,
Barker concludes, God cannot be omnipresent if God is not physically in
every point of the universe. If theists argue that "omnipresence" is understood spiritually, then they are using an incoherent concept because humans
cannot understand what it means to be spiritual.

Moreover, Barker argues that God's eternality causes even more problems for God's omnipresence:

> Those theists who argue that God exists "outside of time" make
> it even worse. If you live "outside" of temporal coordinates, then
> you cannot be present "inside" space-time. You are non-present
> rather than omnipresent. If God is defined as a nonmaterial or
> nontemporal being who is omnipresent—occupying physical
> reality—then God does not exist.[15]

Again, Barker is saying that to be present is to be physically in some place.
If God is outside of time, this means that God is completely outside of the
space-time block that is the universe. But if God is not physically present,
then he is not present at all.

14. Barker, *godless*, 128 (emphasis in original).
15. Barker, *godless*, 128.

Barker on the Incompatibility of God's Attributes

As mentioned, Barker not only argues that many of God's attributes are incoherent, but also that many of God's attributes are incompatible with one another. In "Omni-Aqueous," Barker argues against several combinations of God's attributes including God's omniscience and omnibenevolence; omnipotence and omniscience; free will and omniscience; and omniscience, omnipotence, and omnibenevolence.

First, Barker says that God's omniscience is incompatible with God's omnibenevolence. This is because, Barker argues, God created the world knowing that his creatures would suffer and commit sin. This is "at least criminal negligence, if not malice," he says, and, "This is mean-spirited."[16] Similarly, Barker goes on to argue that God's omnipotence, omniscience, and omnibenevolence are incompatible. However, he makes the same argument as he does regarding God's omniscience and omnibenevolence.

Next, Barker argues that God's omnipotence is incompatible with God's omniscience. He says to be omniscient is to know all future facts.[17] This entails that the future is fixed, and God cannot change the future. If God cannot change the future, then God is not omnipotent. If God changes the future, then God was not omniscient. Thus, Barker concludes, God's omnipotence and omniscience are incompatible.

Finally, this leads to Barker's *Freewill Argument for the Non-existence of God* (FANG). This argument leads to the conclusion that God's free will is incompatible with God's omniscience. Similar to his argument against God's omnipotence and omniscience, Barker says that if God is omniscient, then God cannot have free will. Barker explains,

> In order to make a freely chosen decision you have to have at least two options, each of which can be avoided while the other (or "another," if there are more than two) is selected. To be able to freely choose, there has to be a period of uncertainty or indeterminacy during which the options remain open and during which you could change your mind before it is too late. Free will, if it exists, requires that you not know the future. However, if you are omniscient, you already know all of your future choices and you are not free to change what you know in advance. You cannot make decisions. You do not have a period of uncertainty and flexibility before selecting. You do not have free will. If you do change what you thought you knew in advance, exercising

16. Barker, *godless*, 124.
17. Barker, *godless*, 127.

the prerogative of omnipotence, then you were not omniscient
in the first place. You can't have both free will and omniscience.[18]

"Free will," as defined by Barker, includes being able to choose between alternatives and also being uncertain as to whether one choice will be chosen over the other(s). If God knows all his future choices, then God cannot have free will because God will not be uncertain. Therefore, Barker concludes, God does not exist.

A CLASSICAL UNDERSTANDING OF GOD'S ATTRIBUTES

There have been more positions than just Thomas Aquinas's positions on God's attributes in the history of Christianity.[19] I will mention a few when discussing Aquinas's position. However, here I will mainly focus on Aquinas's writings.

In the *Summa Theologiae*, Aquinas lists his famous arguments for God's existence, known today as the *Five Ways*.[20] Many people have misunderstood Aquinas's arguments because he wrote the *Summa Theologiae* for an advanced audience.[21] He did not explain the philosophical concepts necessary to understand his Five Ways, and he did not fully explain the arguments themselves. Instead, he briefly lists the arguments before he spends a great number of pages in the *Summa Theologiae* discussing what the arguments entail.

Regardless, the Five Ways are five different arguments that reach the same conclusion: God is pure act, existence itself, and has all perfections. It would take an entire book to explain the philosophy behind the Five Ways, and there is not enough space to do so in this chapter.[22] However, as I explain Aquinas's arguments regarding God's attributes, I will occasionally

18. Barker, *godless*, 127–28.

19. For a good resource for the historical development of Christian doctrines including the attributes of God, see Allison, *Historical Theology*.

20. Aquinas, *ST* I, q. 2, a. 3. For an explanation of the Five Ways and the metaphysical background for understanding the Five Ways, see Feser, *Aquinas*; and Klubertanz and Holloway, *Being and God*. All quotes from the *Summa Theologiae* are from Aquinas, *Summa Theologica*.

21. For a discussion of frequent misconceptions, see Buijs, "On Misrepresenting the Thomistic Five Ways," 15–34.

22. For a very brief, but helpful, discussion of the metaphysics behind the Five Ways, see Richard Howe's chapter in this book. Also see note 20.

touch on certain aspects of what it means for God to be pure act, existence itself, and to possess all perfections.

Aquinas on Omnipotence

The first of the Five Ways, the *argument from change*, concludes that there must be an unmoved Mover.[23] This unmoved Mover explains why contingent things in the universe go through change. In the world, we see things that are changing, and in each instance, we see that they are being changed by something that exists and is acting on them. Without the unmoved Mover, contingent things in the universe would never undergo change because there could not be an infinite regress of things that are here-and-now undergoing change that rely on something external to change them. Without an unmoved Mover, the series of changing things would be groundless and would not exist; nothing would be changing. Therefore, there must be something that is pure actuality (i.e., something that has no potential to change) to ground the series of things that need something external to change them.

The First Way is one argument leading Aquinas to the conclusion that God is omnipotent. As mentioned, things in act (i.e., things that exist and have the power to create change) change things that have the potential to change. As pure actuality, God is understood to be infinitely powerful because God is not only the grounding for all change in the universe, but also because God is unlimited actuality itself.[24] For example, think about all of the most powerful forces in the universe such as atom bombs, black holes, gravity, etc. As the unmoved Mover, God is the cause and grounding of all of these forces. All these forces have power as far as they exist and cause things to change. Yet as unlimited actuality, God is infinitely more powerful than all these forces combined.

Aquinas is careful to distinguish what he means by omnipotence, however.[25] By "omnipotent," Aquinas does not mean that God can do anything. This is because believing that God can do anything results in contradictions.[26] For example, believing that God can create a square circle is incoherent because the notions of a circle and a square are contradictory. There

23. Although Aquinas talks about an unmoved Mover, he is not just talking about motion, but also about change. Motion counts as a change, but Aquinas is talking about change in general and not simply motion.

24. Aquinas, *ST* I, q. 25, a. 1.

25. Aquinas, *ST* I, q. 25, a. 4–6.

26. Some Christians, such as René Descartes, have argued that God can do anything including the logically impossible.

can be no such thing as a square circle or a circular square. If something is a circle, then it cannot be a square and vice versa. Accordingly, Aquinas specifically mentions that God cannot do contradictory things like change the past.[27] Thus, Aquinas's definition of "omnipotence" is closer to the idea that God can create anything that is conceivable.[28]

God being unable to create inconceivable things is not a limit to God's power. This is because inconceivable things are non-things; that is to say, they are nothing. So, it is not a limit on God's power if we understand that God cannot make certain non-things. If they are nothing, then to say that God cannot create them is not to place a limit on his power.

Aquinas on Omniscience

The second of the Five Ways, the *argument from efficient causality*, concludes that there must be an uncaused efficient Cause. This uncaused Cause explains why contingent things in the universe exist at each moment in which they exist. Without the uncaused efficient Cause, contingent things in the universe would cease to exist.

The conclusion that there is a Cause for the existence of contingent things in the universe leads Aquinas to argue that this Cause must be omniscient. In the *Summa Theologiae*, Aquinas argues that God must be omniscient because God is the cause of everything that exists (as concluded by the argument from efficient causality and the other Five Ways).[29] Since God created and holds all contingent things in existence at every moment they exist, he necessarily knows everything about them. If God did not have perfect knowledge of something, then God could not create and sustain it. For example, a house cannot exist unless it first exists as an idea in the mind of a builder or architect. In a similar way, if God did not have knowledge of everything in the universe, then God could not be the cause of everything in the universe. However, since the Five Ways show that God is the cause of everything in the universe, it follows that God has knowledge of everything in the universe because he is sustaining everything in the universe in existence.

Similarly to his defense of God's omnipotence, Aquinas is careful to qualify what he means by "omniscience." Aquinas argues that God's

27. Aquinas, *ST* I, q. 25, a. 5.

28. For a detailed discussion of Aquinas's view of God's power and the advantages of Aquinas's view over other views of God's power, see Davies, *Thinking about God*, 173–79.

29. Aquinas, *ST* I, q. 14, a. 5.

omniscience entails that God knows himself, all existing things, and anything conceivable that God could create.[30] It was already explained why Aquinas thinks that God knows everything that exists. Additionally, Aquinas argues that God knows himself. This is because, Aquinas emphasizes, God's pure actuality (i.e., God's essence and existence are identical[31]) entails that if God has knowledge and understanding, then God is his knowledge and understanding.[32] If God is his knowledge and understanding, then God necessarily knows and understands himself.[33] Another way to say this is God knows himself because God is identical to his infinite knowledge. This is certainly a different way of knowing from humans in that knowledge is accidental to humans because knowledge is added to them as they learn, yet a human without knowledge is still a human. Knowledge in God is not accidental and not gained in time. However, this is similar to knowing in humans because "to know" is "when the known becomes one with the knower."[34] Since the forms of all things that have ever existed, exist, will exist, and could exist are in God, God knows all things to an infinite degree compared to humans.

In this last sentence, I mentioned that God knows all things that will or could exist. Aquinas believes this is so because in God knowing himself, God knows all the things that God's power will and could create.[35] In fully knowing himself, God knows everything that he has decided to create. Also, in fully knowing himself, God knows everything that his power could create. Thus, God knows himself, everything that he has or will create, and everything that he could create.

Aquinas on Omnipresence

Understanding the conclusions of the Five Ways and God's omniscience and omnipotence helps with understanding what is meant by God's "omnipresence." To clarify, Aquinas says,

---

30. Aquinas, *ST* I, q. 14, a. 2–3, 5–6, 13. For a detailed discussion of Aquinas's view of God's knowledge and the advantages of Aquinas's view over other views of God's knowledge, see Davies, *Thinking about God*, 180–95.

31. For a discussion of the identity of God's existence and essence, see Richard Howe's chapter in this book.

32. Aquinas, *ST* I, q. 14, a. 2.

33. Aquinas, *ST* I, q. 14, a. 2–3.

34. For Aquinas's understanding of the term "knowledge," see my discussion in my chapter on faith and reason.

35. Aquinas, *ST* I, q. 14, a. 5, 13.

> Since place is a thing, to be in place can be understood in a two-fold sense; either by way of other things—i.e. as one thing is said to be in another no matter how; and thus the accidents of a place are in place; or by a way proper to place; and thus things placed are in a place. Now in both senses, in some way God is in every place; and this is to be everywhere.[36]

The first way "place" is understood, Aquinas is saying, is when something is in another thing, such as when red is said to be "in" an apple. The second way "place" is understood here is when something is physically located somewhere, such as when an apple is said to be "in" a room.

Aquinas argues that God is in every place in both senses.[37] This is because God gives existence and actuality to all things in the universe. In the first sense, God is in every place because he gives the existence that is in things. In the second sense, God is in every place because he gives existence to things that fill every place in the universe.

Another way to explain Aquinas's point here is to emphasize God's knowledge and power.[38] God creates and sustains everything in the universe by God's knowledge and power. God can be said to be everywhere in that he knows everything and every event that is occurring at every place in the universe. Also, God can be said to be everywhere in that his power is upholding the existence of everything and every event that is occurring at every place in the universe. Thus, God is omnipresent in that God is present in and at every place in the universe through his knowledge and power.

ANSWERS TO BARKER'S OBJECTIONS

Now that Aquinas's understanding of some of God's attributes has been explained, we can return to Barker's objections to God's attributes. It should now be obvious just how far off Barker's objections are from Aquinas's understanding of God's attributes. Of course, Barker does not say he is answering Aquinas in *godless*, but as will be discussed, it seems that Barker is not responding to any orthodox Christians at all with his objections.

---

36. Aquinas, *ST* I, q. 8, a. 2.

37. Aquinas, *ST* I, q. 8, a. 2.

38. See Aquinas, *ST* I, q. 8, a. 3.

Barker's Objections to Omniscience

One of the major reasons that Barker is not actually objecting to Christianity is that he usually fails to listen to or understand how Christians define the terms involved with God's attributes. A major case in point is Barker's definition (not Christianity's definition) of "knowledge." As mentioned, Barker defines "knowledge" as a mind containing a true image or idea. Barker thinks this causes problems with God's omniscience because God would have to contain an idea of himself in himself, which would result in infinite regress problems.

First, Barker's definition of "to know" is not a definition held by Christians. It is not clear where Barker gets his definition, but as I explained in my chapter on faith and reason, there have been two major positions on knowledge in the history of Christianity. Following Plato, many Christians have viewed "knowledge" as "justified true belief." Following Aristotle, many Christians, including Aquinas, have viewed "knowledge" as "the thing known becoming one with the knower." Barker's definition seems to be a confused jumble of these two distinct positions on knowledge. His definition does not fit the definition of Plato because it lacks Plato's justification requirement for knowledge. Barker's definition does not fit the definition of Aquinas because it redundantly mentions truth. For Aquinas, "being," "truth," and "goodness" are all interchangeable, and to know something is to possess the form of that thing. It is understood that if someone knows something, then the form (e.g., essence/truth of something) is in that person's mind. When Barker adds truth in his definition, yet does not mention justification, it is unclear whether, if any, of the two classical positions he is referencing.

Regardless, Barker's argument against God's omniscience is very poor indeed. First, it is unclear why Barker has a problem with infinite regresses in God's mind if Barker allows for omniscience to be the attribute that God is all-knowing. If God has infinite knowledge (i.e., unlimited knowledge), then it does not seem to create a problem if God's knowledge of himself necessitates an infinite regress.

Yet even so, Aquinas's understanding of God's omniscience shows why there need not be an infinite regress. As mentioned, "omniscience," to Aquinas, is the understanding that God knows himself, everything that exists, and everything that could exist. God knows himself because God is pure actuality (i.e., infinite existence), and God has knowledge. If God is pure actuality and has knowledge, then God is his knowledge. In knowing his infinite being, God knows himself and everything that his knowledge and power did, has, could, and would create. God's knowledge does not need to regress to infinity because God is his knowledge. There is no necessity of God containing an infinite concept of himself in an infinite concept of himself, ad infinitum. Instead, God is his own understanding.

Before moving on, besides noting that Barker's definition of "knowing" and failure to answer any major position from the history of Christianity, it should also be noted that there are other major problems with his arguments regarding God's omniscience. One major problem is his analogy involving the map and GPS supercomputer. Orthodox Christianity has always viewed God as an immaterial and eternal being. Barker's analogy using an infinite regress of images is completely irrelevant. God cannot have an image of himself since he is immaterial, let alone an image of an image of himself. For the same reason, Barker's analogy using a GPS supercomputer is irrelevant. Space-time or no space-time, God is immaterial. So, God does not need a four-dimensional image of himself. Moreover, God has infinite power and knowledge, so God would never break down like a supercomputer with a virus.

Barker's argument against God's omniscience also assumes that God is temporal. While some Christians believe that God is temporal, many do not, and God has been classically understood as eternal.[39] If God only needs to understand his one pure act of existence, this does not entail that he needs to track an infinite number of decisions at each moment in an infinite regress as Barker suggests. This argument only applies to Christians who believe God is temporal (if it applies to any Christian positions on omniscience at all), and thus it does not apply to all of Christianity as Barker suggests.

Similarly, it is puzzling to read Barker's comment that omniscience is rarely defined or examined within Christianity. This is one of Barker's most demonstrably false statements. Here he must be deliberately misrepresenting Christianity or blatantly demonstrating his ignorance of the history of the Christian understanding of God's omniscience. Besides the wealth of books written on Christian systematic and philosophical theology, a quick internet search of the word "omniscience" shows that there is a sea of websites and articles on this topic. A good place for Barker to start would be the *Internet Encyclopedia of Philosophy*'s article titled "Omniscience and Divine Foreknowledge."[40]

---

39. For a great discussion of classical and contemporary Christian views of God's relation to time, see Davies, *Thinking about God*, 148–70.

40. Borland, "Omniscience and Divine Foreknowledge." The *Internet Encyclopedia of Philosophy* is a great website for beginners. It is a free, peer-reviewed resource written by philosophy PhDs for an undergraduate audience.

Lastly, Barker says that if God's knowing is not the same as human knowing, then it is meaningless. This is simply not true. It could be said that for God to "know" something is for God to "turn things green." In this case, God's knowing and human knowing would be completely different. But we could still understand what is meant by God's "knowing." What Barker means to say is that if God's knowing is not the same as human knowing, then it would be *practically* meaningless because it might be something we could never experience. Regardless, Aquinas's definition shows that God's knowing is analogous to, or something like, human knowing. God's knowledge is infinite because it not only includes himself, but it also includes all things he could or will create. Humans know in a similar manner because we obtain the forms of things we know in our intellects. The difference is that God's knowledge is infinite and that God, as pure actuality, is something that humans will never be. Humans and God know things similarly, but not in identical ways.

Barker's Objections to Omnipotence

Barker's objections to God's omnipotence provide more examples of Barker misrepresenting or misunderstanding the Christian position. Earlier in "Omni-Aqueous," Barker mentions,

> There are some gods—such as the God of the bible—that I claim to *know* do not exist because, like the married bachelor, they cannot exist. Many definitions of "God" are incoherent. They contain mutually incompatible properties that are impossible to reconcile; therefore, they do not exist. This is not dogma—it is simple logic.[41]

Yet Barker does not mention that the definitions of "God" he discusses are his own. For example, he defines "power" in a way that is completely incompatible with Christianity. Again, Barker says that "power" is "the ability to do a certain amount of work in a certain amount of time. Power (or energy) is a physical force, at least." He then goes on to argue that God cannot be omnipotent on the basis of this definition.

It is puzzling as to why Barker would assume that theists view God's power as a physical force. Certainly, throughout the history of Christianity, no orthodox Christian has believed that God is a physically infinite being made of energy. Philosophically, Christians have concluded that God must be immaterial because God is the cause and grounding of all physical reality.

41. Barker, *godless*, 121 (emphasis in original).

Christian philosophers have reached this conclusion on the basis of philosophy and metaphysics, not science, and they have not been constrained
by physical notions of causality.

Barker defines "power" as "energy" and then argues that it is obvious
that an infinitely physical god cannot exist. It might take "simple logic" to
show that such a god does not exist. But this is not the God of Christianity.

As was shown, the classical view of God's omnipotence entails that
God can create anything that is conceivable. God is understood to be all-
powerful because God is the uncaused Cause of the universe. As the Five
Ways demonstrate, without something that is pure actuality, there could be
no contingent things. Notions such as "actuality," "potentiality," and "efficient causality" are metaphysical notions, and there is nothing within them
necessitating that all causes in the universe must be material causes. God is
understood to be an immaterial, infinitely powerful being on the basis of
metaphysics, not science.

Barker, however, argues that God cannot have power if God is immaterial: "By definition a 'spirit' is nonphysical, so a 'spiritual god' should
have no power—no real power—at all. . . . If God is 'directing' nature from
outside, he is still required to do so in a way that causes ordinary matter
to react. There needs to be an energy/mass nexus, or connection, for any
work to be done." Here it is obvious that Barker's conclusion is based in his
definition of "power." If "power" is energy, and God is immaterial, then God
cannot have any power—simple logic.

It should be obvious why this is another argument that fails to object
to the Christian understanding of God's power. The classical understanding
is that God has the power to create anything conceivable. When God creates
and sustains the universe, he is bestowing existence to contingent things.
Barker is failing to consider the classical notion that God is the constant,
moment-to-moment, Cause of all contingent things. Barker seems to assume that after God creates the universe, God must also use his power to
directly move everything within the universe. In the history of philosophy,
there have been Christian and Muslim theologians who have viewed God's
causality in this way. The view that God is the direct cause of all events in the
universe is called *occasionalism*.[42]

However, occasionalism has not been the majority view of Christian
philosophers. Christian philosopher/theologians such as Augustine and
Aquinas argued that while God is ultimately the cause of everything in the
universe, God only indirectly causes events in the universe because events

---

42. See Jordan, "Occasionalism."

in the universe are directly caused by contingent things themselves.[43] The view of Augustine and Aquinas has been called *concurrentism*.[44] It entails that God creates contingent things with causal powers. God is the ultimate cause of everything in the universe because he is sustaining everything in the universe at each moment. However, contingent things cause events according to their inherent causal powers. For example, when I choose to write a sentence on my computer, I am directly causing this event, while God is the indirect cause because he is sustaining me and my computer (along with the earth and all matter and fundamental forces of nature, etc.).

The concurrentist view of God's causality does not entail that God is moving everything in the universe with some immaterial force. Instead, God is sustaining the existence and essences of all things in the universe. Thus, there is no need for a power nexus of any sort for things to interact in nature.

Of course, Barker might object at this point. He says, "If 'all-powerful' does not relate to 'powerful,' as we humans understand the word, then the phrase is incoherent. We may as well say that 'God is rrrghphrrth' instead of 'God is omnipotent.'" Yet again, Barker is wrong. Words can be used in whatever ways language users intend to use them. We could say that for God to have "power" is for God to "think about elephants." This would not be incoherent, although it is not what people usually mean when they talk about power. Again, Barker seems to be indicating that if God's power is not like human power, then the concept of "omnipotence" would be practically meaningless. Although the word "omnipotence" would have meaning, its meaning would be so far removed from our experience that it would be of no practical consequence.

Barker's argument here is weak against the Christian understanding of God's power. Humans are not able to create and sustain things in existence. But this does not mean that we cannot understand what it means for God to have power. It simply means that different beings have different ways of causing their effects.

Barker is obviously presupposing the notion that for God's attributes to be meaningful, they must be physical and human attributes. But Barker never offers an argument for why this is so, and regardless, even if he did, he still would be failing to interact with the Christian understanding of God's power. Just because I cannot create and sustain something in existence does not mean that I cannot understand what it means for God to do so.

---

43. See Aquinas, *Quaestiones disputatae de potentia (De Potentia)*, q. 3, a. 7; Aquinas, *ST* I, q. 105, a. 5; Aquinas, *Summa contra Gentiles (SCG)* III, c. 67.

44. See Jordan, "Occasionalism."

Barker's Objection to Omnipresence

Barker's objections against omnipresence are probably his most pitiful regarding God's attributes. His comments regarding God's omnipresence seem to be more of a discussion of his misunderstanding of the Christian concept of "omnipresence" rather than an argument against it. Once again, he defines "presence" in physical terms and then argues that God cannot be omnipresent. Barker says, "To be 'present' means for matter and/or energy to occupy space-time at some spatial coordinates at a particular point in time," and, "To say that God is present in a 'spiritual' sense is meaningless until 'spirit' is defined." Once again, Barker is wrong.

The word "present" can include more than merely the physical. It was already shown how Aquinas explains the various uses of "presence." Something can be present in something else (e.g., redness in an apple), or something can be located at a particular place (e.g., an apple in a classroom). God is in all things and places in the universe through his knowledge and power because he sustains all things in the universe in existence.

This classical concept of God's "omnipresence" is not a meaningless concept, although God is not understood to be physically in all places. Moreover, this is not practically meaningless either. Since God is sustaining everything in existence with his mind and power, God has complete knowledge of everything and every event that occurs in the universe. Just as sports fans are "present" at a sports event through technology, God is present everywhere through his knowledge and creative activity. Thus, it is not necessary to have a complete understanding of what God is to understand what it is meant for God to be omnipresent.

Barker's Incompatibility Objections

As mentioned, Barker not only thinks that several of God's attributes are incoherent in themselves, but also that several of God's attributes are incompatible with each other. The first set of attributes that Barker mentions are God's omniscience and God's omnibenevolence. Barker argues that God cannot exist if God is omnibenevolent and omniscient because this means he chose to create, knowing that Adam and Eve would sin and that humanity in turn would commit all kinds of evil and suffer. If God knew what would happen to humanity, it was "mean-spirited" and criminally negligent for him to follow through with his choice to create humanity.

This is a strange argument coming from Barker, who has children. Parents all over the world choose to have children, knowing their kids will at one point suffer in some way. Having children in this world is celebrated more often than not, and usually people do not think that it is cruel or mean-spirited to have children.

Barker is talking about God, however, and it is much different for a human parent to decide to have children than for an all-powerful, all-knowing, and all-good God to decide to create humanity. God obviously has more options than human parents. To this regard, the problem of evil and the question of the compatibility of God's goodness, omniscience, and omnipotence have been discussed and debated within Christianity for thousands of years.[45] To properly explain the classical answer to the problem of evil would take much more room than is available at this point in this chapter.

Suffice it to say that many Christians would argue it is God's knowledge of and plan for the future that allows him to create, knowing that his creatures will suffer in various ways. This is because God's plan entails that humanity eventually will live in paradise with him forever. Barker says, "God should have had an abortion rather than bring a child into such misery."[46] Yet it seems hard to understand how it would be better to never exist rather than live in paradise for eternity after suffering through a life of hardships for only sixty to eighty years. A meager human lifespan is almost nothing compared to eternity.

After arguing for the incompatibility of God's omnibenevolence, omniscience, and omnipotence, Barker moves on to say that God's omnipotence and omniscience are incompatible. He says that if God knows the future, then God is powerless to change the future and should not be thought of as omnipotent. On the other hand, if God changes the future, then God is not omniscient.

Barker's problem here is that he is considering omniscience and omnipotence in isolation. Perhaps it would create a dilemma for God if the only two attributes that theists knew of were God's omniscience and omnipotence. However, theists are careful to consider all of God's attributes when trying to solve problems that arise when thinking about God. In this case, it is good to remember that classical Christianity views God as eternal and as the creator and sustainer of the universe. God does not make decisions in time as humans do. The future is fixed, not because God is powerless to stop it, but because God decided from all eternity to create the world and actualize it according to his plan. Because God is omnipotent, his good plan

45. Two great books on Aquinas's philosophy and the problem of evil are Davies, *Reality of God and the Problem of Evil*; and Knasas, *Aquinas and the Cry of Rachel*.

46. Barker, *godless*, 124.

cannot be thwarted. Thus, he has no reason to change his mind if such a thing were possible for him to do.

Also, the inability to change one's mind is not something that counts against the classical understanding of God's omnipotence. Recall that God's omnipotence is God's ability to create anything conceivable. This says nothing about whether God can or cannot change his mind.

Regardless, since Barker's argument is based on the assumption that God is in time, his argument, at best, only applies to a small percentage of theologians who believe that God is temporal. Yet, even considering that his argument applies to a small percentage, there are still many theists who would say that God's knowledge of the future includes knowledge of free-willed beings, including himself.[47] Barker might not know of such positions, however, since he thinks that theists take God's omniscience as a given, without thinking further into it. But even theists who think God is temporal would have an answer for Barker's objection in that it would not make sense to say that God cannot change the future since God knows everything he will freely decide.

Similarly, considering God's eternality shows the problem with Barker's FANG argument. Barker argues that God cannot have free will and be omniscient at the same time. He thinks that if God knows what will happen in the future, then God technically has no choices as to what he can choose. If God does not have choices, then God cannot have free will. Especially important to Barker's argument is his understanding of free will: "To be able to freely choose, there has to be a period of uncertainty or indeterminacy during which the options remain open and during which you could change your mind before it is too late. Free will, if it exists, requires that you not know the future."

Yet, here Barker is once again defining God out of existence and failing to interact with genuine Christian concepts. Of course, God's free will, and the nature of free will itself, have been debated for centuries in Christianity. However, a major view of free will is that it is the ability to have done otherwise in regard to any choice that is made.[48] With this understanding of free will, God is thought to have free will because he could have decided to create any conceivable world he wanted to (i.e., an infinite number of worlds besides our own), or he could have created nothing at all. It is not the indeterminacy that makes it free will, but the ability to do more than one

---

47. See footnote 39 of this chapter.

48. For Aquinas on God's freedom, see Aquinas, *De Potentia*, q. 1, a. 4; Aquinas, *ST* I, q. 25, a. 5; and Aquinas, *SCG* II, c. 23–30.

thing. That is why it is called *free* will. Barker seems to be arguing for a kind of *undetermined* will.

Again, however, Barker seems to fail to consider that God is eternal. Since God is not in time, whatever God creates (if anything) will have been something that God has willed to do from eternity. In other words, there would be no time at which God would not have willed to make what he has made. The God of classical Christianity is not a God who makes decisions like humans make decisions because God is eternal, omniscient, and omnipotent. Barker is not only failing to interact with the Christian understanding of God's free will, but he (intentionally or not) defines "free will" as something that only a temporal being can possess.

CONCLUSION

It seems that Barker should have taken his religion classes more seriously and given "pointless" philosophy a little more consideration. He claims to use "simple logic" to show that God's attributes are incoherent and incompatible, yet he fails to realize that he cannot refute Christianity if he is not actually arguing against it. Barker's basic strategy is to consider one or more of God's attributes, define each attribute in simplistic, non-Christian terms, and then swiftly dismiss them as incoherent and unbelievable. In "Omni-Aqueous," Barker basically argues against a temporal, infinitely physical, undetermined god without realizing that it would be hard, if not impossible, to find a single Christian who believes in such a god.

As shown, there are perfectly coherent explanations of God's omniscience, omnipotence, omnipresence, and others. God is thought to be omniscient in that he knows himself, everything he has created, and everything that he could create. God is thought to be omnipotent in that he can create anything conceivable. God is thought to be omnipresent in that his knowledge and power are everywhere in the universe. And these are only snapshots of the many positions that have been taken on God's attributes out of the thousands of years that Christianity has existed.

In light of Barker's arguments and ignorance of basic Christian doctrines, I think it is safe to say that Dan Barker is a charlatan. His book *godless* mentions that he is "one of America's leading atheists" and flaunts his years of experience as a Christian pastor. Yet it seems to me that he has no clue about what he is arguing against. Barker claims to "know" that the God of the Bible does not exist, yet he shows his ignorance of the God of the Bible in his arguments against the God of the Bible. If this is one of America's leading atheists, then atheism is in trouble.

BIBLIOGRAPHY

Aquinas, Thomas. *Summa Theologica*. First complete American ed. Translated by Fathers of the English Dominican Province. New York: Benziger, 1947.

Allison, Gregg R. *Historical Theology: An Introduction to Christian Doctrine*. Grand Rapids: Zondervan, 2011.

Barker, Dan. *godless: How an Evangelical Preacher Became One of America's Leading Atheists*. Berkeley: Ulysses, 2008.

Borland, Tully. "Omniscience and Divine Foreknowledge." http://www.iep.utm.edu/omnisci/.

Buijs, Joseph A. "On Misrepresenting the Thomistic Five Ways." *Sophia* 48 (2009) 15–34.

Davies, Brian. *The Reality of God and the Problem of Evil*. New York: Continuum, 2006.

———. *Thinking about God*. Reprint, Eugene: Wipf & Stock, 2010.

Feser, Edward. *Aquinas: A Beginner's Guide*. Oxford: Oneworld, 2010.

Jordan, Jason. "Occasionalism." https://www.iep.utm.edu/occasion/.

Klubertanz, George P., and Maurice R. Holloway. *Being and God: An Introduction to the Philosophy of Being and to Natural Theology*. New York: Appleton-Century-Crofts, 1963.

Knasas, John F. X. *Aquinas and the Cry of Rachel: Thomistic Reflections on the Problem of Evil*. Washington, DC: The Catholic University of America Press, 2013.

6

Dan Barker and the Immoral God of the Bible

—Steven Lewis

If you claim to be a good person, then this book should embarrass you and disgust you.
—Dan Barker[1]

A COMMON JAB OFTEN lobbed at the God of Christianity is that of the alleged immorality of the Bible. In his debate with Richard Howe at the 2017 National Conference on Christian Apologetics on the existence of God, prominent atheist author and speaker (and former Christian minister) Dan Barker employed just such an argument. Speaking about the Bible, Barker boldly asserted, "If you claim to be a good person, then this book should embarrass you and disgust you."[2] The purpose of such arguments, of course, is not to prove that God does not exist, or even that the Bible is false, but rather to show that God (as portrayed in the Bible) is not the holy, loving, forgiving Father believers assume, but he is instead evil, hateful, petty, prideful, vindictive, and a host of other horrifying descriptors.

---

1. God Who Speaks, "Is There a God Who Speaks?," 43:12.

2. God Who Speaks, "Is There a God Who Speaks?," 43:12. Though the arguments of several different atheists will occasionally be addressed and included, this chapter will focus primarily on the arguments of Dan Barker in his writings and debates.

This may seem at first more like an emotional outburst than an intelligent argument. After all, Barker is more interested in supporting dinner-table atheism and proselytizing ignorant believers than presenting rigorous academic arguments.[3] However, despite the lack of intellectual pretentions in his claims, the implications for believers remain significant and should not be so quickly dismissed or ignored.

In order to respond to Barker (and others who make similar claims), the Christian apologist may take a number of possible approaches. One common response, for example, is to systematically address each of Barker's examples of divine misbehavior in the Bible while offering various counter-examples and explanations as to why God may have chosen some particular course of action or issued some seemingly nefarious command.[4] This approach answers Barker on his own terms; it concedes Barker's assumption that God's actions must be justified in order to better accord with human moral sensibilities. Though this approach may be intuitive and straightforward, it also proves to be challenging and laborious.

Another possible response questions the veracity of the Bible itself, such as whether all the accounts of God and his actions in the Bible are literally true or accurate.[5] However, this just throws the baby out with the bathwater. If the truth of some part of the Bible is brought into question, then every part of the Bible is suddenly up for debate, including passages that may be critical to the Christian faith. This seems to just concede the point to Barker that his examples of God's immorality necessitate the absurdity of Christianity, and, thus, this approach is of little help to the vast majority of Christians who hold the Bible to be the inerrant, inspired word of God.

A third approach is one of balance—looking more at the "big picture" of the Bible and considering both the good and the bad.[6] This helps to present a unified picture of the God of the Bible from the Old to New Testaments and uses the positive texts to interpret the negatives. While this approach certainly (and rightfully) takes things like context and scope seriously, it can be difficult to turn the whole argument into a balance game. Someone like Dawkins or Barker would likely just turn it around and suggest using the negative texts as the standard instead.

---

3. In the autobiographical book *godless*, Barker explains, "I hope *Godless* will be helpful to atheists and agnostics who are looking for ways to talk with religious friends and relatives, but my real desire is that a Christian reader will finish this book and join us" (Barker, *godless*, xv).

4. For an example of this approach, see Copan, *Is God a Moral Monster?*

5. For an example of this approach, see Seibert, *Disturbing Divine Behavior*.

6. For an example of this approach, see Lamb, *God Behaving Badly*.

Therefore, in response to Barker's arguments, my approach will be a bit different. I will instead take a macro-view of the God of the Bible and ask whether Barker has any case to make in the first place. I will first present atheists' claims concerning the God of the Bible and then examine the underlying assumptions inherent in those claims. I will follow with a brief sketch of the God of classical theism as portrayed in the Bible and conclude by considering how some of the claims of Barker and others can and should be evaluated from this perspective. In the end, I will show that arguments such as those of Dan Barker regarding the goodness of God offer no significant problem if God in fact truly exists.

ATHEISTS AND THE BIBLE

In his infamous attack on the biblical God, atheist Richard Dawkins writes, "The God of the Old Testament is arguably the most unpleasant character in all fiction: jealous and proud of it; a petty, unjust, unforgiving control-freak; a vindictive, bloodthirsty, ethnic cleanser; a misogynistic, homophobic, racist, infanticidal, genocidal, filicidal, pestilential, megalomaniacal, sadomasochistic, capriciously malevolent bully."[7] Dan Barker follows Dawkins with an entire book defending this claim where he adds eight additional descriptors: pyromaniacal, angry, merciless, curse hurling, vaccicidal, aborticidal, cannibalistic, and slavemongering.[8] Barker writes, "The God of the Old Testament destroyed whole civilizations. He drowned the entire population of the planet. He is not the only bad egg in literature, but he is the most unpleasant character in all fiction."[9] Other atheists have followed a similar pattern. Christopher Hitchens claims, "The Bible may, indeed does, contain a warrant for trafficking in humans, for ethnic cleansing, for slavery, for bride-price, and for indiscriminate massacre, but we are not bound by any of it because it was put together by crude, uncultured human animals."[10] Atheist Michael Shermer writes, "The Bible is one of the most immoral works in all literature."[11] Despite this recent slate of atheists attacking the God of the Bible, such claims are not new. Nearly a quarter century before Dawkins, atheist philosopher J. L. Mackie likened Nazi anti-Semitic violence to God's commands to Israel: "The Old Testament itself reports many atrocities as having been not merely approved but positively demanded by God and his

7. Dawkins, *God Delusion*, 51.

8. Barker, *God*.

9. Barker, *God*, 7.

10. Hitchens, *God Is Not Great*.

11. Shermer, *Moral Arc*, 154.

spokesmen."[12] Such claims abound in atheist literature and surface often in the public square at speeches, interviews, and debates. Before engaging and rebutting such claims, however, one must first consider the underlying assumptions and methodology that lead to these conclusions in the first place.

The Problem of Autonomous Authority

As Dan Barker explains, "It is your job as Christian apologists . . . to demonstrate the reliability and the moral worth of the book on which your whole system of faith is based."[13] While this challenge does seem reasonable on the surface, it is the *way* Barker assumes that this must be accomplished that creates a problem—he assumes that the proper way to evaluate the biblical God is to judge the divine acts and commands by Barker's own moral sensibilities, which themselves must function independently of any divine authority. In other words, Barker rejects God's moral authority and then attempts to hold God accountable to Barker's own moral authority. Barker begins by defining morality without any appeal to authority: "Morality implies avoiding or minimizing harm. This is by definition."[14] Further, Barker ties morality solely to human reason. "Morality is in the mind—and reason is in the mind. No matter where you look for morality, it all comes down to the mind."[15] But how does he know that morality begins in the mind? Barker explains the foundational assumption behind his view of morality: humanism. "Humanism is not just better than the bible . . . it is the only way we can be moral."[16] Thus for Barker, morality is *by definition* independent of authority and yet dependent on humanistic principles of reason. As such, Barker claims that God simply punishes those who offend him, as if the offense itself warrants the punishment. "The humanist, on the other hand, looks for some reason or principle independent of authority."[17] Hence, according to Barker, only his own independent estimation of the reasoned principles governing morality can be used to evaluate the actions and commands of the God of the Bible.

However, this is not how believers typically go about establishing the "moral worth" of the Bible. A better approach is to begin not from this

12. Mackie, *Miracle of Theism*, 259.

13. God Who Speaks, "Is There a God Who Speaks?," 36:15.

14. Barker, *godless*, 210.

15. Barker, *godless*, 211.

16. Barker, *godless*, 202. Barker makes the stylistic choice throughout his writings not to capitalize "Bible."

17. Barker, *godless*, 167.

position of autonomous authority as Barker does, but by first establishing (or assuming for the sake of argument) the basic truth claims of theism as well as the historicity and reliability of the Bible.[18] By this approach, the Bible is understood as the authoritative word of God, and, hence, its own "moral worth" should be evaluated by its own standard of morality. In other words, rather than evaluating ancient documents according to modern moral sensibilities, a better way to evaluate the truth of the Bible is by starting with the Bible itself and working backwards from there.

Ironically, this is exactly what Barker himself claims to do, while simultaneously failing to do it. Barker admits, "I am not a professional bible scholar," and, "I'm not claiming to be a great authority," and insists that the Bible "can simply be opened and read."[19] In fact, Barker rejects centuries of biblical and theological scholarship that help us to understand and contextualize many of the problematic passages that constitute his arguments. "I have avoided footnotes, and there is little reference in the text to scholars and authors . . . but you will see them in the Bibliography. I have tried to let the bible speak for itself."[20] In fact, a brief look at Barker's bibliography confirms that he is not interested at all in whatever answers or counterarguments theologians or apologists may propose.[21] However, despite his claims to take the Bible at face value and let it "speak for itself," Barker either mocks or rejects any attempt to use the Bible itself to respond to his arguments. For example, when addressing God's command to slaughter the Canaanites, Barker rejects the Bible's own explanation of the Canaanites' wickedness. "However, the only reason they think the Canaanites were more corrupt than other cultures is because the bible says they were."[22] Thus, Barker is perfectly willing to take the Bible at face value when attacking God's moral character, but he is simultaneously unwilling to take the Bible at face value whenever it purports to explain the very reasons or possible motives for God's acts and commands. Barker cannot have it both ways. Either the Bible can speak for itself, or it cannot.

18. For an introductory treatment of an apologetic approach for the truth of the Bible as argued from basic intellectual and philosophical principles, see Geisler and Turek, *I Don't Have Enough Faith to Be an Atheist.*

19. Barker, *God*, 2.

20. Barker, *God*, 3.

21. Barker's bibliographies are composed entirely of like-minded atheists. This is true of both *godless* and *God: The Most Unpleasant Character in All Fiction* (with the exception of a few biblical concordances). It is a shame that Barker does not at least examine and attempt to refute the many counterarguments posed by theologians and biblical scholars over the centuries. Barker instead proceeds under the false guise that his arguments are definitive, and biblical scholars are silent on the matter.

22. Barker, *God*, 4.

It is in this respect that a contradiction becomes apparent in Barker's "autonomous authority" approach to evaluating the Bible. On the one hand, Barker writes, "I think we should read the bible like any other writings, just like millions of normal people have done throughout the centuries without the aid of scholars by their side explaining what it *really* means."[23] Yet Barker himself spends the rest of his book posing as a scholarly authority, explaining what it really means. Apparently, when reading the Bible, readers should ignore all interpretations and authorities—except Barker's.

The Problem of Context

Another critical aspect of Barker's claims regarding the immorality of the God of the Bible is that of context. Barker himself acknowledges the importance of understanding the context of a verse or passage to help draw out its broader meaning and implications. He writes, "Yes, context is crucial. . . . If something is truly out of context, I would like to know how."[24] However, Barker explains that understanding the proper context of a passage can be tedious and laborious, so he attempts to help his readers by emboldening the most offensive elements of the passages he includes. "Reading the bible can be laborious, especially during long passages. I have tried to make the task easier by boldfacing the relevant words in each verse. If you are in a hurry, simply scan for the boldface and come back later for the context."[25] In other words, Barker treats the importance of context as only a secondary effort. Also, the lack of importance of truly understanding context is perhaps most evident when Barker reduces the entire enterprise of seeking the context of a passage to an act motivated by blind devotion to a cruel deity.

> I think what believers most often mean by "context" is not the broader meaning of a verse as understood by the writers and readers of that time, as the words were used and allusions were grasped in their language and culture, considering the passages before and after the verse as well as the overall purpose of the book within which it resides; I think what they really mean by context is "my theology" . . . Their lives are devoted to their God, and naturally they rush to his defense. They want me to see God the way they do, so that I might accept his atrocities as a small part of a greater holy and righteous plan.[26]

23. Barker, *God*, 6.
24. Barker, *God*, 5.
25. Barker, *God*, 3.
26. Barker, *God*, 5.

But he also wants us to see the way he does.

Here Barker offers nothing more than an *ad hominem* attack by impugning motives rather than answering arguments.[27] As Barker himself rightly explains, "A strong clue that a person is arguing from a position of weakness is when they attack character rather than arguments and facts."[28] In fact, throughout his book of isolated biblical passages on the "atrocities" of God, Barker only rarely includes any mention of the broader context or original meaning of the passages in question; he instead relies upon overwhelming his readers with lengthy lists of isolated passages.

Barker is right that understanding the proper context of a biblical passage can be difficult and laborious; it requires either a good deal of effort on the reader's part or faith in the scholarly efforts of others who have already done the work. Barker seems uninterested in either. As already mentioned, he intentionally avoids consulting any theologians or biblical scholars in his efforts to understand the passages he brings up, and the passages he does use do not appear to be the result of painstaking effort on his own part to read and understand the Bible. In fact, Barker includes in his book a backhanded compliment to a Christian publisher for use of its searchable database: "Zondervan is committed to truth, so I am sure they will be pleased to know that their searchable database of dozens of translations has made it easier to learn the facts about the God of the Old Testament."[29] Thus, it is apparent that for Barker the proper tool to "discover the facts about God" is a searchable database of keywords and phrases—not actually studying the proper context as he describes and evaluating the text on its own merit.

ATHEISTS AND GOD'S NATURE AND EXISTENCE

The proper context of the Bible includes the fact that God exists as creator and sustainer of the universe. God is also said to be omnipotent, omniscient, righteous, benevolent, loving, merciful, longsuffering, and so on. Given this understanding of the God of Bible, the task of evaluating difficult passages must be taken from the context of the whole, including these claims about God. Despite his pretentions to the contrary, Barker expressly ignores this contextual element. When describing his own transition from belief to unbelief, Barker explains that it was not "reading the Bible" that led

27. This type of *ad hominem* argument from Barker is also known as a "genetic fallacy"—when the merits of an argument are ignored, and its origin or motives are attacked instead. Even if it is true that some arguments are motivated by a theist's desire to preserve his own theology, that does not mean that such arguments are false.

28. Barker, *godless*, 88.

29. Barker, *God*, 304.

him to atheism, but rather he began by rejecting the Bible's authority first and then the existence of God. He writes, "If the Prodigal Son is a parable and Adam and Eve are a metaphor, then why is God himself not one huge figure of speech?"[30] It was only then that Barker returned to the Bible and began to read it as if God did not exist. "I was forced to admit that the bible is not a reliable source of truth: it is unscientific, irrational, contradictory, absurd, unhistorical, uninspiring, and morally unsatisfying."[31] All of this is ostensibly true if and only if God does not exist.

Again, the focus of this chapter is not whether or not God exists, but whether the God of the Bible is guilty of Barker's accusations of immorality. If the context of Barker's claims is that God is fiction, then discussing "God's immorality" is nothing more than meaningless conjecture with no basis in reality. But as we have seen, Barker is not writing to like-minded atheists—he is writing to theists who believe that God exists. Thus, in order to make any meaningful case at all, Barker must presume that the God of the Bible truly does exist (even if just for the sake of argument) and then attempt to demonstrate a contradiction given that assumption. This is the only reasonable option for Barker if he wishes to avoid self-defeating circularity or pointless conjecture. As theists Paul Copan and Matthew Flannagan rightly explain, "We have emphasized . . . for the sake of argument, that biblical theism is true and that the existence of a good, commanding God cannot be removed from the biblical narrative without doing serious damage to its coherence and significance."[32]

Furthermore, another problem for Barker is that of the nature of God. Even if Barker truly lets the Bible speak for itself, considers its context correctly, and presumes God's existence in its evaluation, he still must consider God's nature as described in the Bible in order to fairly and accurately evaluate God's acts and commands. The scope of the present project does not permit an exhaustive explanation of the classical view of God and how that view can be argued from a position of foundational metaphysical principles in reality,[33] so for the purposes of this chapter, I will simply assume that God is the infinite, omnipotent, omniscient, perfectly good creator and sustainer of the universe that the Bible claims him to be. This view is consistent both with the biblical view of God and with over two millennia of theological

---

30. Barker, *godless*, 39. He explains that his rejection of the literal truth and historicity of stories in the Bible (such as that of Adam and Eve) led him to question the Bible as a whole, including God's existence.

31. Barker, *godless*, 40.

32. Copan and Flannagan, *Did God Really Command Genocide?*, 240.

33. For an excellent look at God's existence and nature in this regard, see Gilson, *Christian Philosophy of St. Thomas Aquinas*.

scholarship,[34] so it seems to be a fair place to start when evaluating the sort of being Barker is referencing.

The central thesis for Barker is one of morality—that God somehow fails to live up to basic moral sensibilities that are obvious to most humans. Barker asks, "Doesn't it follow that if [God's] actions were cruel, then he was cruel?"[35] The focus here is in what sense God can be said to be a "moral being" beholden to the moral principles Barker appeals for his arguments.

For Barker, God must answer to his apparent violations of Barker's moral code, but where does Barker get his moral code? As we have already seen above, Barker goes to great lengths to deny any need for external authority when it comes to determining morality. But if Barker draws his morality only from his own internal perceptions, then he has lost his case against God. Even if Barker were right, then God would be beholden not to Barker's morality, but to his own. However, Barker believes his own morality is superior to God's. "Why do believers assume that a *higher* power is necessarily a more moral power? How do they know it is not the other way around?"[36] To answer Barker's question, we must consider the nature of God. If God is in fact the perfect creator of humanity and morality, then the very internal sense of morality that Barker perceives in his own mind ultimately has its origin in God's own nature and goodness. Therefore, God would always *by necessity* be the greater moral authority.

But even if God's morality is superior to human morality, Barker asks why God should be the judge of humans. "Why should the mind of a deity—an outsider—be better able to judge human actions than the minds of humans themselves? . . . A human mind feels physical pain. The human mind can know sorrow, grief, regret and embarrassment, while the mind of a perfect deity cannot."[37] Here Barker assumes that a proper moral authority over humans should always be one that best understands what it is like to be human in the first place. However, if God is the presently active creator and sustainer of every human being in every moment they exist (as the biblical view of God affirms), then God would by necessity possess a perfect understanding of every human—and human nature as a whole. Thus, God would

---

34. For an excellent volume summarizing the biblical, philosophical, and traditional support of the classical view of God and his nature as described here, see Geisler, *Systematic Theology*.

35. Barker, *God*, 277.

36. Barker, *godless*, 212. Barker must establish that his own morality is in fact superior to God's morality, or he has lost his entire argument. If Barker's moral sensibilities are not authoritative, he has no case against God.

37. Barker, *godless*, 211.

know *even better than humans* what it is like to be human, and what is in the best interest of humans.

Thus, if God is the perfectly good Creator and Sustainer of all humans (as assumed here for the sake of argument), then human morality *must* begin with God. Even so, it is in this respect that Barker asks, "If the basis for morality rests with a single entity, then what makes that entity accountable? What makes God moral?"[38] For the answer to this question, once again we must return to the proper understanding of God's nature. If God is himself perfectly good according to his nature, then God does not look to some external standard to decide his own actions but rather to himself and his own perfect nature. But in what sense is God a "moral being" if he is not behaving according to some external standard? In short, God can be said to be "morally perfect" only insofar as he acts consistently with his own perfect goodness, which he always does; he is not considered "morally perfect" because he behaves in such a way that is admirable or successful from some outside perspective (such as Barker's).[39] In short, God is not bound by external moral duties, and, thus, he cannot be judged by external moral standards.[40]

Barker himself is aware of this approach. As he explains, "True Christians should not ask if the bible is moral. If God is the source of morality, then asking if God is moral is like asking if goodness is good."[41] He goes on to point out that anyone who believes in God will have no recourse except to just claim that God is good by definition. "If pressed [believers] will have to back off from judging God, and will have to admit that God is moral by definition alone. It doesn't really matter how God acts: God is good because he says he is good, and we should worship him not because he has earned our admiration but because he has demanded it."[42] Putting aside the fact that Barker gets many of the details wrong,[43] he at least gets the result cor-

---

38. Barker, *godless*, 162.

39. For a similar treatment of questions concerning God's nature and divine morality, see Davies, *Reality of God and the Problem of Evil.*

40. More can be said of Barker's own individual sense of morality, which (according to the Bible) is tainted by sin and fleshly passions. Thus, Barker cannot claim that his own moral sensibilities are the same as God's because they have their origins in God. Only what is good and right about Barker's morality is from God—anything imperfect or flawed is from Barker. Once again, according to the Bible, God is the ultimate moral standard.

41. Barker, *godless*, 162.

42. Barker, *godless*, 163.

43. Barker misunderstands the basic reason that God is known to be good and why God is worshiped. According to the classical view, God is not "good because he says he is good"; rather, he is good because it is an essential aspect of his nature—God just *is*

rect: God is good by definition—because goodness is an essential aspect of his nature. Despite his familiarity with this idea of God's essential goodness, Barker offers no further alternative or counterargument in response. He also makes no attempt to show that this is somehow incoherent or contradictory. He simply moves on to criticizing the morality of the Bible.

Barker appears to miss the devastating implications of the view he has just explained and subsequently ignored. Namely, if God exists and is by nature perfectly good (which the Bible affirms), then God is the ultimate moral authority, and all his acts and commands are always consistent with his goodness by absolute necessity. The only way the Bible could possibly contradict this would be a direct negation of God's essential nature with no reasonable alternative explanation. In other words, Barker must show that it is logically impossible that God were in fact perfectly good if the Bible were true.

Furthermore, Barker is right that it makes little sense for a believer to go about "judging God" on the basis of God's actions. God's goodness is just who he is; it is not up for evaluation or debate. In fact, to even consider God as a being who must act according to some greater moral authority is simply nonsense. In other words, if God does not exist, then morality is just whatever Barker (or anyone else) wants it to be. But if God truly exists, then Barker's entire argument collapses. Thus, the entire issue is resolved on the basis of God's existence and nature, not God's actions.

However, even given the correct understanding of God and his nature, Barker may yet think he has a solid case against the God of the Bible. After all, Barker believes that the Bible clearly and unequivocally portrays God as a whole litany of horrifying descriptors that do not result in any sort of being that is perfectly good in its own essence. Once more, Barker must show that the Bible *directly contradicts* God's essential goodness and is thus conclusively incoherent, and as such Barker must show that no reasonable alternative explanation for the examples he offers is forthcoming when taken in context and at face value. No doubt Barker believes his arguments have accomplished exactly that. In the last section below, I will examine and evaluate some of Barker's specific claims in this regard.

---

goodness. Also, God is not worshiped by believers because "he has earned our admiration," nor because "he has demanded it," but rather because he *deserves* it by his very nature.

ATHEISTS AND THE GOD OF THE BIBLE

Barker's list of divine offenses in the Bible—expanded from Dawkins's quote—is too massive to address here in totality, so here I will focus on three of Barker's most virulent and oft-repeated arguments against the God of the Bible: jealousy, slavery, and genocide. In keeping with the approach detailed above, each claim offered by Barker (and other atheists) will be treated only in its original context and always with the assumption that the God of classical theism (as described in the Bible) truly exists. The intent is not to argue here that these assumptions are true, but rather to show that Barker is able to produce no contradiction in any of his most prevalent claims that would cast any reasonable doubt on the existence of God as described in the Bible.

God and Jealousy

The case against God's jealousy is pervasive in atheistic literature. Richard Dawkins accuses God of sexual motives: "God's monumental rage whenever his chosen people flirted with a rival god resembles nothing so much as sexual jealousy of the worst kind, and again it should strike a modern moralist as far from good role-model material."[44] Michael Shermer compares God to a petulant child: "These humanlike emotions reveal Yahweh to be more like a Greek god, and much like an adolescent who lacks the wisdom to control his passions."[45] Dan Barker describes God as a controlling lover:

> The one word that sums up the scenario between Genesis and Malachi is 'jealousy.' Almost every page, every story, every act, every psalm, every prophecy, every command, every threat in those 39 ancient books points back to the possessiveness of one particular god who wanted to own and control his chosen lover by demanding total devotion.[46]

For Barker, God's jealousy flares up, not in response to his people acting in harmful ways, but only when the Israelites try to worship other gods; thus, it is selfishly motivated. As Barker explains, "The God of the Old Testament rarely gets angry when he sees his people doing morally harmful things. . . .

---

44. Dawkins, God Delusion, 276.

45. Shermer, Moral Arc, 177 (emphasis in original).

46. Barker, God, 13. In fact, Barker is so taken by the biblical evidence of God's jealousy that he spends the rest of his book referring to God's name as the "Lord Jealous" in keeping with Exodus 34:14: "For you shall not worship any other god, for the Lord, whose name is Jealous, is a jealous God."

The Lord Jealous becomes enraged when he sees someone loving a god other than himself."[47]

The biblical examples offered by Barker to support this charge of divine jealousy abound. "You shall not worship them or serve them; for I, the LORD your God, am a jealous God, visiting the iniquity of the fathers on the children, on the third and the fourth generations of those who hate Me" (Exod 20:5, NASB). "'They made Him jealous with strange gods; With abominations they provoked Him to anger'" (Deut 32:16). "For they provoked Him with their high places and aroused His jealousy with their graven images" (Ps 78:58). Barker accumulates over twenty such examples of God's jealousy, but to make the case that these pose a contradiction with God's goodness, Barker must show that the proper context and understanding of God's jealousy is evil or bad. As such, he defines jealousy connotatively. "Jealousy is insecurity. . . . It is possessive and controlling, based on an assumed right of ownership. Strong jealousy arises from a desperate need to be validated by the devotion of another, even if (or especially if) that 'love' is forced. It is shaky vanity. It is the terror of losing the property that bolsters your sense of self-worth."[48] What Barker describes here is certainly an example of what sometimes occurs with human jealousy, but is this the most reasonable way to consider jealousy when describing God?

While the word "jealousy" in its typical connotation seems more of a flawed character trait than something to be proudly proclaimed of a good and honorable being (such as God), this is not the only sense in which this word is used. Instead of leaping to conclusions that jealousy is always evil or bad, one must consider in what sense the word is being applied to God. When speaking of a perfect and eternal God, Barker's definition of jealousy makes little sense. Humans often want things for selfish reasons, or even from a sense of loss or incompleteness when a desired object is absent, but an infinite being lacking nothing would be wholly incapable of such desires. If God exists as he is portrayed in the Bible, one must pause to consider whether there is any other reasonable sense in which jealousy could be ascribed to God.

In its most basic sense, jealousy involves a rivalry over the possession or affection of something or someone of value. This involves both *righteous* jealousy (when it is for something that rightfully belongs to you) or *sinful* jealousy (when it is for something that does not belong to you). The question then becomes, "Is God described as 'jealous' because he desires something that is rightfully his, or because he is forcing admiration on something that

47. Barker, *God*, 233.
48. Barker, *God*, 16.

belongs to another?" The context of the Bible makes it clear that the answer is the former. God's jealousy is for Israel to remain devoted and committed to him as the ultimate and perfect source of all that is good. The imagery often mirrors a marriage commitment. "The reason God is jealous is because he binds himself to his people in a kind of spousal intimacy."[49] Just like a husband may be rightfully jealous of a wife who commits adultery, the affection and devotion shown to false gods by Israel provokes God's jealousy because God (as the perfectly good Creator and Sustainer of all that exists) is the *only* being deserving of Israel's religious devotion.

Furthermore, is God somehow *lacking* in himself if he does not rightfully receive the affection of the Israelites, or is he jealous because it is truly the Israelites themselves that are lacking without God? The answer is clear. If the Bible is right, then God's jealousy is never out of some selfish desire or need for self-fulfillment or divine ego-stroking, but **actually out of God's own** *love* **for the good of the those for whom he is jealous.** If God is the perfect, eternal creator that the Bible portrays, then he is by nature the ultimate source of good in all that exists, and, thus, all people who reject God in favor of false alternatives are only harming themselves. For atheists like Barker, the highest good for humans is always full autonomy from God's authority, but if the God of the Bible truly exists, then such a state of affairs would be unquestionably harmful and self-destructive. "In the end, God desires to be known as God, which is only appropriate and the ultimate good for creatures."[50] Thus, when biblical passages describing God's jealousy are taken in context under the assumption that God truly exists, Barker is unable to demonstrate any sort of direct contradiction in the nature of the biblical God.

God and Slavery

Another prominent criticism of the God of the Bible among the atheistic literature is that of his passive permission of (or active participation in) slavery. Michael Shermer writes,

> The spectacularly unreflective authors of the Bible had absolutely no problem with slavery whatsoever, as long as the slave owner didn't actually beat his slave blind and toothless (Exodus 21:26, 27). That was going just too far, although beating a slave to death was perfectly fine as long as the slave survived for a day or two after the beating. Then, when the slave died, it was appropriate

49. Copan, *Is God a Moral Monster?*, 36.
50. Copan, *Is God a Moral Monster?*, 30–31.

to feel sorry for the unfortunate slave owner because it was he who had suffered a loss (Exodus 21:21).[51]

Dan Barker points out that an eternal God should have corrected slavery long ago.

> If the God of the Old Testament were more than a fictional character, he might have been free to rise above the culture of his authors to denounce slavery. Instead, we had to wait millennia to abolish the biblically approved practice on our own, a progress that was hampered by faith in an ancient slavemonger deity. Like the writers who invented him, God had no choice but to endorse and encourage the cruel and inhumane customs of their primitive age.[52]

Richard Dawkins agrees that human morality has evolved and improved beyond the Bible. "The point is that we have almost all moved on, and in a big way, since biblical times. Slavery, which was taken for granted in the Bible and throughout most of history, was abolished in civilized countries in the nineteenth century."[53]

The Bible (particularly the Old Testament) speaks often about slavery. Barker points out that slave ownership extends even to the wives and children of slaves: "'If you buy a Hebrew slave . . . If he comes alone, he shall go out alone; if he is the husband of a wife, then his wife shall go out with him. If his master gives him a wife, and she bears him sons or daughters, the wife and her children shall belong to her master, and he shall go out alone'" (Exod 21:2–4). Beating one's slaves seems to be permitted: "'If a man strikes his male or female slave with a rod and he dies at his hand, he shall be punished. If, however, he survives a day or two, no vengeance shall be taken; for he is his property'" (Exod 21:20–21). Barker even points out a racial component to biblical slavery in that only slaves of other races could be purchased and owned: "'As for your male and female slaves whom you may have—you may acquire male and female slaves from the pagan nations that are around you. . . . they [non-Jewish sojourners] also may become your property'" (Lev 25:44–45). The resulting issue is significant for believers. Does the God of the Bible condone slavery? If so, does this represent a moral failure—or even an act of evil—on the part of God?

Before considering this question, one must carefully define the terms being used, and once again, this requires a look at the context of the biblical

51. Shermer, *Moral Arc*, 194.

52. Barker, *God*, 283.

53. Dawkins, *God Delusion*, 300.

laws involving slavery. Slavery in the modern sense invokes images of kidnapping, bondage, forced servitude, cruelty, rape, racial hierarchy, and overall dehumanization. These potent images of slavery generally reference the international slave trade that ravaged the United States (and other countries) up until the late nineteenth century. The typical American is appalled at the actions of his ancestors in this regard, and, thus, when reading in the Bible where slavery was permitted in ancient Israel under the guidance and laws of God himself, the response is often shock and confusion. However, the error here is a fallacy of equivocation. Simply speaking, slavery in the Bible is not the same as slavery in nineteenth-century America. A few distinctions are important so that one can more clearly see the full picture of what is being discussed in the Bible when it speaks of slaves.

First, biblical slavery was more akin to indentured servitude than forced slavery. It was typically a contract entered into willingly by both slave and owner, usually for the sake of the poor in order to provide for themselves or their families (Exod 21:5; Lev 25:39, 47). Second, kidnapping and the forced servitude of captives were expressly forbidden as capital crimes, which would outlaw the entire nineteenth-century slave trade outright (Exod 21:16). Third, slavery came to a natural end. A number of conditions could occur that would mandate a slaveowner to free his slaves: if a slave was injured (Exod 21:26–27), not adequately provided for (Exod 21:11), or redeemed by kinsmen (Lev 25:48–49); after seven years of servitude (Exod 21:2; Deut 15:1); and at the year of Jubilee (Lev. 25:40–41). As such, a closer look at the context of these laws shows a gradual push *away* from slavery— not further into it. Furthermore, the laws did more to protect the slaves than the slaveowners; the human dignity of the slave is always protected and preserved. "Israel's servant laws were concerned about controlling or regulating—not idealizing—an inferior work arrangement. Israelite servitude was induced by poverty, was entered into voluntarily, and was far from optimal. The intent of these laws was to combat potential abuses, not to institutionalize servitude."[54]

One final objection regarding biblical slavery worth addressing here is the charge that even if biblical slavery was not the same as other forms of chattel slavery that eventually spread throughout the world, God should have known better. Michael Shermer explains, "Imagine how different the history of humanity might have been had Yahweh *not* neglected to mention that people should never be treated as a means to someone else's ends but should be treated as ends in themselves. Would this have been too much to

54. Copan, *Is God a Moral Monster?*, 127.

ask from an all-powerful and loving God?"[55] However, it is irresponsible to make any sort of judgment that God should have outlawed slavery in the Bible from the start to save humanity from centuries of what became such a cruel, inhuman enterprise. Perhaps God knew that such a blanket condemnation of slavery would not be heeded, and so he chose to construct his laws more as a gradual step away from slavery and toward human dignity and equality rather than an ineffective or destructive condemnation from the start. In any case, slavery in world history cannot be blamed on God. Slavery existed long before God's law was given to the Israelites, and it existed long after.

In summary, Barker's condemnation of the modern notion of slavery is admirable and correct, even though the slavery permitted and regulated in the Bible is a vastly different social enterprise than what Barker imagines. A great deal more can be said on this issue than what space here allows, but suffice to say, there are plenty of good and reasonable alternatives to the "slavemonger" view of the God of the Bible proposed by atheists such as Dan Barker. Thus, when the Bible's descriptions of slavery and slave laws are taken in the correct social context under which they were given, a direct contradiction in the existence of the perfectly good God of the Bible fails to materialize.

God and Genocide

Perhaps the most common and potent charge against the moral perfection of God is that of his authorized commands to kill entire settlements of Canaanites in order to clear the land of foreigners for Israelite occupation—what Barker calls "ethnic cleansing" or "genocide." "The God of the Old Testament committed, commanded, and condoned many more human annihilations. Their totals were smaller in number than the flood, but they were no lesser genocides."[56] Christopher Hitchens expresses sympathy for the Canaanites: "One mutters a few sympathetic words for the forgotten and obliterated Hivites, Canaanites, and Hittites, also presumably part of the Lord's original creation, who are to be pitilessly driven out of their homes to make room for the ungrateful and mutinous children of Israel."[57] Richard Dawkins emphasizes the racial element of the slaughter: "The ethnic cleansing begun in the time of Moses is brought to bloody fruition in the book of Joshua, a text remarkable for the bloodthirsty massacres it records and the

55. Shermer, *Moral Arc*, 197–98.
56. Barker, *God*, 136.
57. Hitchens, *God Is Not Great*, 101.

xenophobic relish with which it does so."[58] Finally, Dan Barker pities the Israelites who were compelled to such atrocities: "It appears that in order to win favor in the eyes of the God of the Old Testament, you have to be an obedient and heartless ethnic cleanser. Otherwise, step aside."[59]

Barker provides several examples of acts of genocide commanded by God. Nothing that breathes should be left alive: "Only in the cities of these peoples that the LORD your God is giving you as an inheritance, you shall not leave alive anything that breathes. But you shall utterly destroy them, the Hittite and the Amorite, the Canaanite and the Perizzite, the Hivite and the Jebusite, as the LORD your God has commanded you" (Deut 20:16–17). Infants and animals are to be slaughtered: "Now go and strike Amalek and utterly destroy all that he has, and do not spare him; but put to death both man and woman, child and infant, ox and sheep, camel and donkey" (1 Sam 15:3). Kill everything, but keep the virgins for yourselves: "Now therefore, kill every male among the little ones, and kill every woman who has known man intimately. But all the girls who have not known man intimately, spare for yourselves" (Num 31:17–18).

The problem for believers is the apparent contradiction between God commanding, on one hand, to kill and, on the other, not to kill. "How can we reconcile God's commandment not to kill anyone with his commandment to kill everyone? In light of this account, and many others like it, the Sixth Commandment should probably read thus: *Thou shalt not kill—not unless the Lord thy God says so. Then shalt though slaughter thine enemies with abandon.*"[60] But once again, is the killing of the Canaanites in the Old Testament the same as modern acts of genocide, such as in Nazi Germany, Bosnia, Rwanda, Somalia, Iraq, and others? Dawkins thinks so. "The point is that, whether true or not, the Bible is held up to us as the source of our morality. And the Bible story of Joshua's destruction of Jericho, and the invasion of the Promised Land in general, is morally indistinguishable from Hitler's invasion of Poland, or Saddam Hussein's massacres of the Kurds and the Marsh Arabs."[61]

Here we must return once again to the nature of God as a guide for understanding these commands. Assuming that God exists, and the Bible is his authorized word to humanity, it is clear that these instances of killing were special cases given in specific contexts and authorized by the only one who is truly sovereign over all life and death—God himself. As Copan explains,

58. Dawkins, *God Delusion*, 280.

59. Barker, *God*, 90.

60. Shermer, *Moral Arc*, 179 (emphasis in original).

61. Dawkins, *God Delusion*, 280.

"So what if the facts about the world include a good God who specifically reveals himself and may issue extraordinary commands in specific, unique contexts and with morally sufficient reasons?"[62] In other words, if anyone has the right to end a life, then it is the one who created life in the first place. Thus, God has not broken any laws or stepped outside his moral nature in order to command the killing of the Canaanites. Furthermore, if God commanded these acts as the Bible reports, then the Israelites acted merely as agents under God's authority, not their own. This is a stark distinction between these acts of killing and every modern example of genocide.

Nonetheless, the atheist may yet argue that the question is not whether God or the Israelites had a right (or responsibility) to kill the Canaanites, but rather how such an act or command could be morally justified, considering its brutality if God is truly good. The biblical examples above seem to be chosen often by atheists just for this purpose, as they contain examples of killing innocent women, children, infants, and even animals. Barker asks, "So when Israelites invaded a Canaanite town and they took a sword and they cut off the heads of two-year-olds and they ripped open pregnant women and they destroyed and burned and killed everybody, that could be good?"[63] As Richard Howe points out in reply, Barker here is conflating "good" with "moral good." Considering once more the nature of the God of the Bible as understood from classical theism, God is simply "good" in his essence by necessity in that his being is perfect, complete, and lacking nothing. God is only "morally good" in the sense that he always acts in perfect harmony with his essentially good nature. However, God is not "morally good" in exactly the same way that humans are morally good. Humans must uphold a standard of perfection that is beyond themselves, for humans are not perfectly good in their nature or essence—they must look to a standard beyond themselves. This is not true of God. Hence God's command to kill the Canaanites, for example, cannot be considered a "moral evil" in any reasonable sense of the term if the God of the Bible truly exists. Finite humans can safely assume that God, if he exists as the Bible asserts, is acting according to his perfect nature while giving such a command, and that any seeming contradiction must exist only in the imperfect mind of the human—not in the omniscient mind of God. Whatever God's reasons for such a command, he certainly has them, and they are fully consistent with his infinitely good act of being.

Even though God has no need to reveal the reasons for his actions, he nevertheless often does so within the very texts in which these commands

---

62. Copan, *Is God a Moral Monster?*, 50.

63. God Who Speaks, "Is There a God Who Speaks?," 1:23:54.

occur. This is not necessary to defend the intellectual consistency of God's existence, but it is nevertheless helpful to see what possible reasons or motives may lay behind God's genocidal commands. First, unlike most modern examples of genocide, these commands have nothing to do with race or nationality and everything to do with sin. "'It is because of the wickedness of these nations that the LORD your God is driving them out before you'" (Deut 9:5). Second, the Canaanites are eliminated to spare the Israelites from falling prey to the Canaanites' sinful corruption and idolatry. "'When you enter the land which the LORD your God gives you, you shall not learn to imitate the detestable things of those nations. . . . because of these detestable things the LORD your God will drive them out before you'" (Deut 18:9, 12). In fact, God even promises to destroy the Israelites themselves if they follow in the footsteps of the idolatrous Canaanites. "'For they will turn your sons away from following Me to serve other gods; then the anger of the LORD will be kindled against you and He will quickly destroy you'" (Deut 7:4). Thus, these killings are motivated solely by the unrepentant sin of the heathens in the land—something only God himself is fit to judge. They were not killed because of their nationality or race.[64] Third, it is important to note a distinction in the text that the overarching command in the conquest of Canaan is to "drive out" the inhabitants and clear the land—not necessarily to kill everyone from the start (Deut 7:1–5). "The text therefore continually and repeatedly states that the Canaanites will not be exterminated in the sense that the Israelites are to kill every single man, woman, and child in Canaan. Rather, it states they are to be driven out."[65] Hence, it is possible that the commands to kill the inhabitants of a specific fortress or city are isolated to incidents in which the inhabitants, though warned, refused to leave.

Admittedly, this is a complex and difficult issue given the horrors of genocide enacted against entire nations and people groups in the modern world. But once again, it is important to remember the distinctions that set these biblical commands apart from modern acts of genocide. If the God of the Bible exists, then God alone has the authority to issue these specific, limited commands for humans to act as agents of his judgment against sinful, deserving peoples. Because God alone has this authority, then it is reasonable to conclude that any such commands do not violate any sense of goodness or moral perfection attributable to God.

Also, it could be that God is also trying to keep the bloodline or maintain the rescue plan of the Israelites from ending

64. In fact, some Canaanites, such as Rahab, were spared for their righteous acts. See Josh 6:25.

65. Copan and Flannagan, *Did God Command Genocide?* 80.

to provide the lineage for Jesus?

CONCLUSION

In this chapter, we have looked closely at the arguments of Dan Barker (and others), proclaiming the immorality of the God of the Bible. Barker has offered a litany of verses and commentary to show that God is not as good as believers may think. However, a number of critical problems quickly arise when Barker's arguments are challenged. First, Barker assumes the ineffective position of autonomous authority in his evaluation of God's moral goodness rather than considering God's own moral perfection by his own revealed nature. Second, absent from Barker's arguments are any contextual explanations or justifications within the very Bible he is criticizing—all despite Barker's stated intention to let the Bible "speak for itself." Third, Barker's most glaring contextual error is refusing to consider the actual existence of the being he is criticizing, even though God's existence is an integral and inseparable aspect of the context of the Bible as a whole. Fourth, given God's existence, "jealousy" can only be attributed to God analogically as an aspect of God's love for imperfect creatures who harm themselves by rejecting the ultimate good of God. Fifth, slavery in the Bible is not the cruel enterprise of the nineteenth century; rather, slavery as permitted by God in the Bible is instead more reasonably seen as a temporary solution for a specific ancient cultural context. Sixth, God's commands in the Bible to slaughter Canaanites are nothing like modern acts of racially motivated genocide initiated by human despots; rather, they were special cases in certain circumstances given by the author and sustainer of life as a judgment of wickedness. While there is much more to say about each of these issues, it is clear that Barker's arguments are not without significant difficulties. Given the actual existence of God as described in the Bible, Barker has failed to demonstrate a reasonable contradiction that casts doubt on whether or not the God of the Bible truly exists.

Getting back to Dawkins's well-known critique of God: "The God of the Old Testament is arguably the most unpleasant character in all *fiction*: jealous and proud of it; a petty, unjust, unforgiving control-freak; a vindictive, bloodthirsty, ethnic cleanser; a misogynistic, homophobic, racist, infanticidal, genocidal, filicidal, pestilential, megalomaniacal, sadomasochistic, capriciously malevolent bully."[66] Notice in this list of subjective descriptors and personal judgments about God, Dawkins only includes one actual objective truth claim—the word "fiction." For Dawkins and Barker (and others), this is the crux of the argument. If indeed the Bible is fiction, and God does not truly exist, then Dawkins may indeed have some

---

66. Dawkins, *God Delusion*, 51 (emphasis added).

case to make about the characteristics and motivations of a divine fictional character that cannot be determined or evaluated in reality. But if in fact the Bible is true, and God does exist, as believers assert, then Dawkins's entire complaint is just a dubious impossibility and offers nothing of any reasonable or practical value in understanding God's acts and commands.

Nevertheless, Barker structures his argument, not to provide new philosophical insight into the existence and nature of God, but primarily to persuade believers away from their confidence in the God of the Bible. He attacks what he believes to be a worldwide congregation of ignorant believers who know little about philosophical and theological arguments. He writes, "Church pews are packed with biblically illiterate worshippers. . . . Even the least educated atheist knows enough about the bible to judge its reliability or relevance."[67] It is unclear if Barker truly has a correct understanding of the nature of God and just ignores this intentionally to sway the ignorant masses, or if he himself should be counted among the ignorant. Thus, Barker himself is either deceitful or ignorant when he sets out to demonstrate that God (according to the Bible) is an "unpleasant character" unworthy of the admiration and devotion God is often awarded by believers; Barker simply misunderstands or misrepresents the very nature of the being he is talking about, which precludes the very possibility that God could be any of the things Barker asserts. God, if he exists, is by biblical definition an eternal, perfectly good being—the source of all goodness in the universe, including the good of existence itself. Hence any observation to the contrary can be nothing more than a misunderstanding on the part of the reader of the Bible.

Unfortunately, it appears that despite his claims to the contrary, Barker himself is not really interested in the truth of the matter. He writes, "The bible says that the '*ungodly* are like chaff which the wind blows away.' (Psalms 1:4) That's fine with me. I prefer the winds of freethought to the chains of orthodoxy."[68] But if God does exist, then it is only *truth* that Barker has "freed" himself from, and he is left to be helplessly tossed and thrown about in the dark and destructive winds of autonomous self-authority. Furthermore, for Barker, choosing eternal self-destruction is preferable over acknowledging the truth of the God of the Bible. He writes, "Speaking for myself, if the biblical heaven and hell exist, I would choose hell. Having to spend eternity pretending to worship a petty tyrant who tortures those who insult his authority would be more hellish than baking in eternal flames.

67. Barker, *godless*, 94.
68. Barker, *godless*, 103.

There is no way such a bully can earn my admiration."[69] Even though Barker claims to be fully open to evidence and argument demonstrating that the God of the Bible truly exists, here he explains that he would still choose to reject the truth in favor of his own preferences and perceptions. For Barker, whether he is right or wrong seems to be an entirely secondary issue; the main issue is his willing rejection of the God of the Bible and refusal to consider whether any of his arguments would have any basis in reality if God in fact truly exists. From what is known and understood about the nature of the very God that the Bible portrays, Barker has nothing of value to add to the discussion; his arguments as a whole are just distracting and irrelevant.

BIBLIOGRAPHY

Barker, Dan. *God: The Most Unpleasant Character in All Fiction.* New York: Sterling, 2016.

———. *Godless: How an Evangelical Preacher Became One of America's Leading Atheists.* Berkeley: Ulysses, 2008.

Copan, Paul. *Is God a Moral Monster? Making Sense of the Old Testament God.* Grand Rapids: Baker, 2011.

Copan, Paul, and Matthew Flannagan. *Did God Really Command Genocide? Coming to Terms with the Justice of God.* Grand Rapids: Baker, 2014.

Davies, Brian. *The Reality of God and the Problem of Evil.* London: Continuum International, 2006.

Dawkins, Richard. *The God Delusion.* Boston: Houghton Mifflin, 2006.

Geisler, Norman L. *Systematic Theology.* Vol. 2, *God and Creation.* Minneapolis: Bethany House, 2003.

Geisler, Norman L., and Frank Turek. *I Don't Have Enough Faith to Be an Atheist.* Wheaton: Crossway, 2004.

Gilson, Étienne. *The Christian Philosophy of St. Thomas Aquinas.* Translated by L. K. Shook. Reprint, University of Notre Dame Press, 2013.

The God Who Speaks. "Dan Barker Debates Richard Howe: Is There a God Who Speaks?" *YouTube,* October 14, 2017. https://www.youtube.com/watch?v=LD3-qK-2gu8&t=1s.

Hitchens, Christopher. *God Is Not Great: How Religion Poisons Everything.* New York: Twelve, 2007.

Lamb, David T. *God Behaving Badly: Is the God of the Old Testament Angry, Sexist, and Racist?* Downers Grove: InterVarsity, 2011.

Mackie, J. L. *The Miracle of Theism: Arguments for and against the Existence of God.* Oxford: Clarendon, 1982.

Seibert, Eric A. *Disturbing Divine Behavior: Troubling Old Testament Images of God.* Minneapolis: Fortress, 2009.

Shermer, Michael. *The Moral Arc: How Science and Reason Lead Humanity toward Truth, Justice, and Freedom.* New York: Holt, 2015.

69. Barker, *godless,* 170.

7

Barker's Understanding of Bible Contradictions

—Thomas Baker

Everyone knows that the bible contains accounts of miracles, and that is reason enough to conclude that there may be better uses of one's time than studying Scripture.

—Dan Barker[1]

In chapter 13 of *godless*, Dan Barker presents what he believes to be many Bible contradictions by placing verses he thinks are contradictory next to each other. Outside of a few notes on some, Barker does this without any detailed explanation or exegesis. In addition, most of the verses come from different books with entirely different contexts, but that does not matter to Barker so long as they *appear* contradictory. Moreover, he had previously chastised anyone who thought they could refute him, charging them with lacking logic. He stated in a previous chapter, "We get these tortured point-by-point defenses of the 'inerrant word of God' from fundamentalist preachers and other Christians who think the discrepancies can be explained. What they lack in logic they make up for in length."[2] Ironically,

1. Barker, *godless*, 94.
2. Barker, *godless*, 203.

in these lists of apparent contradictions, he never engages any rebuttals or alternative explanations from well-known Christian apologists. It appears that regardless of what reasoning or evidence a Christian may bring, Barker would disagree. It seems shameful that Barker provides such a lack of exegesis, purposefully ignoring proper context, in order to support his atheistic agenda. Frankly, it is astonishing when looking at the lists because the errors seem so obvious that it reminds me of a small child who is angry with his parents and lashes out irrationally, taking their words out of context.

Since Barker provides thirty-eight different lists with well over 170 verses, it will not be a good use of our space here to provide a detailed treatment for each and every verse given. Instead, like a doctor, it is better to treat the underlying interpretative issues than just the superficial symptoms. This way, even though we do not treat all the lists, one should be able to begin to see the inherent problems, which are repeated throughout. Therefore, I will address these apparent contradictions by primarily surfacing some important interpretative principles and then sampling some of the verses to show that the same interpretative failures occur over and over again. This will be done in three basic steps. First, I will deal with the importance of context for biblical exegesis. Second, I will take the verses he presents in his very first list (a good canonical example of taking verses out of context) by walking through each of them to show how context bears on the interpretation. Third, I will treat some interpretive issues of Barker's largest subject, namely, the nature of God, which consists of twelve lists. Again, we will walk through some important principles that apply to the subject and then sample some of the verses to show their application.

At the outset, one thing should be kept in mind since we are dealing with atheistic critiques of the Bible: attacks against biblical revelation cannot diminish the arguments for the existence of God from natural theology because those arguments are not based on biblical revelation. For those who are swayed by the negative criticisms of the Bible, the most these criticisms can accomplish is to diminish inerrancy, but contrary to atheists' assertions, the biblical criticisms cannot prove that God does not exist. Hence, regardless of the nature or status of the Bible, they do not remove the metaphysical need for a First Cause.

CONTEXT! CONTEXT! CONTEXT!

The proper way to treat interpretative issues is to first look at the context. However, we know that some atheists like Barker want to draw attention away from the actual context and wager the force of their argument on the bare "appearance" of a contradiction in order to sway those who will not look deeper into the issue. Of course, this only works for those who do not honestly want to understand the Bible verses in question.

Now, while the importance of context has been dealt with to some degree already, it is important to delve a bit further into it, given that context is at the heart of meaning. A single word, for example, can be used with different meanings in different contexts. This is why when looking up a word in a dictionary, it often has a numbered list of usages depending on the context. For example, the word "note" has several usages. It can refer to a short, written letter, a sound in a musical composition, an odor or flavor, or to verbally draw attention to a point a speaker or writer is making. Words have usages that show their semantic range, which is directly dependent on their context. The importance of context also applies to events and narratives. For example, the reason why someone goes to the top of the mountain in one passage may not be the same reason found in another passage (cf. Gen 22:2; Exod 19:20). Even phrases have a context in which they should be interpreted. Apologists Norman Geisler and Thomas Howe, in their book on Bible difficulties, provide the example in Psalm 14:1, where it says, "There is no God."[3] In the fuller context, we know that it says, "The fool has said in his heart, 'There is no God.'" Context even applies to larger narratives and their historical development. In Matthew 16:20, it says, "Then He commanded His disciples that they should tell no one that He was Jesus the Christ" (ESV). Yet, in Mark 16:15, and many other places in the New Testament, the disciples are commanded to preach the gospel of Jesus Christ. The difference is context! In Matthew 16:20, Jesus is telling them not to widely spread it now because he had not finished his ministry, not died on the cross, nor rose from the dead yet. He still had other things to do. Now, after he died on the cross and rose from the dead, then it was widely permitted (Matt 28:19–20; Mark 16:15) because now his first advent ministry was completed. Even in commands, which we will deal with more directly below, Geisler and Howe bring up the notable point that Jesus said in Matthew 5:42, "Give to him who asks you," but that does not mean to give loaded firearms to small children.[4] There are even important aspects related to the historical time period and culture in which statements or events take place. Context is key to interpreting any passage in the Bible. While there may be Bible difficulties, most often careful observation of the context can resolve the matter.

---

3. Geisler and Howe, *When Critics Ask*, 17.

4. Geisler and Howe, *When Critics Ask*, 17.

COMMANDS

As briefly indicated above, there are also contexts to commandments. Barker's treatment of murder appears to be one of his favorite objections, and he brings it up again here in chapter 13 of *godless*, showing that the Bible forbids killing in Exodus 20:13 and Leviticus 24:17. This is placed in contrast to verses where God had commanded the taking of life (1 Sam 6:19; 15:2–3, 7–8; Hos 13:16; Ps 137:9). However, there are two major problems with Barker's idea that these passages contradict each other.

First, and perhaps the most obvious, God is not human and is not subject to human morality. It is absurd to think God is a subject to be ruled. God is the creator and lawgiver, not the creature. God can take life because he was the one who gave life. To explain by analogy, it would be wrong for me to pull up the plants in my neighbor's garden, because it is not my garden. However, I can pull up the plants in my own garden because I am the one who planted them. The critics may object with this analogy and suggest by extension that this may imply human parents can take the life of their child since it appears they are the ones who gave it. However, this completely misunderstands the causation involved. There is a difference between an efficient and instrumental cause. The primary efficient cause is that *by which* the effect is produced. Whereas, the secondary or instrumental efficient cause is that *through which* the effect is produced. When a man and a woman have a child, the parents are not the ones who gave life. God is the one who gave life *through* the parents. The parents are only the instrumental cause of the child. This is proven by the fact that when the efficient cause is removed, then the effect does not follow. Without an efficient cause, there can be no effect. If the efficient cause of the child's life were the parents, then when the parents died, the cause would be removed, and the child's life would end also, but this is not what happens. God is the one who sustains the existence and life of each human being, and he is sovereign over it. He is the creator and sustainer of all life. Daniel said it very eloquently in Daniel 5:23b: "the God who holds your breath in His hand and owns all your ways, you have not glorified" (NKJV).

Second, God is sovereign over his creation, and he is the one who can decide when life can or cannot be taken. He is the lawgiver. Similarly, there are laws in our society against murdering the innocent, but the ruling government can issue law enforcement personnel to perform capital punishment to kill individuals convicted of capital crimes. Governments can also issue commands for soldiers to kill other human beings in the defensive or offensive actions of a nation during wars or other national security situations related to enemy nations. This is all for the good of the nation to protect against evildoers inside and outside. In the Old Testament, Israel was under theocratic rule; God was the ruling governor. While we are commanded not to kill, the government can (Rom 13:4) because it has greater scope and oversight for the welfare of the entire group. In general, it should not be surprising that sometimes commandments against certain actions apply to some individuals, but not to others. Even in the context of father-child relationships, there are things that the father prohibits the child from doing but that the father himself can do, such as have a gun, drive a car, or go on a long trip by himself.

In the counter verses that Barker lists against Exodus 20:13 and Leviticus 24:17, this is exactly the situation. His counter verses, Exodus 32:37 and Numbers 15:36, are related to capital crimes that existed in Israel at the time. Individuals who committed capital crimes were punished with death. The other counter verses (1 Sam 6:19; 15:2–3, 7–8; Hos 13:16; Ps 137:9) are all related to defenses and offenses against enemy nations. So why is this so difficult for Barker to understand? We have the same situation in our society today. Citizens are not allowed to kill people on a whim, but the government can decree capital punishment for capital crimes or killing for purposes of national security. Why is Barker not protesting about his own government being contradictory? It is either that he is an extremely poor exegete, or he is purposefully trying to deceive with a biased agenda. It seems perfectly reasonable that individual citizens should not have the right to take life at their own discretion, but governments can for the purposes of enforcing laws and protecting the welfare of the entire group.

Out of the thirty-eight lists given by Barker, several are related to God commanding an action, and then (in a different context) doing what he commanded not to do, or prohibiting an action, and then showing support for it (also in a different context). Prohibition against murder was in the first list, but this is followed by additional lists related to lying, stealing, keeping the Sabbath, and making graven images. Each of these suffer similar contextual issues. I will treat one more to give an additional example of the type of contextual problems that exist.

The next list is about lying. Barker provides verses Exodus 20:16 and Proverbs 12:22 to show that it is wrong to lie. The counter verses listed are 1 Kings 22:23 and 2 Thessalonians 2:11, along with a comparison between Joshua 2:4–6 and James 2:25. The contexts for these counter verses are so gravely different that it is an utter shame that he provides a list like this with no attempt to clarify the context. Barker then adds a parenthetical at the end: "(I don't think telling a lie is always wrong, and neither does the bible)."[5] At first glance, it would appear Barker does not have a problem with it, after all. So then why does he list it? Perhaps to imply that God is contradictory, and thus Barker wants to try and tarnish God's character. What Barker does not explain is that all but one of the counter verses deal with the issue of people who reject the truth over and over again, even after repeated admonishment. Consequently, through punishment, God gives them over to what they desire, namely, falsehood. If a person will not receive the truth, then what else is left? God was trying repeatedly to give the truth, but they rejected it and ended up through judgment receiving the opposite. In the first counter verse, God even told the person what the falsehood was.

To delve into the details a bit, the first is the counter verse 1 Kings 22:23. It should be noticed right from the beginning that it was not God who lied, but the spirit in the false prophets. What is even more striking is that the lie was perfectly made clear to Ahab and not done in secret. Micaiah the prophet plainly told Ahab that a lying spirit was in the mouths of Ahab's prophets and mentioned what the lie was. So much for it being deceptive and done in secret. That was very gracious of God to have his prophet Micaiah share this truth with the rebellious Ahab. Moreover, God had already warned Israel to keep away from idolatry, worshiping the gods of other nations, and false prophecy, but Ahab purposely ignored these directives. God is sovereign and will use both good and evil agents to accomplish his ends. God did not force anyone to lie, for in a fallen world, God will use what is available to him to accomplish his ends, whether it be a spirit lying to Ahab who rejects God and the truth, or some other means. Ultimately, God passed judgment on Ahab using the only thing he would listen to, for Ahab did not want to listen to the truth that Micaiah was giving. Micaiah even explained to Ahab that if he listened to the four hundred false prophets, then he should know that they were telling him lies. Unfortunately, this is what Ahab did, and he paid the price for it.

The next counter verse, 2 Thessalonians 2:11, presents a similar situation: "And for this cause God shall send them strong delusion, that they should believe a lie" (ESV). Biblical commentator Dr. Thomas Constable states, "When people refuse to entertain the truth, He lets them pursue and experience the consequences of falsehood."[6] This is God's judgment against a stubborn heart. Psalm 81:12 states, "So I gave them over to their stubborn hearts, to follow their own counsels." God desires people to believe and follow the truth. But as was stated earlier, when someone rebels and rejects the truth over and over again, then he comes under the judgment of God,

---

5. Barker, *godless*, 224.

6. Constable, "2 Thessalonians," 720.

and God gives that person over to that person's desire to believe a lie. This is not contradictory or inconsistent but shows the sovereign judgments of a holy God, who cannot tolerate stubborn and consistent rejection of the truth. What is so ironic about this truth is that it is all written down for anyone to read in the Bible. It is not being hidden as if God is performing this judgment in secret. No, God is warning the world right now through the Scriptures not to reject the truth. When we typically think of lying and deceit, we think of it being done secretly. The whole point is to hide the truth and not let them know they are being lied to and deceived, but that is not the case here. God is openly telling everyone the truth and the judgment for rejecting it.

The last part of this list deals with a comparison between Joshua 2:4–6 and James 2:25. Barker's point here is that Rahab, like the Hebrew midwives in Exodus 1, lied to save a life, and verses in the New Testament (Heb 11:31; Jas 2:25) appear to have supported them lying. There are two points to make in response. First, it is not clear that God supported and blessed Rahab for lying. Both the book of Joshua and the verses in the New Testament appear to be in response to her faith in hiding the spies. Joshua 6:17 and 6:25 mention the reason for sparing her was "because she hid the messengers." Hebrews 11:31 says the reason was because "she had received the spies with peace." And James 2:25 poses the question, "Was not Rahab the harlot also justified by works when she received the messengers and sent them out another way?" Since there was no explicit mention of support about lying, it has to be inferred. However, it could also be inferred that God was not including the action of lying in his support, but only Rahab's faith in receiving and hiding the spies.

Regardless of whether God gave support for her action of lying or not, my second point is that in our fallen world, there can be true instances of moral conflict between higher and lower moral laws. In Matthew 23:23, Jesus referred to the "weightier matters of the law," indicating that some moral laws are more important. When there is a true moral conflict between obeying a human government (Rom 13:1) or God, especially when it is a matter of life or death, then one should obey God, which is more important. This is the moral conflict that Rahab found herself in when the "king of Jericho" in Joshua 2:3 asked Rahab to bring out the men that had entered her house. Rahab states in Joshua 2:9–11, "I know that the LORD has given you the land . . . for the LORD your God, He is God in heaven above and on earth beneath." Either Rahab was to obey the king of Jericho or God. As Geisler and Howe explain, "It may have been impossible for her to both save the spies and tell the truth to the soldiers of the king. If so, God would not hold Rahab responsible for this unavoidable moral conflict. Certainly a person cannot be held responsible for not keeping a lesser law in order to keep a higher obligation."[7]

Since we did not have space to deal with all of Barker's verses related to commands, there is another contextual point to make as it relates to commands in general, namely that later revelation supersedes previous revelation. The Bible is progressive revelation, and more is revealed to mankind over time. In doing this, there are dispensations or house rules during different periods of time. There was a point in time when God issued a command to only eat fruit and vegetables (Gen 1:29), which was later expanded (Gen 9:3). At one point in time, believers were commanded to sacrifice animals for their sins (Heb 10:11–14), but now they are to believe in the Lord Jesus Christ and confess their sins to God (1 John 1:9). Geisler and Howe offer a good summary, stating,

> Bible critics sometimes confuse a change of revelation with a mistake. The mistake, however, is that of the critic. For example, the fact that a parent allows a very small child to eat with his fingers, only to tell them later to use a spoon, is not a contradiction. Nor is the parent contradicting himself to insist later that the child should use a fork, not a spoon, to eat his vegetables. This is progressive revelation, with each command suited to fit the particular circumstance in which a person is found.[8]

Therefore, when Barker discussed in chapter 13 and elsewhere the Sabbath, necessity of works, or other verses related to commandments, it is important to keep in mind the time, culture, and to whom the commands were given.

THE NATURE OF GOD

As one looks over the thirty-eight lists from Barker (depending on how you classify each of them), there are roughly twelve questions, each with their own lists of verses attempting to show a contradiction about the nature of God. These are:

1. Does God change his mind?

2. Is God good or evil?

3. Is God peaceable?

4. Was Jesus peaceable?

7. Geisler and Howe, *When Critics Ask*, 134.
8. Geisler and Howe, *When Critics Ask*, 25–26.

5. Was Jesus trustworthy?

6. Does God live in light?

7. Does God tempt people?

8. Does God accept human sacrifice?

9. Has anyone seen God?

10. How many Gods are there?

11. Does God know the future?

12. Is God omnipotent?

From this, it would appear that the nature of God is one of his largest categories. Given our space limitation, the benefits of spending time tackling a portion of his largest category will center the rebuttal where Barker apparently has the most issues. It will also provide ample opportunity to highlight the importance of some key hermeneutical principles as they relate to the doctrine of God. Now, I reordered the list slightly, placing importance on God's immutability and his goodness first, since those seem to be central themes for Barker. Unfortunately, we will only be able to treat the first five, but hopefully there will be enough information provided to enable readers to apply the principles to the other verses. Regardless, it is not as if anything I am saying here is entirely new. These questions have been addressed through Bible commentaries and Bible handbooks many times over. Nonetheless, I am hoping to bring some conciseness and tailor my responses more specifically to Barker.

The initial point to reemphasize here is that God is the creator, not the creation. He is not human, or an animal, or anything created (Hos 11:9; John 4:24; Rom 1:23; Acts 17:24–25, 29). Unlike the universe, God is not finite, temporal, material, or spatial. Nonetheless, the critic may rebut here and say that the definition is begging the question because Scripture seems to be conflicting on whether God is Spirit (John 4:24) or material since God is depicted in human form with eyes (Heb 4:13), ears (2 Chr 6:40), and arms (Deut 5:15). So, let us pause for a moment and consider that reason alone tells us that God cannot be those things and still be God. Scripture even states in Romans 1:20, "For his invisible attributes, namely, His eternal power and divine nature, have been clearly perceived, ever since the creation of the world, in the things that have been made. So they are without excuse." Consequently, as we consider the universe and how things exist, we can reason that a being without these theistic attributes would change, have parts, be finite, have a limited existence, and ultimately need a cause for its own existence. Why? To answer this and show why it is reasonable to interpret Scripture theistically, I will present four reasons for why God cannot be temporal, changing, finite, material, or spatial.

First, anything that is temporal is changing, and vice versa, for time is a measurement of change. If something changes, then it has a before and after. So, anything temporal has to have a beginning because there cannot be an infinite regress of moments or changes, for then it would be impossible to ever arrive at the last moment or change. There can be no leap from an infinite past to the present because it is impossible to cross an infinite. It would be like trying to crawl out of a bottomless pit. Therefore, anything that changes or is temporal has a beginning and needs a cause for its existence. If something was caused to exist, then it cannot be God.

Second, all change needs a changer, for an effect cannot arise without a cause. Consequently, you have to get back to a First Uncaused Cause that does not change in order to get the series going. Besides, the fact that something changes implies a change for the better or for the worse: a gain or a loss. Something is gained that was needed, or something is lost that was previously needed. Regardless, this cannot apply to God, who is perfect.

Third, unless something completely changes into something else (i.e., substantial change), then part of it changes, and part of it stays the same (i.e., accidental change), otherwise you would not be able to identify it after its change. But, if part of it changes, then it is composed of parts. Anything that has parts is finite because the nature of a part is to define limits. Adding more parts still does not free something from being limited. You simply cannot have an infinite number of parts because you could always add one more. Being limited is further underscored as soon as we consider something that is material or spatial because you cannot have an infinite amount of matter or spatial extension for similar reasons (i.e., there could be more matter or more spatial extension added). Basically, anything with dimensive quantity is limited, which is what it means to be finite. Besides, to be material would also imply change both at the subatomic level (e.g., motion of an electron) and through consideration of the Second Law of Thermodynamics. Anything material is also spatial, and vice-versa, granting that we are using "material" and "spatial" in the widest sense to include all the modern classifications of material states. This shows the interconnectivity of space, time, and matter or STM for short, which was brought into existence at the moment the universe was created. This is why God cannot be like finite, temporal, and material creation.

Fourth, to be limited requires a limiter. Anything limited is *caused to be in a finite way*. It becomes an effect *with specification*. Consider that "existence" as a notion is unlimited. To say something exists does not say how it exists or that it exists with such and such qualities. However, as soon as one says something exists with specific limits, like a certain length, width, color, etc., then there has to be a cause to explain why it has such limits. Something does not just happen to be circular, three inches in diameter, and red for no reason. Every specification needs a specifier. It is caused to be that way. It is an effect with specification. This is also why, teleologically speaking, every efficient cause ultimately requires a final cause to determine its end. And subsequently, every final cause requires an agent with an intellect to determine the end. The implications of requiring an intellect to determine an end cannot be underestimated. Paul Hoffman, in commenting on motion, argues, "First, something cannot move unless it moves in a determinate direction. Moreover, something cannot move in a determinate direction without being determined to that direction. But to be determined to a determinate direction is to have that direction as an end. Thus, all locomotion is teleological."[9] All matter is in motion, and this motion has to be accounted for. Otherwise, you have the absurd and non-scientific position that everything is random, and there are no physical laws. Anything can move or change its specification at any moment on a whim. But alas, we see there are physical laws that describe the consistent operation of things. Well, physical laws need a lawgiver, just as much as moral laws do. Hence, all limited things, whether speaking about qualities, quantities, and so on, are caused to be that way. They need a cause to explain the specification in the effect.

Consequently, the infinite God of the Bible has no quantitative limits of dimension, states, or changes. Ultimately, one has to get back to a spiritual reality, a First Uncaused Cause that is change-less, space-less, time-less, and immaterial; otherwise, it cannot be the First Cause. This natural theistic reasoning is not new, for it has had a rich history in the writings of Augustine, Anselm, and Aquinas. And so, in accordance with Romans 1:20, "His invisible attributes, namely, his eternal power and divine nature, have been clearly perceived." Therefore, it is not begging the question, and reason alone tells us that God is not finite, temporal, material, or spatial.

Now, the point to be made from this is that when it comes to human language in the Bible that describes God, not everything can be taken literally or metaphysically. As Geisler states,

> There are *anthropomorphisms*, which depict God in human form, such as having eyes (e.g., Heb. 4:13), ears (2 Chron. 6:40), and arms (Deut. 5:15). Next, there are *anthropopathisms*, which picture God having changing human feelings like anger and grief (Eph. 4:30). Finally, there are *anthropoieses*, which attribute

9. Hoffman, "Does Efficient Causation Presuppose Final Causation?," 300.

to God human actions, such as repenting (Gen. 6:6) and forget-
ting (Isa. 43:25; Job 11:6). None of these are intended as literally
true, and to take them as such can lead to serious error.[10]

Human language is plagued with tense and finitude. Therefore, when it
comes to biblical revelation, we have to acknowledge that some things have
to be taken symbolically. Failure to understand these things when interpreting the Bible can lead to many false notions about the nature of God. Even
for Barker, it should be obvious that the predicates used of God in the Bible
cannot all be literally true. For it says that God is Spirit in John 4:24, but as
shown above, it also says he has eyes, ears, and arms. Moreover, it says that
God is a shield (Ps 18:1), a rock, and a strong tower (Ps 144:12). He cannot literally be all these things. Obviously, there is symbolic language in the
Bible, and one needs to take that into account!

The second point is that the Bible is written in time, and God deals with
each person and situation as it happens, which he knows from all eternity as
the First Cause.[11] Consider for a moment if you were omniscient and knew
all things, and you knew that your son would grow up to be a good, honest,
and loving adult, but at this moment your son has lied to you and violated
many rules of the house. What would you do? You would deal with your son
and discipline him for what is happening in that moment. And being omniscient, you would also understand that the discipline you take with him
now will indeed help form the person he will become. Likewise, the Bible is
consistent in stating that God will give to each according to one's works (Ps
62:12; Prov 24:12; Jer 17:10). Furthermore, you may even pose questions,
testing him, or engaging him in certain ways, knowing that the influence
you are having now will be one of the triggering moments in your son's life
that places him on the path you see him become in the future. The very experiences we have can bring about new developmental stages in our growth.
Think of a person who has always been afraid of horses, but, through some
special influence or pressure, rides a horse and loves it. That very experience brought about something in the person that was dormant that now
both that person and others realize. God does this also. We see God come
to people and ask them questions, which he already knows the answers to,
but asks them in such specific ways in order to test them, to evoke some
response that will bring about something in them. Moreover, God also tests

10. Geisler, *Systematic Theology*, 28.

11. As Aristotle argued, knowledge comes through knowing the causes. In other
words, to know a thing is to know its causes. See Aristotle, *Phys.* I.1, 184a10–15. Since
God is the First Cause and knows himself fully, he also knows all the effects that proceed from himself.

people to see if they will indeed trust him in various situations. A simple search of the Bible shows many verses where God tests people (1 Sam 16:7; 1 Chr 28:9; 29:17; 2 Chr 6:30; Pss 7:9; 139:1, 2, 24; Prov 17:3; Jer 11:20; 17:10; 20:12). So, does testing mean that God does not know what they will do? No, again, testing will often bring to light what may be dormant, what is in potentiality, and make it actual. Why would God do this? In order to reveal it both to that person and deal with it in the open. Ecclesiastes 12:14 says: "For God will bring every work into judgment, Including every secret thing, Whether good or evil" (NKJV).[12] And lastly, God does not reveal all that he knows in every situation and in every engagement. God interacts with people in ways that are in accordance with his providential plans. Consider Jesus's interaction with the woman at the well in John 4. From Jesus's first interaction in asking for a drink to the last, Jesus did not reveal everything all at once, but interacted with the woman, asking questions, while obviously knowing a lot more than he revealed to her. In conclusion, and now armed with these two rather expanded points, it is time to treat a few key items in Barker's lists about the nature of God.

God's Immutability

Barker asks, "Does God change his mind?"[13] Barker provides Malachi 3:6, Numbers 23:19, Ezekiel 24:14, and James 1:17 in support of God's immutability. The counter verses attempt to show using the King James Version that God "repented" and changed his mind. These verses are Exodus 32:14, Genesis 6:6–7, Jonah, 3:10, 2 Kings 20:1–7, Numbers 16:20–35, 44–50, and also Genesis 18:32–33, where it provides the narrative of Abraham bargaining with God. So, let us walk though these and show how both context and our understanding of God's nature from natural theology can be utilized in our understanding of these passages.

Change always implies a context and perspective. When we say the sun rises and the sun sets, does this imply the sun is moving around the earth? No, but the early astronomers thought so. The earth moves, and the sun stays. What about when a person says the window is to my left and then turns and now says the window is to my right? Did the window move or did the person? These same sorts of basic implications are at play here. In Exodus 20:14, the circumstances changed, and so the judgment God initially was going to give was changed to mercy. God did not change, but the circumstances changed. God is always unchangeably pleased with righteousness

---

12. Cf. 1 Cor 4:5; 14:25.

13. Barker, *godless*, 227.

and always unchangeably displeased with unrighteousness. Joel 2:13 states, "Rend your hearts and not your garments. Return to the LORD your God, for he is gracious and merciful, slow to anger, and abounding in steadfast love; and he relents over disaster" (ESV). When Moses approached God and interceded on behalf of Israel, the circumstances changed, and God gave mercy. All those events and interactions were known to God from all eternity like a scroll rolled out before him. God deals with each situation individually. He does not extend mercy until it is deemed appropriate. This is just like a father with a son who is now disobedient but will know in the future the son will grow to become an honest and loving person. It would have been strange for God to have said to Moses, "I am going to extend mercy and not judge Israel for these sins because I know in a short moment you will intercede for them." No, God dealt righteously with the situation and expressed his displeasure over their blatant idolatry. It would have been strange to Moses if God did not do this, given that in the Ten Commandments, he had already expressly forbidden idolatry. I have to say at this point that it becomes a bit tiresome to have to remind critics of these basic hermeneutical principles. For Barker, the Bible is guilty before proven innocent. And then, even when reasonable interpretations are provided, they quickly get dismissed given his atheistic agenda. For Barker, the Bible cannot be innocent; it cannot be right. It has to be wrong, and nothing anyone says appears to change that.

Regardless, I am going to continue with the next verse showing that the issue is the same. In Genesis 6:6, depending on the translation, God was "sorry," "regretted," or "repented" he had made man, given that mankind's corruption had become so extensive. This is something God knew from all eternity would come, and while he regretted that it would come, he had a solution to prolong mankind and provide an ultimate plan of salvation through Noah. God did not change, but the situation changed. Mankind had become very corrupt. It would not be much different than if you knew ahead of time of some regrettable future that would require severe action on your part. As we know, God had a plan. Like pruning off the disease and weak parts of a plant to allow for more growth, God chose righteous Noah in which to bring about a more promising future for all of mankind. If God would not have done this, then mankind would have become totally corrupt and thus destroyed itself.

As for the rest of the counter verses, while the situations are slightly different, the pattern is the same. God is like a pillar; God does not change, but the people, situations, and events change in relation to him. God is unchangeably pleased with righteousness and unchangeably displeased with unrighteousness. The Bible shows how God dealt with each situation as it historically unfolded, even though he knew from all eternity it would eventually come (cf. Gen 15:16; Isa 46:10; 2 Thess 2:1–4).

Is God Good? Is He Peaceable? Is He Trustworthy?

Four of the twelve questions deal with God and Jesus's character as to whether they are good, peaceable, and trustworthy. For Barker to argue for a contradiction among the verses given, again shows a great blindness to the context. It is almost unworthy of a response. In the case of whether God is good, Barker supplies the following verses in the affirmative: Psalm 145:9 and Deuteronomy 32:4. Then, he supplies the following counter verses: Isaiah 45:7, Lamentations 3:38, Jeremiah 18:11, and Ezekiel 20:25–26.

Now to begin, I will take his first counter verse, Isaiah 45:7, but what I say about this verse applies in similar fashion to the other counter verses. With Isaiah 45:7, Barker skips the first clause and lists it as in the King James Version as "I make peace, and create evil. I the Lord do all these things." Well, perhaps Barker does not like the fact that God judges sin, for when he does, he may inflict punishment or calamity upon the evildoers, such that from the perspective of those on the receiving end, it will be deemed harmful or evil. Yet, it is righteous and just for God to do it. If you take a closer look at the verse, "evil" is sitting opposite of "peace." What is the opposite of peace? Take for example, 1 Kings 22:8, which says, "And the king of Israel said to Jehoshaphat, 'There is yet one man by whom we may inquire of the LORD, Micaiah the son of Imlah, but I hate him, for he never prophesies good concerning me, but evil.' And Jehoshaphat said, 'Let not the king say so.'" The same Hebrew word *ra*, used in Isaiah 45:7, is also used here. In context, Ahab was an evil king, and when God, through the prophet Micaiah a few verses later, did indeed announce judgment upon Ahab, he called it evil (1 Kgs 22:18). Why is this so hard for Barker to understand? When a parent disciplines a child, it is not joyful for the child (Heb 12:11). The same analogy can be readily seen in his counter verse in Jeremiah 18:11: "Now, therefore, say to the men of Judah and the inhabitants of Jerusalem: 'Thus says the LORD, Behold, I am shaping disaster against you and devising a plan against you. Return, every one from his evil way, and amend your ways and your deeds.'" And also in Isaiah 31:2, "And yet He is wise and brings disaster; He does not call back His words, but will arise against the house of the evildoers and against the helpers of those who work iniquity."

Second, after the counter verses, Barker adds that the "Hebrew word *ra* clearly means 'moral evil,' as it is used in Genesis 3, the most moral tale in the entire bible."[14] However, it is a hermeneutical fallacy to ignore the context where a word is actually sitting and just blindly import the meaning of that same word from a foreign context. This would be like taking the meaning of the word "note" in the description of a musical composition and importing its meaning into the sentence, "The tea had a note of mint." Remember, earlier it was shown how words obtain a more determinate meaning from their context. Case in point, we just showed how it can be a perceived and subjective harm or evil in the case of Ahab's judgment, which is not a moral evil, but a divine judgment. According to one of the most respected Hebrew lexicons, the Hebrew word *ra* has ten usages as an adjective, four as a substantival, and four more as a type of expression.[15] That amounts to eighteen different usages. It is simply poor hermeneutics and frankly poor scholarship to suggest *ra* only ever means one thing regardless of the context.

Third, Barker attempts to capitalize on the word "create" in Isaiah 45:7, stating in his note, "That word 'create,' by the way, is *bara*, used in the first verse of the bible."[16] A similar problem applies here. The word *bara* can be used in other ways besides creation *ex nihilo* of the universe. Apparently, the implication is that evil is something God created. However, evil itself is a privation of some good thing that should be, according to the nature of that thing, whether we are talking about physical or moral evil. A physical evil would be like blindness, the privation of some good thing that should be there, like sight. An example of a moral evil would be a crime, such as stealing, which is the privation of some good thing that should be there, like virtue. Evil itself is not an existential thing. No one walks around and finds a pile of evil. It is not a substance, not material, not spatial. Ontologically, it is the privation of being. To use an analogy, evil is like rust in a car. The car must exist for there to be rust, but a totally rusted car is no car at all. Or to use another analogy, if you were to take all the imperfections out of something, what would you be left with? You would be left with something good and perfect. However, if you were to remove all the perfections out of something, what would you be left with? Absolutely nothing. Hence, good and being are convertible and so is evil and non-being. There is nothing that is pure evil, for it would be non-being. Nor is evil a mere *absence* of good, but it is a *privation* of some good thing that should be there. The point is that the word "create" here cannot apply to evil, *per se*, in the same way God created the universe. God does not create evil directly, out of nothing. God

14. Barker, *godless*, 230.

15. Koehler et al., *Hebrew and Aramaic Lexicon of the Old Testament*, s.v. "*ra*."

16. Barker, *godless*, 230.

is Pure Actuality or Pure Being, and act communicates act. God cannot create evil because evil is not an actuality, not an existential thing. Evil cannot and does not come from God. Instead, as indicated above, *bara*, as it relates to *ra* in Isaiah 45:7, pertains to God bringing about calamity and harm *to evildoers* because of his divine justice.

Why would God perform actions that would result in the loss of goods? We have already touched on the answer, namely, divine justice. Yet, there are some deeper truths here that perhaps can provide a bit more help. Thomas Aquinas notes, "But regarding the one who inflicts punishment, punishment has the nature of justice and right order, and so moral wrong is made less evil by the connection of good."[17] This connection of good (justice and right order) is God's gracious corrective to the divine ordered ends missed.[18] Aquinas explains, "And the order of justice likewise has a connected privation of the particular good of one who sins, since the order of justice requires that the person who sins should be deprived of a good that the person desires."[19] In other words, Aquinas is making the point that justice may involve depriving a person of some good (i.e., causing a privation). Callan and McHugh make a similar point in that "punishment is virtuous only in so far as it restrains from evil those who cannot be restrained by love of virtue, but only by fear of penalty. Hence, penalties should consist in the deprivation of goods that are more prized than the satisfactions obtained through delinquencies."[20] Aquinas argues that God graciously does this to prevent further evil when he states, "But divine wisdom inflicts pain to prevent fault."[21] God's justice in this sense is a teleological corrective. We even see this principle at play in amoral situations, such as accidentally touching a hot stove and receiving temporary pain in order to prevent a more serious burn.

Along with attempting to impugn God's goodness, Barker attempts to show an inconsistency in claims to peace. He quotes Romans 15:33, stating, "The God of peace," and Isaiah 2:4, "and they shall beat their swords into plowshares, and their spears into pruninghooks: nation shall not lift up sword against nation, neither shall they learn war any more" (KJV). The

---

17. Aquinas, *Quaestiones disputate de malo* (*De Malo*), q. 1, a. 5, ad. 12; all quotes from *De Malo* are from Aquinas, *On Evil*.

18. Further deterrence will cause a continual response, where hell represents the eternal response to evil.

19. Aquinas, *De Malo*, q. 1, a. 1, ad. 1.

20. Callan and McHugh, *Moral Theology*, 2384. See his examples of divine and human laws punishing through loss of bodily goods.

21. Aquinas, *ST* I, q. 48, a. 6, s.c.; all quotes from the *ST* in this chapter are from Aquinas, *Summa Theologica of St. Thomas Aquinas*.

counter verses follow with the quoting of Exodus 15:3, where he leaves off the last phrase: "The Lord is a man of war . . ." (KJV). Now, before I give you the next counter verse, did you catch the word "war" here and also in the previous verse? Something should already be apparent as out of context. Isaiah 2:4, which was given after Exodus, includes "learn war *any more*" (KJV), implying that there may have been war, but a state is coming in the future where that will not be the case. There is a temporal context to the verses that Barker is ignoring. The other counter verse is Joel 3:9–10, where he skips the first phrase and quotes the King James Version: "Proclaim ye this among the Gentiles; Prepare war, wake up the mighty men, let all the men of war draw near; let them come up: Beat your plowshares into swords, and your pruninghooks into spears: let the weak say, I am strong." Apparently, Barker is trying to show the inconsistencies between taking plowshares and pruninghooks and beating them into swords and spears versus taking swords and spears and beating them into plowshares and pruninghooks. Does Barker really think this cannot happen at different times? Surely it can. The whole context for not learning war any more is after the battle mentioned in Joel 3:9–10. It is a time of peace in the far future. This is just yet another reason why I find Barker disingenuous, with a very biased agenda; he does not even seem to try to be honest to the text.

As far as the relationship of war and peace, one should know that in a fallen world, where there is evil at work, "freedom is not free," and thus "peace is not free." Sometimes peace follows after conflicts are resolved, but those conflicts can be very costly with blood. Military personnel give their lives to defend their country to protect certain freedoms, peace, and investments. Jesus himself gave his life and shed his blood on a cross to pay the penalty of our sins so we could obtain ultimate peace with God. There is absolutely no contradiction between war and peace in any of the verses.

In very similar fashion, Barker's other question—"Was Jesus peaceable?"—attempts to play off of different contexts to show inconsistencies. It is important to keep in mind that peace is contextual. A person can have peace with God, knowing his sins are forgiven, and he has eternal life, but that does not mean he has peace with those who are trying to harm him for his faith in God.

Lastly, Barker questions Jesus's trustworthiness by contrasting two verses in the King James Version against each other. He first gives John 8:14, which says, "Jesus answered and said unto them, Though I bear record of myself, *yet* my record is true: for I know whence I came, and whither I go; but ye cannot tell whence I come, and whither I go." He then gives John 5:31: "If I bear witness of myself, my witness is not true." Again, there are two different contexts going on here. First, it is crucially important to point out that an individual person can make a true statement, if by "true" we mean his statement corresponds to reality. A person can say, "My car is black," and it truly can be black. And furthermore, there is nothing absolutely wrong about a person claiming that his own statement is true. However, if the black car could not be found and verification testimony was needed for legal or court proceedings, then more witnesses would be needed to help establish that truth. It is not that it was not true when that individual person made the statement, but in order for it to be convincing, it needed to be strengthened before others that have no way of making verification. And hence, more witnesses will help establish the truth of the claim. That is exactly what is at play here. Biblical commentator Gerald Borchert explains,

> The defense here began with a restatement of the issue in prepa-
> ration for the calling of witnesses. There is first an admission
> of a presupposition that is based on the accepted legal code of
> the Torah, the foundation book of the Jews who were Jesus' op-
> ponents. In cases where there is a need for verifiable testimony,
> it is necessary that there be two or three witnesses to provide
> corroboration of the matter (cf. Deut 19:15). That principle was
> expected to be firmly observed, particularly in capital cases
> (Num 35:30; Deut 17:6; cf. Heb 10:28), and that principle was
> accepted as a basic thesis by Jesus (Matt 18:16; John 8:17) and by
> the early Christians like Paul (2 Cor 13:1). It was assumed that
> corroboration would assure the courts and others that the ninth
> word of the Decalogue (Exod 20:16) had been safeguarded be-
> cause bearing false witness was regarded as an act of personal
> treason (Prov 25:18).[22]

The Jews were expecting this type of supporting witness for Jesus's state-ments in order to safeguard Exodus 20:16. But again, even if there were no witnesses, it does not mean what Jesus said was not true. Truth is defined as "that which corresponds to reality." This is the difference between John 5:31 and John 8:14. In John 5:31, Jesus is following the Jewish legal code in providing supporting witnesses, which he indeed immediately followed with not just two or three, but four witnesses: John the Baptist (John 5:33), the works of Jesus (John 5:36), the Father (John 5:37), and the Scriptures (John 5:39), which includes Moses (John 5:45; e.g., Deut 18:15). Now, in John 8:14, the Jews did not want to receive Jesus's witness, which he gave earlier in John 5:31, because of their own selfish ambitions (John 11:48). So, Jesus essentially told them that what he is saying is indeed true despite their rejection of the previous witnesses he gave them. Nonetheless, he tried

22. Borchert, *John 1–11*, 243–44.

again to give them what they wanted according to the law for verifying testimony by referring again more simply to the Father, but alas they still did not want to receive it. So as can be seen, there is no contradiction. The difference between the two verses is essentially Jesus pleading with the Jews, first along legal lines, but then after their refusing to hear that, a personal plea.

CONCLUSION

Above, I highlighted some of the underlying contextual issues behind many of the apparent contradictions. While I did not review all lists, due to space, the others are not entirely different in their underlying interpretive issues. There is a sense in which Barker is charging Scripture as guilty before being proven innocent. I would like to propose the opposite. The literal, historical-grammatical method that is so often referred to in textbooks for hermeneutics really centers on the importance of context. There are both historical and grammatical contexts under which the given words should be understood. The importance of context cannot be underestimated. Now, it should be obvious, but my efforts in this chapter were never intended to provide a systematic course in hermeneutics. Consequently, there are many other valuable principles that are useful for proper interpretation. Gaining a better understanding of these principles and forming a habit of employing them will help provide a good and consistent way to interpret Scripture. A great resource to begin to inoculate yourself is to review Norman Geisler and Thomas Howe's list of seventeen mistakes that many critics' interpretations suffer from, as described in their book, *When Critics Ask*.[23]

The other thing to keep in mind is that whenever there appears to be a contradiction, always check your biases. Just because one interpretation may superficially fit, this does not mean there may not yet be another that yields equal or greater explanatory power. What makes a person choose one over the other should be analyzed to ensure his presuppositions, or any prior commitments, are themselves reasonable.

Finally, my hope is that this brief treatment will give you pause before considering any apparent contradiction. Do not be quick to judge the Bible with errors. Many great minds throughout history have read, studied, and have accepted the Bible as the word of God. While most issues in the Bible dissolve easily under further study, there are some that do require a deeper analysis into the original languages. Over the past two decades, I have yet to

---

23. In the latest publication, the book has been renamed to *The Big Book of Bible Difficulties: Clear and Concise Answers from Genesis to Revelation.*

meet an issue in the Bible that does not have a reasonable interpretation that is consistent with biblical inerrancy.

BIBLIOGRAPHY

Aquinas, Thomas. *On Evil.* Translated by Richard Regan. Edited by Brian Davies. New York: Oxford University Press, 2003.

————. *The Summa Theologica of St. Thomas Aquinas.* Translated by Fathers of the English Dominican Province. Notre Dame: Christian Classics, 1981.

Barker, Dan. *godless: How an Evangelical Preacher Became One of America's Leading Atheists.* Berkeley: Ulysses, 2008.

Borchert, Gerald L. *John 1–11.* The New American Commentary 25A. Nashville: Broadman & Holman, 1996.

Callan, Charles Jerome, and John A. McHugh. *Moral Theology: A Complete Course Based on St. Thomas Aquinas and the Best Modern Authorities.* Rev. ed. New York: Wagner, 1958. http://www.gutenberg.org/cache/epub/35354/pg35354.html.

Constable, Thomas L. "2 Thessalonians." In *The Bible Knowledge Commentary: An Exposition of the Scriptures: New Testament,* edited by J. F. Walvoord and R. B. Zuck, 713–26. Wheaton: Victor, 1985.

Geisler, Norman L. *Systematic Theology.* Vol. 2, *God, Creation.* Minneapolis: Bethany, 2003.

Geisler, Norman L., and Thomas A. Howe. *When Critics Ask: A Popular Handbook on Bible Difficulties.* Wheaton: Victor, 1992.

Hoffman, Paul. "Does Efficient Causation Presuppose Final Causation? Aquinas vs. Early Modern Mechanism." In *Metaphysics and the Good: Themes from the Philosophy of Robert Merrihew Adams,* edited by Samuel Newlands and Larry M. Jorgensen, 295–312. New York: Oxford University Press, 2009.

Koehler, Ludwig, et al. *The Hebrew and Aramaic Lexicon of the Old Testament.* 1st English ed. 5 vols. New York: Brill, 1994.

8

Moral Outrage or an Outrageous Morality

A Critique of Dan Barker's Ethics

—JOHN D. FERRER

> Human values are not absolutes—they are relative to human needs. The humanistic answer to morality, if the question is properly understood, is that the basis for values lies in nature.
>
> —DAN BARKER[1]

FOR MANY YEARS NOW, Dan Barker's public speaking, writing, and debating have maintained a unifying theme of moral indignation. The story of God's providence, according to Barker, is not just a fairy tale, but a horror story, where the Christian God should be scorned and rejected as a villain, entirely undeserving of worship or religious belief. This moral indignation is not uncommon among contemporary atheists like Barker as it sharpens the aggressive anti-religious edge of militant atheism.[2] In Barker's creedal

1. Barker, *godless*, 210.

2. According to moral psychologist Jonathan Haidt, New Atheists consider religion to be an overall negative influence on society. See Haidt, *Righteous Mind*, 285–95. Illustrating Haidt's point are the titles by New Atheist stalwarts, Hitchens, *God Is Not Great*; Harris, *End of Faith*; Dawkins, *God Delusion*; and Dennett, *Breaking the Spell*.

monograph, *God: The Most Unpleasant Character in All Fiction*, he proposes over a "thousand examples of the badness of God," arranged like an exhaustive Bible commentary on the famed quote by Richard Dawkins:

> The God of the Old Testament is arguably the most unpleasant character in all of fiction: jealous and proud of it; a petty, unjust, unforgiving control freak; a vindictive, bloodthirsty ethnic cleanser; a misogynistic, homophobic, racist, infanticidal, genocidal, filicidal, pestilential, megalomaniacal, sadomasochistic, capriciously malevolent bully.[3]

Barker is not just annoyed—he's angry. He is outraged at biblical morality personified in the Christian God. Barker is not just emoting either. He is trying to weave together a sustained evidential case against God's existence on the basis of moral objections. Barker's outrage, however, might be more bluster than substance. Unless he can show that his antagonism has truth-value or, at least, points toward truth, then his boiling scorn could evaporate down to nothing more than a personal problem.

To be sure, Barker raises some challenging questions about God's behavior, for example, in Holy War, slavery, and the sacrifice of Isaac.[4] Those questions and more are addressed in chapters 6 and 7 in this book, so they don't need repeating here.[5] But if Barker is launching a morally-charged assault on the biblical God, he needs the kind of machinery that can launch those flaming volleys. He needs a moral framework qualified to identify and evidentially weaponize moral objections to God's existence. It could be that Barker's moral indignation stems from his misunderstanding or disliking God's ways. But ignorance and opinion are not a serious objection to the Christian God.

In this context, the first question we'll be answering is: "Does Dan Barker have the moral machinery in place to launch damaging assaults on the character of God?" This first line of critique tests the integrity of his ethic, namely the harm principle and the three moral minds. Then we measure his influences, notably naturalism, materialism, evolution, and determinism.

---

3. Barker, *Mere Morality*, 105. See also Barker, *God*, 1. The quote originates in Dawkins, *The God Delusion*, 51.

4. Barker, *God*, 87, 121–5, 135–45. See 1 Sam 15; Gen 22:1–19; and Col 3:22, respectively.

5. Those sorts of problem passages are addressed at length in Copan, *Is God a Moral Monster?*; Copan and Flannagan, *Did God Really Command Genocide?*; Lamb, *God Behaving Badly*; Ferrer, "Common Biblical Objections to God's Goodness"; and The Bible and Beer Consortium, "Does the Bible Advocate Slavery?"

After evaluating his moral system, this critique shifts focus towards his effort to undermine God-belief on moral grounds. The question then becomes: "Does Barker succeed in discrediting God's existence on the basis of morality?" The conclusion of this chapter is that Barker fails to morally discredit God's existence. It will be shown that Dan Barker's ethical system is a clunky mishmash of just-so stories, materialism and determinism, with no metaethical foundations to speak of, thus failing to show that it qualifies as ethics at all. The end result is that Barker's ethic crumbles to the ground, and his assault on God's character dissipates.

DOES DAN BARKER HAVE THE MORAL MACHINERY IN PLACE TO LAUNCH DAMAGING ASSAULTS ON THE CHARACTER OF GOD?

Barker's primary work on ethics is his 2018 imprint *Mere Morality*. It is an expansion of his chapter, by the same name, in *Life Driven Purpose*. In these works, he lays out a minimalist ethic wherein, he believes, secularists can lay claim to moral knowledge, moral goodness, and some measure of meaning. He alludes to a larger ethical framework than his "mere morality" but does not devote much energy there.[6] His objective is *mere* morality, highlighting just the basics for a secular normative ethic.[7] And he does keep it basic, with just two ideas anchoring his ethic: the harm principle and the three moral minds.

The Harm Principle

Central to Barker's ethic is what he calls the "harm principle." A common-sense general rule, it is the claim that "the way to be good is to act with the intention of minimizing harm."[8] This harm principle is not original with Barker. It's roughly synonymous with the principle of non-malfeasance in medical ethics and traces at least as far back as the Hippocratic Oath from the fourth to fifth century BC. Barker's notion of "harm," however, is narrower than that of malfeasance.

6. Barker, *Mere Morality*, 150–51.

7. According to Julia Driver, normative ethics "is concerned with the articulation and the justification of the fundamental principles that govern the issues of how we should live and what we morally ought to do" (Driver, "Normative Ethics," 31). In other words, it is the study of ethics as a framework for guiding moral living.

8. Barker, *Mere Morality*, 19.

In Barker's view, "harm" refers to anything that is a "threat to survival," impeding survival, and or causing pain.[9] Barker would do well to expand his harm principle to address a wider array of harms besides just "threats to survival." Nevertheless, we can grant that the harm principle is generally a good idea, even if Barker is working from a narrowed sense of "harm."

Also, while Barker focuses this harm principle on the survival of humanity, he does note that our instincts are "goal" oriented toward "the minimization of harm to biological organisms."[10] We can charitably assume he is applying the harm principle to plants and animals, so that would include farming practices, animal abuse, deforestation, over-fishing, and various ecological concerns. Plus, harming animals and the environment can indirectly threaten the collective survival of humanity.

How did Barker arrive at this harm principle? He doesn't say how he arrived at this knowledge or whether this principle is the kind of thing that nature can generate. Presumably, he would try to justify the harm principle by appealing to common sense, natural reason, or something like that, so long as there's no special revelation involved. Unfortunately for him, he offers no metaethics or moral epistemology to speak of. In his view, the harm principle is just something he "knows," and he does not bother with *how* he knows it or how it could arise from a godless universe, or whether its truth undermines other tenets of his worldview (i.e., materialism, naturalism, etc.). For Barker to accomplish his task of a secular ethic, he needs to show that his ethic doesn't imply God's existence via the moral argument.[11] But to do that, Barker would have to venture deeper into metaethics than what is found in his ethics writing.

The Three Moral Minds

Besides the harm principle, there is also what Barker calls the "three moral minds" of instinct, reason, and law.[12] He understands these to be the three authorities that people would be wise to consult in making ethical decisions.

He treats "reason" in the popular and general sense of "natural reasoning," "thoughtful discernment," "fact-finding," etc. In his words, reason is "what makes you feel you are a free volitional agent. . . . It is the part that

9. Barker, *Mere Morality*, 23.

10. Barker, *Mere Morality*, 35.

11. The moral argument for God's existence has many phrasings, sharing a common conclusion that God-belief is credible given the evidence of morality. See, Baggett and Walls, *Moral Argument*.

12. Barker, *Mere Morality*, 16–52.

makes deliberate conscious decisions. Reason is clear thinking and logical judgment."[13] In his view, reason seems to be the most important of the three moral minds as he says, "In reason we trust."[14] But he is fairly respectful towards the other two.

The "law," as one of the moral minds, refers to societal laws.[15] These seem to include not just formal rules and regulations, but also informal guidelines, such as taboos, "house rules," and other cultural norms, but it is not clear just how far his notion of "law" extends. At minimum, "law" includes formally codified statutes, such as state and federal laws, constitutions, civil rights, international law, and so forth. He does not seem to be fundamentalist about human law codes. In his view, laws are conventional agreements on preferred behavior.[16] Often, they are deeply mistaken (such as the Dred-Scott decision), but, more often, they are at least helpful guidelines. Law is an imperfect inheritance of collective wisdom from generations past.

Besides reason and law, Barker also identifies instinct as one of our moral minds.[17] Instinct includes innate urges, reflexes, "gut" reactions, and otherwise primitive or thoughtless predispositions. Instincts, it would seem, are a controversial inclusion, with some instincts being horrific, violent, and sociopathic. But Barker is virtually required to install instincts in a prominent position in his ethic since he affirms materialism (i.e., everything that exists is matter and its properties), naturalism (i.e., nature is all that exists), evolution (i.e., universal common descent), and determinism (i.e., no free will).[18] In his worldview, instincts are not a side-note; they are an entire explanatory dimension for humankind. Instincts are, for Barker, the acquired traits written in our human nature through the coercive forces of natural selection. Just as laws reflect the wisdom of past civilizations, instinct reflects the utility of our primitive past. In this way, Barker believes instincts have practical value just as they helped our ancestors survive long ago.

Critiquing the Harm Principle

Taken on its own merits, the harm principle is somewhat respectable, but it leaves a lot to be desired if it is to serve as the central guiding principle for

13. Barker, *Mere Morality*, 36.

14. Barker, *Mere Morality*, 52.

15. Barker, *Mere Morality*, 44–52.

16. Barker, *Mere Morality*, 44.

17. Barker, *Mere Morality*, 28–35.

18. Barker, *Free Will Explained*, 11, 21, 22, 40, 43, 93.

Barker's ethical system. Plus, while he claims the harm principle is a moral category, he has not *shown* that his godless, materialistic, deterministic landscape permits morality at all.[19] His system would benefit from some meta-level defenses, but he offers no serious metaethic or moral epistemology.

It's not unusual to base one's ethics on a single guiding principle. Christian ethics has the golden rule, for example.[20] Joseph Fletcher has his "love principle," Immanuel Kant has his categorical imperative, Jeremy Bentham has the principle of utility, and so on.[21] Those examples may or may not succeed as independent ethical systems, but they illustrate that it's plausible for a single moral principle to tie an entire ethical system together. But not just any principle will suit such an ambitious task. Barker's harm principle needs to be robust enough to span the greatest heights and the deepest depths of our many moral quandaries. And Barker's harm principle doesn't seem to do all that.

For one thing, he has mis-defined "harm" as a "threat to survival."[22] His definition is too narrow. There are other kinds of harms, like destruction of property, theft, slander, cheating, non-lethal pain, and suffering, which do not necessarily bear upon survival.[23] His restricted definition reduces harm to a "quantity of life" metric, when there is also quality of life and perhaps sanctity of life to consider.[24] Morality is more than just a matter of survival; the quality of life matters too. Charitably, I would assume he affirms other morally valuable criteria besides survival. But I cannot admit those charitable assumptions into his system, since he defines his own moral system, not me. Survival just does not seem to be the sole criterion for distinguishing harms.

---

19. Atheists, of course, can be moral and sometimes morally superior to theists. But when atheists like Barker behave morally, they may be using stolen ideological goods smuggled in from theism.

20. Lev 19:34; Matt 7:12; Luke 6:31; 10:27; Gal 5:14.

21. Fletcher, *Situation Ethics*; Bentham, *Deontology*, 23–24; Kant, *Groundwork of the Metaphysics of Morals*, 31.

22. Barker, *Mere Morality*, 23.

23. Barker offers a list of harms that mentions "theft," but the rest of that list, including disease, predators, parasites, and floods, are all life-threatening circumstances (Barker, *Mere Morality*, 23). So, we cannot assume that the *kind* of theft Barker has in mind includes cases that are innocuous and otherwise non-threatening to survival. Barker's list, even with "theft" included, aligns with his notion that "harm" is defined as "a threat to survival" (Barker, *Mere Morality*, 23).

24. "Sanctity of life" can be a religious concept, but it doesn't have to be. It can also refer to a secular legal sense of "inviolability," especially in the context of human rights. See Bouvier, *Law Dictionary*, s.vv. "Sanctity of Life" and "Inviolability."

Perhaps Barker can interpret these other moral values as entailments or implications within his survival sense of "harm," or as derivatives of the three moral minds, but since it's his system, it's his job to show that at least a sample of these sorts of values are included already. Otherwise, he needs to admit that his *mere* morality is too paltry to be plausible as it stands. In assembling his ethic, he left too many unused parts on the table, suggesting he either didn't put it together right, or it's too unfinished to be a reliable instrument just yet.

To be fair, Barker clearly has *the beginnings* of an ethical system. But if he wants to keep his harm principle as the single guiding idea for the rest of his ethic, then he risks a kind of reductive fallacy in the form of a lowest-common-denominator ethic. He has found a generally good idea that's likely to be found in most every popular-level ethic. It's a common denominator between different ethical outlooks. Perhaps some militant anarchist won't affirm the harm principle, but it's still a common denominator for most everyone's ethic.

Unfortunately, it's minimalist. It's the *lowest* common denominator, offering sparse guidance. Just imagine if a set of parents morally trained their children with that one rule: "reduce threats to survival." Those children would not learn basics like sharing is caring, love others as yourself, speak respectfully, etc. And they would not be positioned to learn many of the mature moral lessons about facing one's fears and being a hero. They'd be morally handicapped. They may avoid certain violent pathologies, but they wouldn't have the moral framework in place to navigate well in civil society as we know it. Lowest-common-denominator ethical systems are the moral equivalent of a spare tire; they can work for a short while but will burst under pressure if they aren't traded-in soon for something more roadworthy.

Another problem for Barker is his contradictory stance regarding "intention." He tries to incorporate intentionality into his moral framework, saying one should "intend to lessen harm," and, "Intention is crucial when determining the legality or morality of an action."[25] But this nuance greatly complicates his "mere" morality. Intentions precede actions and outcomes because they are causes (final causes) not to be mistaken for effects (outcomes/results).[26] Yet in the next paragraph of *Mere Morality*, Barker nullifies intentionality saying, "In assessing harm, it is the overall consequences that matter, not just personal desires."[27] If overall consequences are what matter, then causal priors (intentions) do not matter. Perhaps Barker is just showing

25. Barker, *Mere Morality*, 24.
26. Aristotle, *Phys.* II, 3; *Metaph.* V, 2.
27. Barker, *Mere Morality*, 24.

his philosophical inexperience, but if he wants to incorporate intentionality as a morally weighted component in his system, then he cannot rule them out in the next paragraph. He cannot have his proverbial cake and eat it too.

Barker's harm principle is also burdened by negative framing. While ethics broaches positive and negative values, with good things to promote and bad things to discourage, the harm principle relies on the negative—reduce harm. What should be done about helpful or neutral options? It's not clear. His ethic only addresses these matters insofar as they bear upon harm. In Barker's defense, he is well aware that his "mere morality" is not a fully formed ethical system.[28] But even as a minimalist system, the absence of directly positive values is conspicuous.

Positive goods are not all "above and beyond" behaviors either, what ethicists call "supererogatory goods." Besides the soldier who falls on a grenade, or selfless parents sacrificing years of self-interest and liberty to raise their children, there are scores of morally weighted behaviors like avoiding gossip, telling the truth, forgiving someone for their trespass, letting a friend have a taste of food, etc. These actions are all too subtle for Barker's harm principle. Barker has not shown that the harm principle can entail the rest of the moral values, notably those on the positive end of the spectrum.

Perhaps Barker sensed this line of objection. At one point, he smuggles in positive goods when discussing New Atheist Sam Harris's *The Moral Landscape*, saying, "Sam Harris identifies the 'well-being' of conscious creatures as the aim of morality." Then Barker surprisingly says, "I think that is right. 'Well-being' is perhaps a more positive way to characterize the harm principle, but it boils down to the same avoidance of some kind of harm or limitation."[29] Barker shows his philosophical shallowness here, since "well-being" does not clearly equate to his survival metric in the harm principle. A person can survive, free of harm, yet have a low quality of life. That state of affairs would be good according to Barker's harm principle but bad according to Sam Harris's notion of "well-being." Barker owes his readers an explanation for how he can frame the harm principle in a negative way (reducing threats to survival) and then suggest that's the same as "well-being," a positive concept. He needs to show that the harm principle includes quality of life somehow within its quantity-of-life metric. Otherwise, he is comparing apples to dehydrated oranges. Well-being is much richer, perhaps an all-encompassing category, in ethics variously identified

28. Barker, *Mere Morality*, 150.
29. Barker, *Mere Morality*, 42.

with "human flourishing," "happiness," and *eudamonia*, whereas "reducing harm" is shriveled and simplistic by comparison.[30]

Barker also seems conflicted on the scope of his harm principle. Sometimes he sounds absolutist, using sweeping universal claims like, "Ethics is simply concerned with reducing harm," and "humanistic morality is the attempt to avoid or lessen harm."[31] Across his *Mere Morality*, he describes the harm principle as if it is everywhere and always true that we should aim our behavior in ways that, as far as we can tell, will ultimately reduce harm. So, Barker seems to be asserting an absolute moral guideline, true for everyone everywhere. Any relative differences would emerge in applying that universal guidance in particular situations. In this way, Barker's ethic qualifies as absolutist, despite his own protestations. He disparages absolutism, saying there is no "absolute standard," decrying "fundamentalists" for their "absolute morality."[32] He says approvingly, "Most of us . . . act as if we embrace situational ethics in our daily lives."[33] Then he criticizes the absolutism of religious "fundamentalists" saying, "A religiously polarized brain cannot see that an ethical decision is often a compromise, a lesser of two evils, a contextual assessment of the relative merits of consequences, a practical matter."[34] Barker is correct about how ethical decisions can be complicated, but ironically, since he admits a fundamental operating principle and applies it universally, then his own system isn't sophisticated enough to escape the fundamentalism and absolutism he rails against. His system is not absolutist in the sense of asserting heavy-handed, dogmatic, religious-type law irrespective of context. But it is still absolutist unless he can offer some other way to understand the harm principle that is not for everyone everywhere.

Still another problem with the harm principle is that Barker sidesteps his harm principle to affirm autonomy, even to the point of excusing self-harm.[35] He says that "it should be none of my business what you do to yourself . . . if a man cuts off one of his fingers . . . that is certainly harmful and destructive, and may be unhealthy, but the act is only immoral if it affects other people."[36] In his words, "morality is social," and autonomy is morally valuable.[37] This departure, however, contradicts Barker's founding

30. On *eudamonia*, see Aristotle, *Eth. nic.*, I.

31. Barker, *Mere Morality*, 19.

32. Barker, *Mere Morality*, 151; Barker, *Life Driven Purpose*, 117.

33. Barker, *Life Driven Purpose*, 116.

34. Barker, *Life Driven Purpose*, 117.

35. Barker, *Mere Morality*, 23.

36. Barker, *Mere Morality*, 23.

37. Barker, *Mere Morality*, 23.

moral principle. Either self-harm is permissible, or it's forbidden by the only explicit principle in his system. Rather than doing the work of identifying, explaining, and defending autonomy as a moral value within his system, he snuck it in and threw it on the pile, apparently hoping his audience would assume it belongs there. Of course, Barker is entitled to hold whatever moral values he wants to, and he can assemble them however he likes into whatever system he wants. But as long as he is outlining a basic ethical system for his readers, he would do well not to contradict his founding principle six pages later.[38] Perhaps if Barker's *mere* morality graduated to an intermediate or advanced morality, then he may find room for other moral principles besides the harm principle, but as it is now, Barker has not explained how self-harm can be both morally forbidden (by the harm principle) and morally permitted (on grounds of autonomy). As long as Barker leaves this tension between harm and autonomy underdeveloped, it suggests a crack in his engine, a pensive fissure foreboding explosion under the pressure of competing values.

Critiquing the Three Moral Minds

Barker's one moral basic, the harm principle, has a lot of problems. But maybe it can stand up to scrutiny if it's buttressed by the rest of his moral system: namely, the three moral minds of reason, instinct, and law. These elements serve as authorities whom people can consult for answers about how to best implement the harm principle. They do help his system a great deal, at least at a practical level, but they are still quite limited. They have practical value for determining courses of action, but *practical* value does not necessarily equal *moral* value. The only (purported) moral fixture in his system so far is the harm principle. But that principle is fraught with problems, as Barker never establishes that the harm principle is morally weighted, or that naturalism has sufficient grounds for *anything* to be moral. Unfortunately, for Barker, the three moral minds do not rescue his system.

The first moral mind, reason, is fine for what it is, and generally speaking, I have no qualm with appealing to reason. Now Barker tends to treat "reason" like it's a strict antagonist to faith, but he and I can disagree on that aspect, and still agree, broadly, that reasoning is a valuable tool in identifying moral courses of action. Barker does not establish that reasoning can *ground* moral value. He is proposing human reason as a practical tool, not a

---

38. He first states the harm principle in *Mere Morality* on page nineteen, but on page twenty-five grants gratuitous self-harm as morally permissible, so long as no one else is hurt.

metaethical grounding. So, Christian theists can readily grant that Barker's point that human reason offers real, albeit limited, value in making moral judgments.

It should be noted, however, that even reasonable people can disagree. When people have essentially the same level of intelligence and the same information (including law and instinct), they can still reach different conclusions about what is the best moral option. In that event, Barker's system can grind to a standstill. He has no transcendent reference point—such as God or the Bible—to adjudicate between moral dilemmas (where two or more options are equally weighted). Nor is there a transcendent reference point for deciding between two people in reasonable disagreement. This objection is serious but might not be devastating for Barker, however, since he could respond that true dilemmas are rare if they happen at all, and most of the time, people who disagree are not equally informed (by reason, law, and instinct). He could add that even if a true dilemma or impasse occurred, the decision could be resolved by a coin flip, since the available choices are morally or practically equivalent.

Reasoning, however, poses a serious epistemic problem for Barker. How does one come to know any moral facts whatsoever? We can grant, with Barker, that some moral facts exist, like the harm principle. But if we are to achieve reliable moral knowledge, we would need a reliable means of knowing. In Barker's worldview, this function is served by the human brain, which he thinks is identical with the mind.[39] So, moral awareness, moral reasoning, and moral knowledge, being mental exercises, are all entirely functions of the brain. This creates a problem since, for Barker, the only way of knowing whether the brain is reliable is by using the same brain. It's a circularity problem where he is left saying, "My brain is reliable, according to my brain." That's not an argument; that's a stutter. This circularity problem is a potential defeater for Barker's whole system, not just for his moral knowledge, but for all his knowledge claims. If we are all just products of blind, pitiless material forces, then our lying survivalist brains are the only way we can "know" anything. Yet these same brains interfere with everything we might otherwise use to correct the mistakes of our brains. Every question we ask, every answer we find; every book, article, or post we read; every observation, or experiment we conduct; every fact-checking effort we might attempt is filtered through these same brains.

Charles Darwin realized this disturbing problem at the foundation of his evolutionary epistemology when he said that "with me the horrid doubt always arises whether the convictions of man's mind, which has been

39. Barker, *Life Driven Purpose*, 66–67.

developed from the mind of the lower animals, are of any value or at all trustworthy." Then, with rhetorical force, he adds, "Would anyone trust in the convictions of a monkey's mind, if there are any convictions in such a mind?"[40]

The second moral mind, law, is another fine point. Barker is wise to admit that laws offer helpful guidance for moral decisions. He does not seem to be using "law" in a terribly strict way, so it can include various rules and regulations so long as they are human conventions.[41] He does not, however, include uniquely religious laws. In his view, "purely religious teachings are most often divisive and dangerous," and, any "good values that a religion might profess are not religious values. They are human values . . . what makes them good is their humanism, not their theology."[42] His anti-religious cynicism is too vast and complicated to address here. Nevertheless, it can be agreed that civil laws, human rights, and various prescriptive conventions in society are worth consulting for moral decision-making.

Instinct is a little more controversial. At one level, Barker is correct here too. We are wise to consider our instincts in the course of moral decision-making. In Barker's usage, "instincts" include natural urges, basic needs, subconscious appetites, and so forth.[43] There is practical value in heeding our instincts so we know when to take potty breaks, eat regularly, stretch sore limbs, relate with others, hydrate, start families, take a nap, and so forth. At that level, Barker's "instinctive" moral mind is non-controversial. But, in Barker's account, "instinct" is naturalistic terminology, revealing a crippling failure in his system: namely, a fallacious appeal to nature.

The appeal-to-nature fallacy refers to claims that something is good, preferable, beautiful (etc.) only because it's natural. Just because something occurs, however, doesn't mean it *should* occur. And just because something is natural, doesn't mean it's moral. Barker could respond by saying that while instincts alone don't suffice, reason and law can come to the rescue, helping distinguish good instincts from bad ones. With the sex drive, for example, he can say that laws distinguish rape from consensual sex. And reason can distinguish between compatible and incompatible romantic partners. But Barker hasn't shown that there is anything to distinguish since he hasn't shown that *any* instincts are good or even morally weighted at all. He *stipulates* that threatening survival is bad, reducing threats to survival is good, and we know that instincts can vary along that spectrum—some aid

40. Darwin, "Letter to William Graham."

41. Barker, *Mere Morality*, 44–52.

42. Barker, *Mere Morality*, 22, 21.

43. Barker, *Mere Morality*, 28–35.

survival, others hinder survival. But nowhere in all of his literature does he *demonstrate* that his harm principle is indeed a moral fact derived from the facts of nature. He holds tight to naturalism without ever showing that a godless natural world can produce any morality whatsoever.[44]

Another glaring problem for Barker is that he commits a kind of genetic fallacy. Genetic fallacies are mistaken inferences based on the source, or apparent source, of something. Even if we find that morality occurs in nature, this would not prove that nature caused it. The location of where something is found does not itself demonstrate how the thing came about in the first place. That is why we cannot infer that a wristwatch found in the forest was caused by the forest or that a battleship found on the bottom of the ocean was created by the ocean. In this way, morality found in nature is not itself proof that morality comes from nature. And because of the naturalistic fallacy, mentioned above, Barker still needs to show that nature is capable of producing morality.

General Critique of Barker's Ethics

The problems for Barker's system do not stop there. Barker's commitment to evolutionary naturalism, materialism, and determinism pose additional threats to his mere morality.

Naturalism

Barker's naturalism threatens his efforts at ethics via the naturalistic fallacy. Besides the informal fallacy of an appeal to nature, there is also a meta-ethical problem at work here, known as the *naturalistic fallacy*. Associated most famously with David Hume and later G. E. Moore, this problem can be summarized as a challenge to show it is possible to derive moral oughts strictly from natural facts.[45] The entire realm of instinct, natural dispositions, physiology, and so forth, are natural facts. They are "what is." But Barker thinks he can derive moral facts, "what ought to be," from those natural facts. If Barker hopes to bridge into the realm of morality, he needs

---

44. Barker's brand of naturalistic ethics, by all appearances, is oblivious toward more sophisticated atheological options in the form of non-naturalism, such as that of G. E. Moore (see Moore, *Principia Ethica*) or Erik Wielenberg (see Wielenberg, *Robust Ethics*).

45. See David Hume's "is-ought" fallacy and G. E. Moore's "open question argument"—both identified as examples of the "naturalistic fallacy" in Hume, *Treatise on Human Nature* III.1.1; and Moore, *Principia Ethica*, 1.13.

to show that it's rationally coherent, and metaphysically possible, to derive moral facts from natural facts alone. Short of this, Barker's ethic is an underwhelming just-so story or, worse, a case of blind faith.

Evolution

Barker's commitment to naturalistic evolution poses another problem, and a decidedly bloody one too. Evolution makes for a bad judge of moral character. Evolution is "red in tooth and claw," in most cases describing a bloody competition for survival that does not map well into our modern notions of "good" behavior. In Barker's view, evolutionary processes shaped our current moral framework so that we people are, or feel as if we are, morally charged beings responsible to reduce harm.[46] But Barker would be hard pressed to show that evolution can generate moral facts as such since the evolutionary process has not just permitted a smattering of altruistic (i.e., selfless) cases among dolphins, dogs, and dudes, but it has also permitted cannibalism, slavery, tribal warfare, mass extinctions, and so forth. If evolution "generates" altruistic and barbaric behaviors alike, there would need to be something untainted by evolutionary bias whereby we could morally distinguish between those outcomes. Naturalistic evolution, unfortunately, is an aimless shifting tide that, if true, washes across the entire biological history of the globe. It leaves no firm or unchanging dividing line whereby to distinguish between its "good" and "bad" outcomes. If spousal abuse happens to aid the survival of the species better than not, then spousal abuse is okay—according to evolutionary ethics.

Evolutionary naturalism also commits Barker to the pragmatic fallacy. This fallacy refers to the mistaken idea that says just because something "works," it must be good, right, or true. Something may work in aiding survival, and technically qualify as "moral" in Barker's ethic, yet still be grotesquely immoral. History is replete with horrific social experiments where people tried to help evolution along, pursuing the "greater good" for humanity.[47] Outstanding examples include scientific racism and eugenics legislation in the early twentieth-century United States and Northern Europe, but one could also apply the "survival of the fittest" rationale to most any war, skirmish, tribal dispute, assault, or even to bullies asserting their physical superiority.[48]

---

46. Barker, *Mere Morality*, 28–35.

47. West, *Darwin Day in America*.

48. West, *Darwin Day in America*.

Evolutionary ethics also renders morality arbitrary. For example, violent rape is morally prohibited in many cultures today, but if evolutionary change has a determining influence on ethics, then the next climate fluctuation could generate a new moral landscape where violent rape is morally permitted—so long as it produces a higher chance of survival. Within Barker's evolutionary naturalism, not only could it have been the case that evolution made violent rape good, under different circumstances, but it could have *already* made violent rape good in some cultures today—so long as it aids survival. That logical possibility suggests that evolution should not be allowed in the courtroom of moral deliberation. As long as the arbitrary outworkings of evolutionary change are allowed a deterministic say in morality, then our ethics are arbitrary accidents of a "universe [that] has precisely the properties we should expect if there is, at bottom, no design, no purpose, no evil and no good, nothing but blind, pitiless indifference."[49]

Materialism

Still another problem for Barker is his commitment to materialism, meaning that the only things that exist are material, along with their properties and relations.[50] This worldview commitment poses an immediate metaphysical problem since morality is not clearly a material thing nor a property or relation between those things. Morality is a prescriptive category. It does not describe how things are, per se, but rather how things *should* be. These shoulds or oughts are hypotheticals. They don't have to describe any *actual* state of affairs, only possible, theoretical, or potential states. Materialism seems handicapped in addressing any hypothetical states whatsoever, not just moral hypotheticals. For example, consider the moral exhortation, "We should promote peace on earth." Peace on earth has never existed in all of recorded history, so there's no material reference point to which that "peace on earth" can refer.[51] Barker could respond, perhaps, that people generate the idea of "peace on earth," and in that way, it exists as a material property, but that doesn't solve the problem either. The claim that "we should promote peace on earth" is not referring to the *idea* of "peace on earth," it refers to a state of affairs where peace on earth occurs, but no global harmony has happened in recorded history. It only exists as a hypothetical, if it exists at all. Materialism, at least in Barker's hands, isn't equipped to grapple with hypotheticals like that.

49. Dawkins, *River Out of Eden*, 133.
50. Barker, *Life Driven Purpose*, 144–48, 153.
51. This is not counting Genesis 1–2, assuming those chapters are historical.

Determinism

Perhaps the most glaring and devastating threat to Barker's ethics is his own commitment to biological determinism. Morality, normally understood, includes some sort of free ability to choose between morally weighted options. If a man is in a coma, for example, and his nurse used his hand to do something evil, he would not be morally liable. The comatose man was just an instrument of evil. He is morally innocent, having had no choice in the matter. In this way, free will is needed for morality. In Barker's account, there is no libertarian free will (i.e., the power of contrary choice) nor agent causality (i.e., to be a sufficient cause of one's action). He tries to explain free will in naturalistic terms in his book *Free Will Explained*, but, rather than explain free will, he tries to explain *away* free will. If determinism were true, after all, then Barker is not a reliable witness to that fact since he was *forced* to write that book. Coerced testimony isn't trustworthy.

DOES BARKER SUCCEED IN DISCREDITING GOD'S EXISTENCE ON THE BASIS OF MORALITY?

Weighing the merits of Barker's mere morality, it proves to be a failure. Despite the salvageable value of the harm principle and the usefulness of his three moral minds, the system is worth more for its parts than the whole. Besides an array of unresolved problems and internal issues, his "ethical" system isn't clearly ethical at all since he never shows that naturalism can bridge from the material facts of nature into the moral facts of what should and should not be. Add into the mix his commitment to evolutionary naturalism, materialism, and determinism, and his attempt at ethics is a self-defeating mess. Perhaps a more competent philosophical ethicist could salvage his work and make a functional ethic out of it, but in Barker's hands, this mere morality is a wreck.

Notwithstanding, Barker still might have a way to morally discredit God's existence. Failing in a straightforward competition of naturalistic ethics versus Christian ethics, he still could discredit God by demonstrating internal inconsistency within the Christian concept of a "good God." Perhaps the strongest line of argument Barker offers to this effect is his litany of accusations against God's character, most notably in *God: The Most Unpleasant Character in All Fiction*. For people unschooled in the principles of interpretation, in Ancient Near Eastern culture, or otherwise unfamiliar with the problem passages he lists, that onslaught can seem emotionally overwhelming. The details of that material are addressed in chapters 6 and

7 and won't be rehashed here. But some general notes can be added to show that Barker fails here too.

First, Barker cannot justify any accusations against God because he is a hard determinist. He believes that free will is illusory.[52] In denying free will, he's rejecting not just libertarian free will (i.e., the power of contrary choice), but also agency (i.e., to be a sufficient cause of one's action). The closest he comes to affirming free will is to say that "you are an animal whose behavior is determined by the laws of nature, but after you act, your mind retroactively loops around and judges that you were free."[53] Barker's commitment to biological determinism does not just plague his own ethic (see above), but can likewise derail his moral judgments about Christianity.

According to biological determinism, every action and decision Barker has ever made was forced on him so that he is not himself a sufficient cause for any of them. In judicial terms, he's a coerced witness. And coerced witnesses aren't credible. They *might* be right, or they might be wrong, but since they have no locus of deliberation or independent conviction, or any means to weigh competing views, they are reduced to tools at the mercy of outside forces. For Barker, determinism undercuts his efforts to identify God as an evil character. He might be correct or incorrect, but his testimony is tripe since he's only spitting up what was force-fed to him. He *thinks* he can judge between good and evil; he *thinks* he made a moral judgment, decrying an immoral God, but it wasn't *him* making that judgment since he's not a free agent. That supposed "judgment" might not be a judgment at all, but just another useful illusion that happens to exist for its survival benefits. Barker's raging moral indignation towards God is looking like hot air.

Second, the possibility of different levels of moral authority deflates Barker's argument. In Christian thought, God occupies the highest status, being the creator, uncaused cause of all things, perfect in knowledge and foresight, giver of life, etc. God has rights fitting his status, just as a king has special rights, or even a police officer, or a parent. Every level of authority in a civilized society carries its own rights or privileges balanced by responsibilities. Parents have the right to send their children to their rooms. The children do not have the same right towards their parents to say, "Go to your room, Mom and Dad." A police officer has the right to forcibly detain a suspect, but an average citizen does not. A judge has the right to send people to jail, but a parent or police officer does not have that right. What sort of rights and responsibilities would God have?

---

52. Barker, *Free Will Explained*, 11, 12, 23, 57.
53. Barker, *Free Will Explained*, 25.

God is responsible for the entire universe, the whole earth, with every person and people group across all of time, past, present, and future. And God can have operating purposes and plans far surpassing our terrestrial goals of pleasure and long life. God would have the rights fit for the highest level of authority because he also has the highest level of responsibility. Consider how parents may let children fight till they learn to get along. Or a government official may let crime go unchecked in part of the city till the police union goes off strike. Or a military officer may let hundreds of his men die in battle in pursuit of a costly victory. As difficult as it is to say, God would have the rightful authority to make even weightier judgments than those. He is not just responsible for a few children, a city, or a battalion. He is responsible for all humanity, and more.

This admission about God's exalted status is not intended to resolve the full force of Barker's moral argument against God. But it should help guard against mistaken moral identities, where God is faulted for acting within his own authority instead of limiting himself to man's lower-level authority.

Third, Barker consistently violates the principle of charitable interpretation, preferring instead a hostile and maliciously biased reading.[54] More specifically, he fails to interpret moral claims in Scripture according to its native context but in starkly negative terms according to a contemporary secular-humanistic ethic. This point is subtle but critically important. Barker treats his own preferred cultural norms as if they are the universal standard for judging right and wrong across all other cultures. Elsewhere, Barker talks like a relativist when he tries to describe his own ethical system.[55] But, when he rants against God with a steamrolling onslaught of Bible verses, he sounds decidedly absolutist.[56]

Fourth, Barker hasn't done his due diligence to show that his hostile readings of Scripture are responsible, credible, and scholarly. He's entitled to interpret Scripture however he wants. But reasonable onlookers don't owe his unsupported interpretations any credence until Barker offers sufficient evidence to support his interpretations.

In his most focused attack on God's character, his book *God: The Most Unpleasant Character in All Fiction*, Barker just prooftexts, citing verse, after

54. Feldman, "Charity, Principle of."

55. Barker, *Life Driven Purpose*, 70–71, 77, 94, 116–17; Barker, Mere Morality, 20, 24, 40–43, 52, 133, 151.

56. For example, he claims the God of the Bible condones eating kids according to Levi 26:27–29; Deut 28:53; Jer 19:7–9; Ezek 5:8–10; Lam 2:20; 4:9–11 (see Barker, *God*, 280–81). But he fails to note that those are not *prescriptive* (do this) but *descriptive* (this happened), likely referring to the dire circumstances in siege warfare.

verse, after verse, without context and without any evidence that he interacted with the experts on those verses.[57] To be fair, some Scripture passages are fairly straightforward, accessible to any reader. And many other passages may seem difficult at first but need only a little amateur sleuthing. The Bible can be read, meaningfully, even by beginners. But it also challenges even the most seasoned scholars and anyone willing to seriously weigh competing interpretations. That difficulty is expected since the Bible is ancient literature, written across centuries by many different authors, spanning dozens of different regions and cultures, utilizing three ancient languages (two Semitic: Hebrew and Aramaic; one romantic: Koine Greek), filtered through textual criticism and scribal transmission, bridging between ancient Middle Eastern and Hellenic epochs, and addressing matters of inestimable breadth and depth. It would be naïve to think that there's no learning curve involved when modern Americans try to study the Bible in depth.

Fifth, and finally, the moral argument for God's existence poses a direct threat to Barker's whole project. Theists have long argued that morality itself testifies to God's existence.[58] Undoubtedly, Barker considers that argument unsound, but it remains a direct rebuttal to his naturalistic ethic. In Barker's literature, so far, he only skirts the moral argument, discussing how atheists can be moral, theists can be immoral, and how religious ethics can overlap with humanistic ethics, etc.[59] But if Barker hopes to establish his moral case against God, he needs to show that his own appeals to morality are not smuggling God back in the house in through the backdoor via the moral argument.

REVIEW

It has been shown that Barker fails (1) to erect a viable atheistic ethic and (2) to morally discredit God. Barker's whole moral project collapses under the weight of its many problems, including

1. There is little or no metaethical account offered in this system.

---

57. Barker's *God: The Most Unpleasant Character in All Fiction* is 310 pages total, yet has no significant scholarly discussion, no footnotes, no endnotes, no paragraph notes (besides Bible versions), or any such citations suggesting he interacted with biblical scholarship. He has a two-page bibliography which, apart from reference works (concordances and Bibles), includes only antagonistic sources like Hector Avalos, Michael Shermer, Steven Pinker, Richard Dawkins, and himself (see, Barker, *God*, 305–6).

58. Baggett and Walls, *Moral Argument*.

59. Barker, *Life Driven Purpose*, 19–101; Barker, *Mere Morality*; Barker, *godless*, 161–202.

2. There is little or no moral epistemology offered in this system.

3. The harm principle isn't robust enough to anchor a whole ethic, even with the assistance of his "three moral minds."

4. "Harm" is defined too narrowly as "threats to survival."

5. He commits a reductive fallacy in the form of lowest-common-denominator ethics.

6. Barker contradicts himself, saying only consequences matter, but intentions do too.

7. The harm principle is handicapped by negative framing, leaving out positive goods.

8. Ambiguity between quality of life (well-being) and quantity of life (survival).

9. Ambiguity between moral absolutism and moral relativism.

10. Barker contradicts the harm principle by affirming autonomous self-harm.

11. He commits a circular appeal to natural reason, wherein "my brain is reliable according to my brain."

12. He commits an appeal to nature fallacy (*argumentum ad naturam*).

13. He commits a pragmatic fallacy (*argumentum ad practicum*).

14. He commits a naturalistic fallacy or is-ought fallacy.

15. He commits a genetic fallacy or fallacy of origins.

16. He fails to account for different levels of authority, namely God's higher authority.

17. Biological determinism is incompatible with moral responsibility.

18. Biological determinism is incompatible with moral judgment.

19. Biological determinism is incompatible with moral knowledge.

20. Evolutionary naturalism renders ethics arbitrary; it could change morality on a whim.

21. Evolutionary naturalism renders moral knowledge suspect.

22. Materialism renders moral oughts to nonexistent hypotheticals.

23. Barker violates the principle of charity (preferring a consistently hostile interpretation).

24. By avoiding hermeneutics, Barker leaves his audience to trust his interpretations despite a general lack of corroborating evidence.

25. Barker's moral objections *against* God are directly undermined by his general failure to address or rebut the moral argument *for* God's existence.

BIBLIOGRAPHY

Baggett, David, and Jerry L. Walls. *The Moral Argument: A History.* Oxford: Oxford University Press, 2019.

Barker, Dan. *Free Will Explained.* New York: Sterling, 2018.

———. *God: The Most Unpleasant Character in All Fiction.* New York: Sterling, 2016.

———. *godless: How an Evangelical Preacher Became One of America's Leading Atheists.* Berkley: Ulysses, 2008.

———. *Life Driven Purpose: How an Atheist Finds Meaning.* Durham: Pitchstone, 2015.

———. *Mere Morality.* Durham: Pitchstone, 2018.

Bentham, Jeremy. *Deontology; or, the Science of Morality: in Which the Harmony and Co-Incidence of Duty and Self-Interest, Virtue and Felicity, Prudence and Benevolence, Are Explained and Exemplified.* Edited by John Bowring. London: Longman et al., 1834.

The Bible and Beer Consortium. "Does the Bible Advocate Slavery?" *YouTube*, July 26, 2019. https://www.youtube.com/watch?v=ahZVGzZ-uog.

Bouvier, John. *A Law Dictionary Adapted to the Constitution and Laws of the United States of America and of the Several States of the American Union with References to the Civil and Other Systems of Foreign Law.* Philadelphia: Childs and Peterson, 1856. https://legal-dictionary.thefreedictionary.com/.

Copan, Paul. *Is God a Moral Monster?* Grand Rapids: Baker, 2011.

Copan, Paul, and Matthew Flannagan. *Did God Really Command Genocide?* Grand Rapids: Baker, 2014.

Darwin, Charles. "Letter to William Graham." Self-published, July 3, 1881.

Dawkins, Richard. *The God Delusion.* New York: Houghton Mifflin Harcourt, 2006.

———. *River Out of Eden.* New York: Basic, 1995.

Dennett, Daniel. *Breaking the Spell: Religion as a Natural Phenomenon.* New York: Penguin, 2006.

Driver, Julia. "Normative Ethics." In *Oxford Handbook of Contemporary Philosophy*, edited by Frank Jackson and Michael Smith, 31–62. Oxford: Oxford University Press, 2007.

Feldman, Richard. "Charity, Principle of." https://www.rep.routledge.com/articles/thematic/charity-principle-of/v-1.

Ferrer, John. "30 Common Biblical Objections to God's Goodness." https://intelligentchristianfaith.com/2018/04/26/30-common-biblical-objections-to-gods-goodness/.

Fletcher, Joseph. *Situation Ethics: The New Morality.* Philadelphia: Westminster John Knox, 1966.

Haidt, Jonathan. *The Righteous Mind: Why Good People Are Divided by Politics and Religion.* New York: Vintage, 2012.

Harris, Sam. *The End of Faith: Religion, Terror, and the Future of Reason.* New York: Norton, 2005.

———. *The Moral Landscape: How Science Can Determine Human Values.* New York: Free, 2011.

Hitchens, Christopher. *God Is Not Great: How Religion Poisons Everything.* New York: Hachette, 2009.

Hume, David. *Treatise on Human Nature: Being an Attempt to Introduce the Experimental Method of Reasoning into Moral Subjects.* London: Noon, 1739.

Kant, Immanuel. *Groundwork for the Metaphysics of Morals.* Translated and edited by Allen W. Wood. London: Yale University Press, 2002.

Lamb, David T. *God Behaving Badly: Is the God of the Old Testament Angry, Sexist, and Racist?* Downers Grove: InterVarsity, 2011.

Moore, George E. *Principia Ethica.* London: Cambridge University Press, 1903.

West, John. *Darwin Day in America: How Our Politics and Culture Have Been Dehumanized in the Name of Science.* Wilmington: ISI, 2007.

Wielenberg, Erik J. *Robust Ethics: The Metaphysics and Epistemology of Godless Normative Realism.* Oxford: Oxford University Press, 2014.

9

Did Jesus Rise From the Dead?

—J. Thomas Bridges

The Gospel stories are no more historic than the Genesis creation accounts are scientific. They are filled with exaggerations, miracles and admitted propaganda. . . . Taking all of this into account, it is rational to conclude that the New Testament Jesus is a myth.

—Dan Barker[1]

INTRODUCTION

In Dan Barker's book *godless*, he includes two chapters in which he argues that Jesus Christ never existed and that the Gospels of Matthew, Mark, Luke, and John cannot be trusted because they contain accounts of miracles. One of Barker's main arguments is that if a story contains an account of a miracle, it cannot be historical. Barker says that

> if a miracle is defined as some kind of violation, suspension, overriding or punctuation of natural law, then miracles cannot be *historical*. . . . In order for history to have strength at all, it must adhere to a very strict assumption: that natural law is regular over time.

1. Barker, *godless*, 275.

> Without the assumption of natural regularity, no history can be done. There would be no criteria for discarding fantastic stories. Everything that has ever been recorded would have to be taken as literal truth.
>
> Therefore, if a miracle did happen, it would pull the rug out from history. The very basis of the historical method would have to be discarded. You can have miracles, or you can have history, but you can't have both.[2]

Barker emphasizes here that it is the regularity in nature that makes history possible. If there is no regularity, then we cannot make sense of history because there would be no way to tell if stories are reliable or not.

I agree with Barker that history needs regularity, although I do not agree with his conclusion that stories cannot be historical if they contain miracles. This is because, as will be explained below, I believe that God is the source of the laws of nature. God made a world that acts in regular ways so that reality would be intelligible for human beings and also so that humans would realize when he is trying to speak with them through miracles. It is not necessary for a Christian to entertain every single story containing supernatural claims but only those stories that claim to be from God.

An alternate title for this chapter could have asked, "Is it reasonable to believe that Christ's resurrection is a historical fact?" This is probably more precise but does not make for as catchy a chapter title. Regardless, this chapter will approach the question (as it is alternately stated) in phases to show how someone can believe the Gospels are objectively and historically true. I have sketched out a case where we first look at preliminary issues. These are issues that deal with the "reasonable" part of the question and address what would push an individual one way or the other in answering "yes" or "no." Next, we will look at the main arguments for a "yes" response. As with any chapter, this one can either be comprehensive or concise, but it cannot be both. We will not deal with all the preliminary issues, arguments, or objections. What this chapter is intended to do is to introduce you to these areas, give you some things to think on, and point you to further resources on this topic. At the least, this chapter aims to show that Barker is wrong to say that we must explore every possible natural explanation for the origin of Christianity as a world religion. If God exists, and the Gospels we have today are reliable, then there is nothing wrong with believing that Jesus's resurrection is a historical fact.

---

2. Barker, *godless*, 274.

PRELIMINARY ISSUES

The Existence of God and the Possibility of Miracles

The first of the preliminary issues, since it reaches the broadest scope, is whether or not miracles are possible. The reason this is a preliminary issue is that the belief that Jesus rose from the dead is a belief that a particular miracle, the resurrection, happened. If miracles are not possible, however, then this particular miracle is also not possible, and other considerations are moot.

I define "miracle" as "an event that has solely God as its cause." This definition is important because often times "miracle" is defined as "a rare event." This latter definition would allow any number of highly improbable but wholly natural events to count as miracles. My definition avoids this problem and sets the boundaries of what can and cannot count among the miraculous. Note, given my understanding of what a miraculous event is, by definition, it requires God to exist. I am not arguing that miracles happen, therefore God exists. I am simply pointing out the obvious fact that if a miracle is an event that solely has God as its cause, then belief in miracles entails a belief that God exists. If one does not believe the theistic God exists, then one will not believe in the possibility of miracles.

The broader question touching on the resurrection is "Are miracles possible?"—this question therefore demands us to answer a previous question, "Does God exist?" This question about God's existence is addressed in chapter 4, but I raise it again here because the belief in or denial of God's existence does play a role in how we judge historical evidence for events claimed to be miraculous. William Lane Craig summarizes this point nicely:

> Naturalism, in contrast to supernaturalism, holds that every effect in the world is brought about by causes that are themselves part of the natural order (the space-time world of matter and energy). . . . [When] inferring to the best explanation, one chooses from a pool of live options a candidate that serves as the best explanation of the evidence. For the naturalistic New Testament critic confronted with evidence concerning the empty tomb, the hypothesis that Jesus rose from the dead would not even be a live option.[3]

So, if one answers the question of God's existence with a "no," then there is no further basis on which to argue that Jesus rose from the dead. At the same time, this fact does not rule out the possibility that an individual, upon

3. Craig, "Did Jesus Rise from the Dead?," 141–76.

examining the historical evidence for Jesus's resurrection, might simultaneously come to believe both that God exists and that he raised Jesus from the dead. It is still the case, however, that there is a logical priority of the existence of God, and this typically plays a significant role in how one even weighs the historical evidence itself.

The Objectivity of History

Though the objectivity of history is not the main focus of this chapter, the claim that it is reasonable to believe in the resurrection of Jesus presupposes history's objectivity. Later in this chapter, historical testimony will be brought forward as evidence for this unique and central claim of Christianity. If historical testimony is hopelessly subjective or rationally unacceptable on other grounds, then this testimony cannot possibly give us reasons to believe in the resurrection. So, the question is, "Can we have objective knowledge of historical events?"

Several criticisms are raised against the possibility of objective knowledge of history. Some say, for example, the historian has at his disposal only fragmentary evidence for his historical thesis. What follows from this, the subjectivist says, is that the historian must select, collate, and interpret his data and reproduce for his audience some account that is greater than the original data that he first possessed. Therefore, history is more created than it is "objectively known."

Another criticism motivated by a subjectivist view of history is that every historian is himself situated in a specific time and place. Being removed from the times and places of the events upon which he is commenting, the historian can only give us an account as seen from his present perspective or "historical conditioning." The result is that anything a twenty-first-century historian might say about events in first-century Palestine is hopelessly littered with his own interpretive framework that is largely informed by his own historical situation.

Norman Geisler offers several concise responses to these criticisms of the possibility of the objectivity of history. He writes, "If by 'objective' the subjectivists mean absolute knowledge, then of course no human historian can be objective. On the other hand, if 'objective' means an *accurate and adequate* presentation that reasonable people should accept, then the door is open to the possibility of objectivity. . . . Objectivity resides in the view that best fits all the facts into the overall system, that is, into systematic consistency."[4] Responding to the objection from the historian's situatedness, Geisler writes,

> It is true that every historian is a product of his time; each person does occupy a relative place in the changing events of the spatio-temporal world. However, it does not follow that because the historian is a product of his time, his history is also purely a product of the time. That a person cannot avoid a relative place in history does not mean his perspective cannot attain a meaningful degree of objectivity. This criticism confuses the content of knowledge and the process attaining it . . . Further, if relativity is unavoidable, then the position of the historical relativist is self-refuting, for either their view is historically conditioned and therefore unobjective, or else it is not relative but objective.[5]

A final observation should suffice to bring this section to a close. Geisler also notes that "the very fact that one can know that some histories are better than others reveals that there must be some objective understanding of the events by which this judgment is made."[6]

As all other versions of thoroughgoing relativism, historical relativism ends up being self-defeating. Geisler's last observation is most telling. He notes that since we can look at two historical accounts and judge that one of them is objectively better than the others, there are some facts of the matter (as well as a grasp of the psychological and sociological issues surrounding the events) that make a particular historical account reasonably objective. This is not to say the events are known with absolute certainty, but with a degree of reasonability. This is all we need to preserve the possibility of objective historical evidence for a purportedly miraculous event.

The Integrity of the Gospels

The integrity of the Gospels is an important preliminary issue, as well as being an apologetics issue worthy of book-length treatment. Here we can only briefly address the question of whether the New Testament documents, and specifically the Gospels, are reliable regarding their 1) authorship and 2) contents. If the authorship of the documents is questionable, or the content has been horribly corrupted, then the testimonies of the New Testament writers about the resurrection are not reliable evidence. In recent years,

4. Geisler, *Systematic Theology*, 189–92 (emphasis in original).

5. Geisler, *Systematic Theology*, 192.

6. Geisler, *Systematic Theology*, 202.

some critical New Testament scholars, such as Bart Ehrman, have deemed the New Testament documents unreliable for elucidating historical facts because they are corrupted and of later authorship. But as is true of nearly every area of scholarship, where there is a liberal reading of the data, there is also a conservative reading. We will look at a conservative reading of the data and offer some justification for this reading.

New Testament documents scholar Craig Blomberg gives us insight into the issue of the authorship of the Gospels and Acts. The following provides a somewhat lengthy, but excellent, summary of the issue. Blomberg writes,

> Modern biblical criticism has made two different kinds of claims about the authorship of the gospels and Acts. On the one hand, it has rightly pointed out that these five books are, strictly speaking, anonymous. None of the gospels or the Book of Acts originally had a writer's name attached to it. Titles (for example, "The Gospel according to . . .") were likely added early in the second century when the fourfold gospel collection circulated as a unit. On the other hand, modern scholarship has more speculatively also questioned the accuracy of the traditional ascriptions of the authorship of these books to Matthew, Mark, Luke, and John. There are no dissenting traditions whatever in the first centuries of the Church's history concerning the authorship of the first three gospels and Acts and concerning the repeated claims that these books were indeed written by Matthew, Mark, and Luke. Given that two of these men were not apostles (Mark and Luke), and that Matthew would have been one of the most "suspect" of the apostles, in light of his background as a tax collector, it seems unlikely that the first Christians would have invented these authorship claims if they were merely trying to enhance the credibility of the documents attributed to these writers. Later apocryphal gospels and acts are consistently attributed to less suspect writers—for example, Peter, James . . . even Mary. There *is* some uncertainty in the early centuries about the Gospel of John, but it surrounds which "John" was behind the Fourth Gospel (John the apostle or a later John the elder), not whether or not the book was written by someone named John. And the clear majority opts for the apostle.[7]

The most telling observation that Blomberg offers, besides the historical data of the early church's witness to the authorship of the texts, is that later apocryphal works, like the Gospel of Peter, attribute authorship of the

---

7. Blomberg, "Historical Reliability of the New Testament," 203–4.

writing to the well-known leader of the early church. This is in stark contrast to the strong tradition that attributes the synoptic Gospels to Matthew (a tax collector and relatively minor figure in the early church), Mark (not an apostle), and Luke (also not an apostle). The tradition is that Mark and Luke are reliable because Mark wrote down what he heard from Peter (an eyewitness) and that Luke interviewed early believers for the eyewitness source material of his Gospel account.

The fact that the early writings were anonymous can be likened to the fact that some small towns are completely without street signs. Why? The community is so small and the terrain so familiar that no one needs to name the streets to know where everything is. In a similar way, the early church was small enough and the copies of authoritative writings so apparent in terms of their sources that they didn't need to place names on them. It was only later, as Blomberg says, when the Gospels were collected as a unit that it became necessary to distinguish them by their authorship. The idea of the authors of the Gospels being eyewitnesses or derivative of eyewitness accounts is directly related to the manuscript evidence for the text itself. After all, an eyewitness account is not much good if its contents have been radically corrupted. But it is important to note also an observation by New Testament scholar Gary Habermas, "Even though he says he would argue for the traditional Gospel authors, R. T. France makes the point that it is not essential whether their identity is known. These books should be judged the way most historians judge historical accuracy—by their early date and the tradition behind them."[8] So, even though church tradition identifies the Gospel authors, the crucial historical question is whether the accounts themselves have been radically corrupted or well-preserved.

The question of assessing the reliability of the New Testament documents must fall under the broader question, "How does one assess the reliability of ancient documents?" The reason we want to ask this question is that it would be unfairly biased to submit the New Testament documents to rigor that far exceeds that submitted to other ancient documents. After all, the question here is not whether the original authors were truly inspired by God to pen what they did. Rather, the question is, "Are the New Testament documents, as ancient documents, reliable in terms of their authorship and contents (leaving aside theological considerations)?"

A well-known scholar, the late F. F. Bruce helps us in this regard. He provides a glimpse into the world of Ancient Near Eastern (ANE) documents and the manuscript evidence upon which rests their reliability. He writes,

8. Habermas, "Did Jesus Perform Miracles?," 132.

> For Cæsar's *Gallic War* (composed between 58 and 50 BC) there
> are several extant MSS [manuscripts], but only nine or ten are
> good, and the oldest is some 900 years later than Cæsar's day.....
> The History of Thucydides (c. 460–400 BC) is known to us from
> eight MSS, the earliest belonging to c. AD 900 . . . The same
> is true of the History of Herodotus (c. 488–428). Yet no classi-
> cal scholar would listen to an argument that the authenticity of
> Herodotus or Thucydides is in doubt because the earliest MSS of
> their works which are of any use to us are over 1,300 years later
> than the originals.[9]

Bruce has given us a small picture of what it is like to test the reliability of
ancient manuscripts. Greek scholar Bruce Metzger offers his own comparison, writing,

> In evaluating the significance of [the] statistics of the amount of
> Greek evidence for the text of the New Testament, one should
> consider, by way of contrast, the number of manuscripts which
> preserve the text of the ancient classics. Homer's *Iliad*, for ex-
> ample, the 'bible' of the ancient Greeks, is preserved in 457 pa-
> pyri, 2 uncial manuscripts, and 188 miniscule manuscripts. . . .
> The works of several ancient authors are preserved to us by the
> thinnest possible thread of transmission. . . . In contrast with
> these figures, the textual critic of the New Testament is embar-
> rassed by the wealth of his material. . . . Instead of the lapse of a
> millennium or more, as is the case of not a few classical authors,
> several papyrus manuscripts of portions of the New Testament
> are extant which were copied within a century or so after the
> composition of the original documents.[10]

What Bruce and Metzger have given us is an incomplete, but very telling,
contrast between the typical numbers of available manuscripts for examination by the textual scholar and the typical gaps for ancient documents
between the original writing and extant copies. These are important facts
if one is going to grasp the relative strength of the documentation for the
text of the New Testament; if someone is going to doubt the reliability of the
New Testament based on the number of extant manuscripts and the time
gap between the original writing and the earliest extant manuscripts, then
he must also doubt all ancient works including Homer's *Iliad*.

---

9. Bruce, *New Testament Documents*, 16–17. Since Bruce published *The New Testament Documents*, the number of discovered, extant manuscripts of Homer's *Iliad* has
grown to over 1,900 (McDowell and McDowell, *Evidence that Demands a Verdict*, 57).

10. Metzger, *Text of the New Testament*, 33–35.

Metzger further expounds on the sources available for getting back to the content of the original manuscripts. He says, "Three classes of witnesses are available for ascertaining the text of the New Testament; they are the Greek manuscripts, the ancient translations into other languages, and the quotations from the New Testament made by early ecclesiastical writers."[11] This latter point is important because not only do we have copies of New Testament documents in the original Greek (over 5,600[12]), but we also have the contents of the originals from copies translated to other languages (e.g., Coptic and Latin), and we have the contents quoted in the letters written by early church fathers. F. F. Bruce notes, "Fortunately, if the great number of MSS increases the number of scribal errors, it increases proportionately the means of correcting such errors, so that the margin of doubt left in the process of recovering the exact original wording is not so large as might be feared; it is in truth remarkably small."[13] When comparing the overwhelming number of documents, even if there are errors in every single one, it is also true that the same error will not be repeated in every one. There will, consequently, be evidence from the manuscripts as to which variant is likely the original reading. This gives us reasonably high confidence that the content of the New Testament documents that we have in our modern Bible does not differ significantly from the words of the original authors.[14]

EVIDENCE FOR THE RESURRECTION

As has been noted throughout the chapter, the purpose here is to give the reader a sketch of the issues surrounding one's belief that Jesus in fact rose from the dead. So far, we have touched on the preliminary issues of the possibility of miracles, the objectivity of history, and the integrity of the New Testament documents. We have finally come to the point of examining some of the evidence that makes it reasonable to conclude that the resurrection is a historical fact. There are many book-length treatments of

11. Metzger, *Text of the New Testament*, 36.

12. McDowell and McDowell, *Evidence that Demands a Verdict*, 47.

13. Bruce, *New Testament Documents*, 19.

14. As an aside, it is clarifying to note the difference between the history of the New Testament documents and the history of the Islamic Qur'an. In the history of the Qur'an, there were times where copies of the book that had what we would call today "textual variants" were collected and burned. This significantly shaped the genealogies of the manuscripts so that the possibility of getting back to the original from one's current copies becomes less likely. In contrast, the New Testament documents were not similarly treated, and they retain textual variants that are "pure," that is, show a distinct genealogical pathway that helps scholars trace a reading back to the original.

the myriad of evidences along with detailed analyses of the thesis for and against each point related to the historicity of the resurrection.[15] Here I have selected from this list a handful of evidences either because they are the more commonly referenced or because I find them particularly persuasive. What follows is in no way an exhaustive treatment.

Expert on the evidences for the resurrection of Christ, Gary Habermas, lists elements in the Gospel accounts for which there is overwhelming consensus among scholars on the historical Jesus. That is, virtually every historical fact on the list is considered largely undisputed by the men and women who study the historical evidence professionally. Of the dozen historical facts, I'll list while retaining their original numeration:

1. Jesus died by Roman crucifixion.

2. He was buried, most likely in a private tomb.

4. Jesus' tomb was found empty very soon after his interment.

5. The disciples had experiences that they believed were actual appearances of the risen Jesus.

6. Due to these experiences, the disciples' lives were thoroughly transformed.

7. The proclamation of the resurrection took place very early, at the beginning of church history.

8. The disciples' public testimony and preaching of the resurrection took place in the city of Jerusalem, where Jesus had been crucified and buried shortly before.[16]

Individually or collectively, this simple list of historical facts is insufficient to prove that Jesus died and rose again from the dead. But it is enough to argue that the resurrection of Jesus as an actual historical event is the *best explanation* of the facts we have in hand, according to William Lane Craig's explanation previously discussed. What history gives evidence of is that Jesus was actually killed (i.e., his death was not faked) and that days after his confirmed execution, he was seen again by his disciples. Why believe this is the best explanation? This is where subsequent lines of evidence come along

15. Scholarly treatments defending the truth of the resurrection include Craig, *Son Rises*; Habermas, *Historical Jesus*; and Licona, *Resurrection of Jesus*. Though Licona's *Resurrection of Jesus* raises some "in-house" debate over the issue of inerrancy, it nevertheless provides a strong case for the historicity of the resurrection. A great beginner's guide to defending the truth of the resurrection is Habermas and Licona, *Case for the Resurrection of Jesus*.

16. Habermas, *Risen Jesus and Future Hope*, 9.

to support the resurrection as the best explanation of the data. At this point, I will begin selecting those elements of that vast sea of data that are to me most provocative.

The first compelling piece of evidence is the fact that the earliest recorded testimony for Jesus's resurrection is sourced from a group of mildly hysterical women. Living at the beginning of the twenty-first century in the Western world, we live in an age that highly values egalitarianism (the equal rights of men and women), but for most of human history, and in many cultures, this was not the case. In first-century Palestine, women did not have the same rights as men. Women could not own property, which meant that a daughter could not inherit her father's estate (a factor motivating the plot in *Pride and Prejudice*). And more significantly related to the present issue, women could not give public testimony. That is, their testimony had zero weight under the law. This strikes me as having a distinct ring of truth. After all, the most ardent skeptic regarding the truth of Christianity, including Dan Barker, must admit that if the disciples were doing anything in writing down the accounts of Christ's life and ministry, they were trying to persuade others to join their religion/community of belief. In light of this fact, the disciples' claim that unreliable women, rather than men, were the first witnesses to the resurrection would render their account less socially acceptable and, thus, more likely true. It would be unexplainable as to why the Gospel writers would invent women as the earliest source about Christ's returning from death.

A second line of evidence is the combination of Habermas's facts (6), (7), and (8) from the above list. Namely, the disciples proclaimed this resurrection event 1) shortly after it happened, 2) among the persons who would have been most aware of and able to verify it, and 3) with the result that their lives were radically transformed. In other settings, Habermas has reminded audiences that though the Gospel accounts tell us about the life of Christ, which occurred chronologically before the events of the early church, the Gospels themselves were written later than most of the other New Testament documents, the Gospels being written from the mid-AD 60s (for Mark) to the mid-AD 70s (for Matthew and Luke), to the mid-AD 90s (for John). It is important to remember that most of the New Testament documents are letters Paul, Peter, and John wrote to various churches or groups. It is in these writings (e.g., 1 Corinthians and Galatians) where we get a glimpse into what the church believed within the first few decades of its founding. In terms of evidences for a particular belief in the ancient world, this is incredibly early.

The other facet, that the disciples advocated the resurrection event within the very same city in which the event purportedly took place is enormously important. This is in contrast to, say, proclaiming in Egypt, Rome, or Persia that an obscure Jewish rabbi died and rose again. Some religions, such as Mormonism or Islam, are based on an account of an individual that is unverifiable. In these cases, an individual has a *private*, purportedly supernatural experience and asks a community of individuals to believe his account simply on blind faith. The disciples of Christ, however, were a group of men and women all testifying publicly about an event (the details of which were open to investigation and verification) among those who 1) knew about the events surrounding the event and 2) were in a position to immediately investigate the claims.

As a working philosopher, I want to make an observation on the nature of belief based on testimony. One may be skeptical about a particular report or a particular source of a report, but one cannot adopt wholesale skepticism about belief based on the testimony of another. The reason is simple: most of what we know is based on the testimony of what we believe to be a credible witness or authority. If I were to ask you how far is the nearest large spiral galaxy to the Milky Way galaxy, you would probably pull out your phone, perform a quick internet search, and open one of the more reputable astronomy sites and tell me that it is the Andromeda Galaxy, and you would be correct. But how do you know that, and why are you so confident about that belief? The answer is that if you go to a site run by NASA or an online magazine called *Universe Today*, you can be reasonably sure that the answer you get will not be a hoax or the information deliberately falsified. So, the issue is, do you think the early Gospel accounts are a hoax or the information is deliberately falsified? This is why Habermas's list is so important. It is a list of agreed upon historical details about the resurrection event. Is it plausible that the disciples were trying to deceive people and included the testimony of women in their account given the social trends of the day? Is it plausible that the disciples were willfully propagating a hoax when they gave early public testimony among those who would be most familiar with their story and most able to refute its claims? It is certainly possible, but it is not a reasonable response.

This brings us to the last element from Habermas's list that I find compelling: the way the resurrection event changed the lives of the disciples. The most compelling evidence is not that they were willing to die for their beliefs and that none of them recanted their testimony on pain of torture, death, or exile. I know that many defenders of the resurrection point to these facts and certainly these assertions are consistent with the disciples wholeheartedly believing their testimony about Christ, but what I find compelling is a bit more primitive than this. Let me elaborate.

When I watch a movie, the thing that is most concerning to me is the development of the characters. Is the main character changed by what he experiences, and in what ways is he changed? Are those changes psychologically plausible? For example, I was watching a movie in which one of the main characters says she was abandoned by her father at an early age and couldn't care less where he is or what has happened to him. Just a few minutes later, when another character finds out her father was involved in some sort of black-market dealings that ultimately led to his murder, her response is, "I'm coming with you because I want to know what happened to my father." My reaction was to roll my eyes and whisper to my wife, "I thought she didn't care about him." It was obviously a reaction calculated to move the plot along, but it was wholly contrary to the character as she had been presented to that point. This element of psychological plausibility is what gives fiction a sense of reality and what gives historical accounts their ring of truth.

In this vein, what I find compelling in the disciples' reaction is that they seem *genuinely shocked* by the resurrection. We tend to have an image of ancient folks as slightly moronic or highly gullible. After all, these were people who thought that thunder was a result of the anger of the gods. But this is faulty thinking, since as early as the sixth century BC, there were natural philosophers (the earliest scientists) who were looking for natural explanations of natural events. These ancient people may not have understood how nature functioned in the ways that it did, but they were familiar with common versus uncommon events. We see this in the disciples' reaction to, for example, Jesus walking on water in the midst of a storm. They were awed by this because, whatever else they knew about the world, they knew that men do not walk on water.

In a similar way, the disciples' reaction to the resurrection strikes me as psychologically plausible. That is, they understood Jesus as a brilliant rabbi (with his unique explanations of the Mosaic law) or a miracle-working prophet (e.g., raising Lazarus from the dead or making the blind see), but when he was dragged off by the local Jewish authorities, placed on trial before the highest Roman official in the land, and handed over for flogging and execution, they realized that he was subject to all the normal political and juridical powers of the day. Then came Sunday morning. The tomb was empty, the crazy women were telling of angels and seeing Jesus . . . then Jesus appeared. "It can't be him!" the disciples may have said. "It must be his ghost!" Then, upon his meeting them on the beach, they might have said, "Nope, it's not a ghost—he's eating with us." The disciples' reactions to Christ are exactly what I would expect from a real event; they are completely psychologically plausible.

The final piece of compelling evidence is directly related to my study of philosophy. Beginning in graduate school, I started reading the earliest pre-Socratic philosophers (those before Socrates) and then worked my way over several years through the history of Western philosophy. When studying the history of ideas, it becomes clear how one thinker is influenced (either positively or negatively) by a tradition of thinking. For example, one can trace (and this is an exercise I set for my history of philosophy students) the influence of Immanuel Kant from the late eighteenth century, through the existentialism of the nineteenth century, and even forward into the work of some early twentieth-century thinkers. Studying the history of ideas makes one more acutely aware of how ideas emerge and evolve over time.

So, this last evidence, making belief in the resurrection reasonable, is the unique idea among early Christians that a single individual rose from the dead, that this event was somehow a picture of our own eventual resurrection, and that both of these have enormous theological import. This evidence was made clear to me by an article written by biblical scholar N. T. Wright. The blessedness of this article is that it was partly adopted from about fourteen pages in Wright's summary of his seven-hundred-page book, *The Resurrection of the Son of God*. In this article, Wright demonstrates that the Christian idea of the resurrection was absolutely unique. He writes:

> One of the things I really enjoyed when I wrote that book [*The Resurrection of the Son of God*] was going back to my classical stomping grounds and researching ancient beliefs about life after death, Greek and Roman and Egyptian beliefs about life after death. And there's a huge range of beliefs, but "resurrection" doesn't feature in the Greco-Roman world. . . . We can track the way in which *resurrection* belief occurs in Judaism. Resurrection is a two-stage sequence: right after you die you're immediately in this holding pattern or waiting state; and then you have this entirely new life called *resurrection*. . . . The Pharisees believed in resurrection, and this seems to have been the majority belief in Palestinian Judaism at the time of Jesus. The Sadducees didn't believe in life after death at all, certainly not resurrection. And people like Philo and perhaps the Essenes (though that's controversial) believed in a single-stage disembodied immortality, in which, after death, you simply go wherever you are going and stay there.[17]

17. Wright, "Appendix B," 196–97.

Wright has done us the service of painstakingly comparing the idea of a personal resurrection among four different cultures—Egyptian, Roman, Greek, and Jewish—then looking deeper into the Jewish tradition on the subject.

We should keep in mind the following question: Is there any history of ideas or previous conception of the resurrection that would have reasonably influenced the ideas of the early church? Wright gives seven unique distinctions about the early Christian view of resurrection. Here are several of the most interesting:

> First, instead of resurrection being something that was simply going to happen to all God's people at the end, the early Christian said it had happened to one person in advance. Now, no first-century Jew, as far as we know, believed there would be one person raised ahead of everybody else. . . . Second, they believed that the resurrection would involve the transformation of the physical body. Those Jews who believed in resurrection seem to have gone in one of two directions. Some said it would produce a physical body exactly like this one all over again, and others said it would be a luminous body, one shining like a star. The early Christians didn't say either of those things. They talked about a new sort of physicality . . . that picture of the resurrection is not in Judaism. . . . Seventh, and finally, we find that in early Christianity there is virtually no spectrum of belief about what happens after death. In Judaism there were several different viewpoints, and in the pagan world there were a great many, but in early Christianity there was only one: resurrection itself. . . . All this forces us as historians to ask a very simple question: Why did all the early Christians known to us, from the earliest times for which we have evidence, have this very new, but remarkably unanimous, view of resurrection?[18]

Wright's observations are interesting for several reasons. For about the first twenty years, the entire community of early Christians was Jewish. This means their religious views were largely Jewish in nature. The early debates over whether or not gentile believers were required to be circumcised or follow the Mosaic Law serve as testimony to this fact. Also, in the history of Christianity, there was a trend toward widespread theological debate as the well-trained and intelligent of the church attempted to understand the meaning of a particular doctrine (e.g., the incarnation). If Wright is correct with his final point, there was no such widespread debate leading to a spectrum of beliefs about the nature of the resurrection. The unanimity of the early church on this topic is uncommon, to say the least. What is

18. Wright, "Appendix B," 199–201.

the best explanation of this novel view of the resurrection being suddenly introduced into Jewish culture by a group of largely unschooled men and women and then held unanimously by the early church? The historical fact of Jesus's resurrection provides the most reasonable explanation. Further, the reality of the resurrection explains the nature of the apostle Paul's subsequent ministry. Something so novel, and Messianic and supernatural, had happened that it required the Jews to understand its ramifications for their traditional views of Judaism. This would not have been the case if the early Christian view of the resurrection had been substantially rooted in previous Judaic traditions.

CONCLUSION

Our original question was, "Is it reasonable to believe that Christ's resurrection is a historical fact?" We looked at preliminary issues related to the possibility of miracles in light of the existence of the theistic God, the objectivity of history, and the integrity of the New Testament text. Finally, we examined compelling lines of evidence that Jesus's resurrection can be reasonably believed to be a historical fact.

These evidences show why it is reasonable to believe that Jesus Christ rose from the dead. If God exists, it does not follow that we must exhaust all naturalistic explanations when questioning the historicity of the Gospels, as Barker suggests. God certainly wants reality to be regular, otherwise there would be nothing special about Jesus rising from the dead. In fact, if there were no natural law, we could not recognize an exception. But so that we can know that God is talking to us, God acts in history in ways that only he has the power to act, especially when God wants to provide evidence that he will one day raise everyone from the dead.

Of course, there are those, including Barker, who object to nearly every one of the above points. Some believe that God cannot possibly exist, and therefore miracles are not possible. Some think that history is too subjective to give us historical fact. Others think that history, as history, is incapable of attesting to a miraculous event. Some who are aware of even more evidences than those sketched above remain unconvinced. But the question was not, "Is the evidence so overwhelming that even one who wants to be skeptical simply cannot be?" The question was, "Is belief in the resurrection as a historical fact *reasonable*?" That is, "Is it possible for one to have a scholarly understanding of all of the relevant historical data and conclude that Jesus did in fact rise from the dead?" The answer is, "Yes, it is perfectly reasonable." Many intelligent and highly educated individuals are persuaded that a balanced view—not a biased view—of the historical evidence leans heavily in favor of the resurrection as the *best* explanation of all the relevant historical facts. The Christian need have no fear that this central belief is somehow based on blind faith or without any evidential support.

BIBLIOGRAPHY

Barker, Dan. *godless: How an Evangelical Preacher Became One of America's Leading Atheists.* Berkeley: Ulysses, 2008.

Blomberg, Craig L. "The Historical Reliability of the New Testament." In *Reasonable Faith,* by William Lane Craig, 193–231. 2nd ed. Wheaton: Crossway, 1994.

Bruce, F. F. *The New Testament Documents: Are They Reliable?* Grand Rapids: InterVarsity, 1998.

Craig, William Lane. "Did Jesus Rise from the Dead?" In *Jesus Under Fire: Modern Scholarship Reinvents the Historical Jesus,* edited by Michael J. Wilkins and J. P. Moreland, 141–76. Grand Rapids: Zondervan, 1995.

———. *The Son Rises: The Historical Evidence for the Resurrection of Jesus.* 1981. Reprint, Eugene, OR: Wipf & Stock, 2000.

Geisler, Norman L. *Systematic Theology.* Vol. 1, *Introduction, Bible.* Minneapolis: Bethany, 2002.

Habermas, Gary R. "Did Jesus Perform Miracles?" In *Jesus Under Fire: Modern Scholarship Reinvents the Historical Jesus,* edited by Michael J. Wilkins and J. P. Moreland, 117–40. Grand Rapids: Zondervan, 1995.

———. *The Historical Jesus: Ancient Evidence for the Life of Christ.* Joplin: College Press, 1996.

———. *The Risen Jesus and Future Hope.* New York: Roman & Littlefield, 2003.

Habermas, Gary R., and Michael R. Licona. *The Case for the Resurrection of Jesus.* Grand Rapids: Kregel, 2004.

Licona, Michael R. *The Resurrection of Jesus: A New Historiographical Approach.* Downers Grove: IVP Academic, 2010.

McDowell, Josh, and Sean McDowell. *Evidence that Demands a Verdict: Life-Changing Truth for a Skeptical World.* Nashville: HarperCollins, 2017.

Metzger, Bruce. *The Text of the New Testament: Its Transmission, Corruption, and Restoration.* 3rd ed. Oxford: Oxford University Press, 1992.

Wright, N. T. "Appendix B: The Self-Revelation of God in Human History: A Dialogue on Jesus with N. T. Wright." In *There Is a God: How the World's Most Notorious Atheist Changed His Mind,* by Antony Flew, 185–213. New York: Harper One, 2008.

———. *The Resurrection of the Son of God.* Minneapolis: Fortress, 2003.

10

Dan Barker's Objections
to the Resurrection of Jesus

—Brett A. Bruster

I am now convinced that the Jesus story is a combination of myth and legend, mixed with a little bit of real history unrelated to Jesus. . . . The Gospels, written many decades after the fact, are a blend of fact and fantasy—historical fiction—and although the proportions of the blend may differ from scholar to scholar, no credible historians take them at 100 percent face value.

—Dan Barker[1]

The bodily resurrection of Jesus Christ is one of the fundamental doctrines of Christian orthodoxy. God's word makes it clear that mankind has a serious problem—that is, that our sin has separated us from God. As sinners, we are not able to resolve our problem. The writer of Hebrews tells us that it is our destiny to die, and when we do, we will stand before a holy God to face judgment (Heb 9:27). However, God in his great mercy offered his Son who took on flesh, lived without sin, and died on the cross in our place. God then raised him to new bodily life as a demonstration of his power to forgive us and resurrect us to new and eternal life.

1. Barker, *godless*, 251–52.

In an era when many do not believe in the supernatural intervention of God in the material world, the truth that the resurrection of Jesus can be shown to have actually happened as a real historical event seems impossible. However, not only is it demonstrable through historical study that Jesus was resurrected from the dead, it is essential that individuals believe this truth in order to receive eternal life.

Dan Barker is a prominent atheist and skeptic of the biblical account of the resurrection. In this chapter, I will analyze and critique Barker's objections to the historicity of the resurrection. First, I will discuss the strengths of the Gospel accounts in relation to a historical criterion formulated by Michael Martin. This will provide a helpful background that readers can reference when I am answering Barker's objections. After explaining this criterion and highlighting the strengths of the Gospels, I will unpack Barker's objections to the historicity of the resurrection and then provide answers to those objections. It will be shown that his criticisms are without merit and that, in fact, the historical evidence for the resurrection of Jesus is sufficiently strong for us to place our complete faith in the biblical account of Jesus's resurrection.

MICHAEL MARTIN'S FIVE FACTORS

According to atheist philosopher Michael Martin, there are five factors affecting the strength and reliability of the evidence put forward to support the historical facticity of the resurrection of Jesus as presented in the New Testament. These factors are first, the consistency of the various accounts; second, whether or not the accounts are eyewitness accounts versus secondhand accounts; third, the known reliability and trustworthiness of the eyewitnesses; fourth, the extent of independent testimony concerning the New Testament accounts; and finally, the extent to which the author's purpose for writing his account may have influenced his reliability.[2] Before addressing the biblical view of the resurrection, one must note that Martin has constructed this list of factors with the end in mind. In other words, this is not a list developed from a widely agreed-upon historical methodology, but rather a list of categories based upon the objections that Martin will present to the biblical view of the resurrection. Therefore, it is important to understand that this list contains underlying premises that may not be true. Nonetheless, this list can be addressed quite well by the biblical, orthodox view of the resurrection.

2. Martin, *Case Against Christianity*, 76–77.

Consistency of the Various Accounts

Multiple authors of books of the New Testament agree that Jesus died from crucifixion and was raised to new life and that the risen Jesus was seen and spoke with his followers (Matt 28; Mark 16; Luke 24; John 20–21; Acts 2). We also have the testimony of Paul and his reference to what the church was teaching very early on (1 Cor 15:3–8). There is absolute consistency in all the primary facts concerning the resurrection. So-called inconsistencies are really not contradictory and must be seen in the light of the various perspectives of the individual authors.

Accounts from Eyewitnesses or Secondhand?

The Gospels, as well as much of the New Testament, present themselves very much as the testimony of eyewitnesses. Though it is popular in modern critical scholarship to suggest the New Testament is not written by eyewitnesses, there is little reason to hold that to be the case. Peter states in 2 Peter, "For we did not follow cleverly devised tales when we made known to you the power and coming of our Lord Jesus Christ, but we were eyewitnesses of His majesty" (2 Pet 1:16, NASB). And Luke says in the beginning of his Gospel that he was among many who received testimony from the eyewitnesses who were with Jesus from the very beginning. He writes of himself in the first person as being in the company of Paul, thereby giving evidence that he had received the testimony of Paul as a direct eyewitness of the risen Jesus. Richard Bauckham presents a very thorough and convincing case that the Gospels are eyewitness testimony. He writes, "They [the Gospels] embody the testimony of the eyewitnesses, not of course without editing and interpretation, but in a way that is substantially faithful to how the eyewitnesses themselves told it, since the Evangelists were in more or less direct contact with eyewitnesses, not removed from them by a long process of anonymous transmission of the traditions. In the case of one of the Gospels, that of John, I conclude, very unfashionably, that an eyewitness wrote it."[3]

Known Reliability and Trustworthiness of the Eyewitnesses

With regard to the reliability and trustworthiness of the biblical witnesses, we have reason to believe they were reliable. First of all, one cannot ignore the teachings of Jesus. Repeatedly, the Old Testament, New Testament, and

---

3. Bauckham, *Jesus and the Eyewitnesses*, 6.

the specific words of Jesus deal with the importance God places on truthfulness. So it would be counter to the teachings of all the authors of the New Testament books to be less than truthful in their accounts. Secondly, the writings of Luke, in his Gospel and in the book of Acts, provide evidence that he was a very careful historian, who has been shown to be very accurate in his representations of geographical and historical facts.[4] Not only do we have evidence that Luke was trustworthy, but we have his explicit statements concerning his intent to be truthful. He writes that his intent is to document the account of Jesus's life, death, and resurrection "so that you may know the exact truth about the things you have been taught" (Luke 1:4). We also have Paul writing 1 Corinthians at a time when there were still many living witnesses to the risen Christ (1 Cor 15:6). It would have been impossible to carry out such a fraud in a time when travel between Corinth and Jerusalem, as two Roman colonies, would have been quite common.

Extent of Independent Testimony Concerning the New Testament Accounts

The Gospels are confirmed both within the New Testament as well as outside. Writing in 1 Corinthians 15:3–8, Paul relates what is certainly an oral formula, which dates back to at least within three years of the death of Christ.[5] This means that not only is Paul writing of his own experience with the risen Christ, but he is also revealing an oral tradition that was being used to relate the events of Christ's death and resurrection before the Gospels were written. Furthermore, Peter, as has already been previously mentioned, confirms his witness of the events of Christ's life (2 Pet 1:16). Beyond the Bible, there are very early church fathers who were quite likely to have had direct personal contact with at least some of the apostles. Clement, Bishop of Rome, for example, has written about the resurrection of Christ.[6]

Extent of Influence of Author's Purpose on His Reliability

The first thing to note about this particular point of Martin's is that it is self-refuting. The implication that one cannot trust an account written by someone who is attempting to promote a particular point of view means that Martin's assessment of the historical evidence should not be given any

4. McDowell, *New Evidence That Demands a Verdict*, 63–66.
5. Blomberg, *Historical Reliability of the Gospels*, 147–48.
6. Habermas and Licona, *Case for the Resurrection of Jesus*, 53–54.

weight, since he makes it clear that he is promoting a point of view: "My claim is simply that in the light of my discussion rational people should give up these beliefs."[7] This self-defeating logic aside, it is clear that the writers of the New Testament are indeed trying to convince their readers of the truth of their account of the events. But if they were doing so by misleading or even lying, then they would not have written that women were the ones who discovered the empty tomb. These and other embarrassing details are a very strong indication of the reliability of their witness.

THE OBJECTIONS OF DAN BARKER

Dan Barker writes of several objections to belief in the biblical view of Christ's resurrection in his book, godless.[8] Barker gives four primary objections to the resurrection account as held in Christian orthodoxy. First, he claims that if the resurrection occurred, then it is a miracle and that history is not able to establish that which is "impossible or highly unlikely" (which he says defines a miracle).[9] Barker relies on the argument (citing Thomas Paine and David Hume) that the probability of a miraculous occurrence is far less than the probability that those claiming the miraculous event are lying. He then goes on to quote Carl Sagan, who said, "Extraordinary claims require extraordinary evidence."[10] However, Barker does not define what would qualify as "extraordinary evidence" (It seems a non sequitur to say that a miracle claim is impossible to prove and then follow with the statement that it could only be proved with *extraordinary* evidence; but there are many such non sequiturs in Barker's writings).

Barker's second objection to the resurrection of Jesus is that there are many naturalistic explanations of what might have happened in lieu of a literal physical resurrection. Barker specifies several of the naturalistic explanations that have been offered by critics, including the swoon theory, the hallucination theory, the theory that Mary went to the wrong tomb, that the body was stolen by the disciples who then conspired to deceive, that Jesus was temporarily placed in the tomb and then buried later in a common grave, and that someone else was crucified in his place. Barker does not offer any analysis of these individual theories. He simply states, "In my opinion, none of them seem overly likely, but they are at *least* as credible as a corpse

---

7. Martin, *Case Against Christianity*, 5.

8. Barker, *godless*, 277–304.

9. Barker, *godless*, 279.

10. Barker, *godless*, 279.

coming back to life and they do fit the biblical facts."[11] He goes on then to say that the main problem he has with the naturalistic explanations is that they give the Bible too much credit.

A third objection that Barker states applies not only to the biblical view of the resurrection, but also to the entire life of Jesus. Specifically, Barker believes that "the life of Jesus is not corroborated. Not a single word about Jesus appears outside of the New Testament in the entire first century, even though many writers documented firsthand the early Roman Empire in great detail, including careful accounts of the time and place where Jesus supposedly taught."[12] According to Barker, even when we look at the books of the New Testament, we cannot see any independent confirmations of the life of Jesus. He bases this claim on the fact that Paul, who wrote the oldest books in the New Testament, never wrote about Jesus's life. Barker even claims that Paul never makes reference to any of the twelve Apostles by name (a bizarre and patently erroneous claim in light of Galatians 1:18–19, where Paul details his spending time with Peter and James!).[13]

Finally, the objection which seems most prominent to Barker (based upon the amount of ink spent on it), is his emphasis that the resurrection accounts are inconsistent. According to Barker, "When we compare the accounts, we see they don't agree. An easy way to prove this is to issue this challenge to Christians: Tell me what happened on Easter. I am not asking for proof at this stage. Before we can investigate the truth of what happened, we have to know what is being claimed to have happened."[14] Barker issues this challenge with the one condition that "not one single biblical detail be omitted."[15] Barker then claims that he himself has tried to do this and failed. The first problem Barker cites is that Matthew 28:2, according to Barker, insists that the stone was rolled away *after* the women arrived at the tomb. Barker contrasts this with the accounts of both Mark and Luke, who describe the stone as having already been moved. Barker writes, "Some bible defenders assert that Matthew 28:2 was intended to be understood in the past perfect, showing what had happened before the women arrived. But the entire passage is in the aorist (past) tense and it reads, in context, like a simple chronological account."[16] However, Barker, having no advanced

11. Barker, *godless*, 281.

12. Barker, *godless*, 252.

13. Barker, *godless*, 264.

14. Barker, *godless*, 281. This is another interesting statement given that he has already claimed that historical investigation of a miracle is impossible.

15. Barker, *Losing Faith in Faith*, 178–79.

16. Barker, *godless*, 282.

degree in biblical Greek, offers no footnotes or explanations as to why his translation of this verse is more correct than, say, the New American Standard Bible translation.[17] So, we are apparently to take his word for it.

Barker goes on to cite many of the other supposed inconsistencies within the resurrection accounts. He writes, "It is not just atheist critics who notice these problems. Christian scholars agree that the stories are discrepant."[18] Barker then quotes three people whom he calls "Christian scholars" as agreeing that the differing accounts of the resurrection cannot be harmonized.[19] He asserts that the "religiously independent (though primarily Christian) scholars at the Westar Institute" agree.[20] However, he does not cite any contrary opinions, such as John Wenham's *Easter Enigma*, published in 1992, which answers the very challenge Barker finds unanswerable by Wenham, offering a chronological harmonization of the various resurrection accounts.[21] Nor does Barker ever mention that the views of the Westar Institute are considered extreme by the vast majority of both critical and conservative Bible scholars.

DAN BARKER'S ALTERNATIVE HYPOTHESIS

Given that Dan Barker rejects the biblical view of the historicity of the bodily resurrection, it is incumbent upon him to give his alternative hypothesis for the biblical accounts and for the growth of the Christian faith. Accordingly, Barker believes that the story of Jesus as told in the New Testament is clearly a legend. He writes:

> A legend begins with a basic story (true or false) that grows into something more embellished and exaggerated as the years pass. When we look at the documents of the resurrection of Jesus, we see that the earliest accounts are very simple, later retellings are

17. In *God: The Most Unpleasant Character in All Fiction*, which he wrote eight years after *godless*, Barker admits, "I am not a professional bible scholar; I was just an ordained minister with a degree in religion from an evangelical university, who preached from every book of the bible as a pastor, missionary, and evangelist for nineteen years. I took two years of biblical Greek and learned something about Hebrew literary styles. I know my way around concordances, lexicons, bible dictionaries, and commentaries, and have consulted academics more knowledgeable than myself while preparing for the more than 120 public debates I have done as an atheist since leaving the ministry in 1984" (Barker, *God*, 2).

18. Barker, *godless*, 289.

19. Barker, *godless*, 289–90.

20. Barker, *godless*, 290.

21. Wenham, *Easter Enigma*.

more complex and the latest tales are fantastic. In other words, it looks exactly like a legend.[22]

Barker bases his conclusion that the resurrection accounts are legendary on his theory that there are an increasing number of "extraordinary" events as one moves through the New Testament accounts from what he holds to be the earliest books to the last to be written. Barker claims that Paul has zero extraordinary events in 1 Corinthians, Mark has one in his Gospel, Matthew has four, Luke has five, the Gospel of Peter has six, and John has at least six.[23] According to Barker's reasoning, the New Testament resurrection accounts were written in the following order: Paul: AD 50–55 (1 Cor 15:3–8); Mark: AD 70 (Mark 16); Matthew: AD 80 (Matt 28); Luke: AD 85 (Luke 24); the non-canonical Gospel of Peter: AD 85–90 (fragment); John: AD 95 (John 20–21). After citing these books and dates, Barker writes:

> This is the general dating agreed upon by most scholars, including scholars at the Westar Institute. Some conservative scholars prefer to date them earlier, and others have moved some of them later, but this would not change the *order* of the writing, which is more important than the actual dates when considering legendary growth. Shifting the dates changes the shape but not the fact of the growth curve.[24]

According to Barker, there are many reasons to doubt what Paul wrote in 1 Corinthians 15:3–8. He acknowledges that what Paul wrote in this formula or hymn quite possibly "originated just a few years after Jesus lived."[25] But, he argues, its poetic form provides evidence against the common position of many who hold to the authenticity of the New Testament, due to its "simple narrative style." Rather, contends Barker, "the very first account of the resurrection is written in poetic, legendary style."[26] He goes on to say it doesn't matter that Paul claims many of the five hundred were still living, since the distance between Corinth and the place where the five hundred lived would have prevented anyone from checking the story. He also states that, because Paul does not mention a tomb, it is unreasonable to conclude that Paul was thinking of an empty tomb in 1 Corinthians 15.

Barker then continues his theory by postulating that Paul never meant a physical resurrection. If Paul had, he would not have used the word

22. Barker, *godless*, 291.
23. Barker, *godless*, 292.
24. Barker, *godless*, 291.
25. Barker, *godless*, 293.
26. Barker, *godless*, 293.

"raised," but rather would have used the word "resurrection."[27] Then Barker cites 1 Corinthians 15:50, where Paul writes that "flesh and blood cannot inherit the kingdom of God" as further proof that Paul never intended to communicate a physical resurrection of Christ. When we read of Paul's experience of the "risen Christ," we can see, believes Barker, that it was clearly not a physical appearance. Therefore, given the above "proof" that Paul's references to the risen Christ were only referring to a spiritual resurrection, we can see that the oldest account was without the resurrection. This would provide the foundation upon which the legend grew.[28]

Then, according to Barker's timeline, Mark was written fifteen years later in the year AD 70, so the theory goes, and there would have been virtually no one alive by this time who was an adult during the time of Jesus's resurrection. Barker claims this proves that Mark was not written by an eyewitness, and this second-generation writer began the process of legend-building. He writes, "Mark's story is more elaborate than Paul's, but still very simple, almost blunt. If we consider the young man at the sepulcher 'clothed in a long white garment' to be an angel, then we have one extraordinary event. Just one."[29] Barker believes that Mark's account is still not describing a bodily resurrection, given that the "young man" in Mark 16:6 uses the phrase, "He has risen," rather than "resurrected." According to Barker, this is proof that Mark is not describing an empty tomb.[30]

Barker proceeds, stating that Matthew was written ten years after Mark. Barker believes that the ten-year span between Matthew and Mark (according to Barker's timeline) allows enough time for a fantastic leap forward in the legend. He argues that it is only after this span of time that the earthquake, rolling stone, and "Halloween" story appear for the first (and only) time, and also at this time there are "bonafide" angel and postmortem appearances.[31]

Following Matthew by five years, Luke's Gospel was written in AD 85. The growth of the legend now results in "now you see him, now you don't" appearances and disappearances of Jesus, and there is a bodily ascension. The one angel has become two.

27. Barker, *godless*, 294.

28. Barker, *godless*, 296.

29. Barker, *godless*, 297. Earlier Barker begs the question claiming that the resurrection was not an extraordinary event, since the event was never a bodily resurrection anyway (see Barker, *godless*, 292).

30. This is another astonishing assertion, given that following the phrase "He is risen," the angel says, "He is not here; behold, here is the place where they laid Him" (Mark 16:6).

31. Barker, *godless*, 297.

Barker then cites the non-canonical Gospel of Peter as further proof that the legend is growing.[32] After summarizing the contents of this non-canonical book, he writes, "This is fantastic stuff."[33] Yes indeed (but it seems quite telling to use a non-canonical text and a highly disputed dating of that text to support his critique of the canonical Gospels and the orthodox view of the resurrection accounts).

The Gospel of John follows in Barker's attempt to build a case for the legendary growth of the story of Jesus. He writes that John was written in AD 90–95, with examples of continued growth in the extraordinary events attributed to Jesus's resurrection. Evidence for this growth is seen in that there is in John a resurrection with real angels (i.e., not referenced as "young men"), bodily appearances, the "fish story" miracle, and an ascension. Barker writes, "By now the legend has become—legendary."[34]

Barker concludes his theory of the explanation of the historical accounts of the resurrection of Jesus with a proposal for how this legend might have begun. According to Barker, one sensible scenario is that Peter's state of mind led him to say that Jesus appeared to him. Peter's guilt over the denial of Jesus before his crucifixion led Peter into such a state of remorse that Peter imagined a conversation with Jesus in which Jesus forgave him. This led Peter to exclaim that Jesus had appeared to him, and, therefore, Paul lists Peter as the first person to whom Christ "appeared" in 1 Corinthians 15.[35]

ANSWERING BARKER'S OBJECTIONS

Barker's first objection is that, if indeed a miracle has occurred, then it is beyond the scope of historical inquiry. Barker writes, "The fact that [the resurrection] is impossible or highly unlikely is what makes it a miracle. And that is what removes it from the reach of history. History is limited; it can only confirm events that conform to natural regularity."[36] However, there are several problems with this view. With regard to a miracle being that which is "impossible," Barker commits the fallacy of begging the question. One cannot claim that what makes a miracle is its impossibility as the demonstration of the fact that it cannot be proven. The second problem with Barker's argument is his idea that a miracle is impossible. If one acknowledges that

32. Of course, Barker here contradicts the vast majority of scholarship in asserting that the Gospel of Peter can be dated in the same year as Luke.

33. Barker, *godless*, 298.

34. Barker, *godless*, 298.

35. Barker, *godless*, 302.

36. Barker, *godless*, 279.

there is a God who created both the physical universe and all the laws that govern the behavior of those physical objects, then there is no reason to suppose that the Creator cannot intervene in ways that are contrary to the normal functioning of the physical universe. Finally, Barker's argument that one cannot use history to prove a miracle is incorrect. Barker admits that "miracles may have happened, but in order to *know* they happened, we need a different tool of knowledge."[37] He cites Hume's argument that "No testimony is sufficient to establish a miracle unless that testimony be of such a kind that its falsehood would be more miraculous than the fact which it endeavours to establish."[38] However, as philosopher William Lane Craig points out, there are two independent claims in Hume's statement, both of which are mistaken. Craig notes that one of these claims is that "no amount of evidence can serve to establish a miracle."[39] But if that were true, writes Craig, "then we should be led into denying the occurrence of events which, though highly improbable, we reasonably know to have happened."[40] The other claim here is that miracles are improbable. But to suggest that improbability equals impossibility is to simply beg the question.

As regards Barker's reference to Carl Sagan's claim that "extraordinary claims require extraordinary evidence," New Testament scholar Michael Licona writes,

> If the evidence for the occurrence of a particular miracle is strong—that is, the historian can establish that the authorial intent of the sources is to report what was perceived as a miracle, the event occurred in a context that was charged with religious significance, the report possesses traits that favor the historicity of the event and no plausible naturalistic theories exist—then a requirement for extraordinary evidence is unwarranted. Some historians may require additional evidence supporting supernaturalism before believing since the event is foreign to their present horizon, but no greater burden of proof is required for a miracle-claim.[41]

Barker's second objection is that there are many naturalistic explanations of what might have happened in lieu of a literal physical resurrection, each of which are at least as probable as a corpse coming back to life and each

---

37. Barker, *godless*, 279.

38. Barker, *godless*, 279, quoting Hume's *Enquiry concerning Human Understanding*, 10.1.10.

39. Craig, *Reasonable Faith*, 270.

40. Craig, *Reasonable Faith*, 270.

41. Licona, *Resurrection of Jesus*, 196.

of which fit the biblical facts. However, Barker makes this statement without supporting it. And he needs to support it because it is contradicted by Gary Habermas and Michael Licona's "minimal facts approach" from their 2004 work, *The Case for the Resurrection of Jesus*. The minimal facts approach, a method for evaluating the historicity of Jesus's resurrection, "considers only those data that are so strongly attested historically that they are granted by nearly every scholar who studies the subject, even the rather skeptical ones."[42] Habermas and Licona contend that there are four main facts that are well evidenced and to which nearly every scholar agrees (including those who are skeptical). These facts are that Jesus died by crucifixion, his disciples believed that he rose and appeared to them, the church persecutor Paul was suddenly changed into a believer, and the skeptic James, the brother of Jesus, was suddenly changed into a believer. Habermas and Licona note a fifth fact of which it can be said that roughly seventy-five percent of scholars who write on the subject agree: namely, that the tomb was found empty. Habermas and Licona conclude that, in contrast to Barker's claim, there is no natural hypothesis that can account for all five of these facts with the same explanatory scope, power, and plausibility without resorting to nonevidenced assumptions. For example, if Jesus faked his death or if his disciples stole his body, this would not account for the sudden changes in behavior of Paul and James. In other words, the only way the naturalistic explanations can explain all of the evidence is to rely on a very ad hoc approach. Moreover, since the minimal facts approach shows that naturalistic explanations are highly improbable, then combining these explanations (as some opponents of the resurrection have done) only serves to exponentially increase the improbability of the resulting combined explanation.

Barker's third objection is that neither the resurrection nor Jesus's life in general are corroborated outside of the New Testament within the first century. Nor does the fact that there are different books with presumably different authors within the New Testament offer any independent confirmation of the resurrection. However, Barker is simply ignoring the evidence on both counts. Habermas and Licona note that there are "nine early and independent sources that fall into three categories [confirming the apostles claim that Jesus rose from the dead and appeared to them]: (1) the testimony of Paul about the disciples; (2) the oral tradition that passed through the early church; and (3) the written works of the early church."[43] Paul's first letter to the Corinthians makes it clear that he understood the resurrection to have been real and bodily, not simply spiritual (1 Cor 15). And in 1

42. Habermas and Licona, *Case for the Resurrection of Jesus*, 44.
43. Habermas and Licona, *Case for the Resurrection of Jesus*, 51.

Corinthians 15:3–8, Paul relates an oral formula that is universally acknowl-edged to have been used by the church as a tradition before the Gospels were written. In referring to Jesus's burial, Craig states that it "is multiply attested in extremely early, independent sources."[44] Craig continues,

> The account of Jesus' burial in a tomb by Joseph of Arimathea is part of Mark's source material for the passion story. This is a very early source which is probably based on eyewitness testimony and which the commentator Rudolf Pesch dates to within seven years of Jesus' crucifixion. Moreover, Paul in 1 Corinthians 15:3–5 quotes an old Christian tradition that he had received from the earliest disciples. Paul probably received this tradition no later than his visit to Jerusalem in a.d. 36 (Gal. 1:18), if not earlier in Damascus. It thus goes back to within the first five years after Jesus' death.

and, additionally,

> For further independent testimony to Jesus' burial by Joseph is also found in the sources behind Matthew and Luke and the Gospel of John, not to mention the extra-biblical *Gospel of Peter*. The differences between Mark's account and those of Matthew and Luke suggest that the latter had sources other than Mark alone. These differences are not plausibly explained as Matthew and Luke's editorial changes of Mark because of their sporadic and uneven nature, the inexplicable omission of events like Pilate's interrogation of the centurion and the agreements in wording between Matthew and Luke in contrast to Mark.[45]

In addition to the independent nature of the various Gospels, Paul's testimony, and the oral formula found in 1 Corinthians 15, there are the early church fathers, who confirm the disciples' account of the resurrection. Just one example would be that of Clement of Rome (c. AD 30–100), whose letter *1 Clement* is widely regarded as genuine and dated to the mid-90s.[46]

Finally, Barker seems most obsessed with his objection that the Gos-pel accounts of the resurrection are internally inconsistent. As noted above, Barker cites only critical scholars on the far-liberal fringe of the spectrum. It is shockingly disingenuous of him to pretend that this subject has not been dealt with in a contrary way. Relatedly, New Testament scholar Michael Blomberg writes that

44. Craig, *Reasonable Faith*, 362.
45. Craig, *Reasonable Faith*, 363.
46. Wright, *Resurrection of the Son of God*, 481.

it is remarkable to observe how often the alleged contradictions among the Gospels are cited without a discussion of the many proposed solutions that can fit them together in a very plausible and natural manner. John Wenham devoted an entire book to a harmonization of the accounts and few of his proposals are entirely new. There is scarcely room to summarize all his main points, but in the case of the sample 'contradictions' mentioned above, one can offer the following brief replies: (1) angels generally appear in Scripture as men, and if one of the two was the primary spokesman, it would not be surprising if sometimes only he were mentioned; (2) it is likely that Jesus appeared to the eleven in Jerusalem, then later in Galilee when they had gone home after the Passover, and then once again in Jerusalem upon their return in preparation for the feast of Pentecost, (3) if Salome is both the 'mother of James and John' and the sister of Mary, Jesus' mother, there is no irreconcilable problem with the lists of women; and (4) it is fair to describe the world as still dark at the first glimpse of morning daylight.[47]

Blomberg notes further that N. T. Wright has made the point that some divergence in parallel narratives is an indicator of reliability.[48] Wright states,

> The surface inconsistencies between Mark 16:1–8 and its parallels, of which so much is made by those eager to see the accounts as careless fiction, is in fact a strong point in favour of their early character. The later we imagine them being written up, let alone edited, the more likely it would be that inconsistencies would be ironed out. The stories exhibit, as has been said repeatedly over the last hundred years or more, exactly that surface tension which we associate, not with tales artfully told by people eager to sustain a fiction and therefore anxious to make everything look right, but with the hurried, puzzled accounts of those who have seen with their own eyes something which took them horribly by surprise and with which they have not yet fully come to terms.[49]

Following Barker's explanation of his objections to the biblical view of the resurrection, he offers what he apparently considers a likely alternative hypothesis to explain how and why the bodily resurrection came to be part of Christian orthodoxy. According to Barker, it is quite probable that the

47. Blomberg, *Historical Reliability of the Gospels*, 140.

48. Blomberg, *Historical Reliability of the Gospels*, 141.

49. Wright, *Resurrection of the Son of God*, 612.

story of Jesus is a legend, or as he defines it, "a basic story (true or false) that grows into something more embellished and exaggerated as the years pass."[50]

However, what follows is a brief review of why the legend hypothesis in general is considered inadequate as an explanation for the known and generally accepted body of "historical bedrock," to use Licona's terminology,[51] which will also refute the basis of Barker's theory. Habermas and Licona note that, though there is much evidence and widespread agreement on the textual purity of the New Testament, many of today's critics deny that eyewitnesses wrote the Gospels. Therefore, the critics argue, the stories are embellished. And "Therefore, in order to use the biblical records to refute the legend/embellishment theory, one must either establish that the specific Gospel texts are early and/or that the traditions contained in them are early."[52]

In answering the critics, it is important to note that Paul wrote 1 Corinthians around AD 55. Within that letter is what is widely accepted to be one of the earliest traditions regarding Jesus's resurrection. Josh McDowell and Bill Wilson list evidence that shows 1 Corinthians 15:3–8 is a very early creed, which Paul did not author and that, rather, this creed was "received" from the first witnesses, and Paul is passing on the tradition:

1. Vocabulary, sentence structure, and diction are clearly not Pauline.

2. The parallelism of the three individual statements is biblically formulated.

3. The threefold "and that" characterizes the Aramaic and Mishnaic Hebrew way of narration.

4. The "divine passive" of "being raised" paraphrases God's action of salvation in order not to mention God, in accordance with the Jewish fear of the name.

5. The Aramaic form of the name "Cephas," not Simon, as Luke gives it in the parallel passage 24:32, sounds more original.

6. The double reference "in accordance with the Scriptures" supports twice in three lines both the death and resurrection of Jesus—as it probably corresponds with the faithfulness of the early church to the Hebrew Bible.

7. "The twelve" [signifies] . . . a closed group of the first witnesses. . . .

50. Barker, *godless*, 291.
51. Licona, *The Resurrection of Jesus*, 277.
52. Habermas and Licona, *The Case for the Resurrection of Jesus*, 292.

8. Finally, the statement, which in its basic features is repeated in almost all later reports of the resurrection, narrates the course of four events which were understood as salvation bearing: He died for our sins . . . was buried . . . was raised . . . and appeared.[53]

It is also compelling that Paul put his reputation on the line in noting that many of the five hundred witnesses mentioned in verse 6 were still alive. Despite Barker's suggestion that "None of the readers . . . would have been able to confirm the story," it would not have been difficult to contact these witnesses.[54]

Another issue with Barker's legend theory, and legend theories in general, is that they don't account for the conversion of Paul, who was a persecutor of the church, and James, who was not a believer during Jesus's lifetime but became the leader of the church in Jerusalem. And not least of all, the empty tomb cannot be accounted for by a legend.

Barker has a few more specific criticisms of the biblical view of the resurrection with regard to his legend hypothesis. He claims that Paul used the word "raised" rather than "resurrection" because he was referring to a "spiritual resurrection" and not to a "bodily resurrection." Though Barker tries to argue that the use of the Greek makes this clear, he cites no scholarly support for his theory.[55] Contra Barker, Wright goes to great lengths to demonstrate that there is no possibility that Paul could be arguing for a "*non*-bodily resurrection."[56]

Barker also makes an oft-repeated case that Paul couldn't have meant a bodily resurrection, given his statement in 1 Corinthians 15:50: "flesh and blood cannot inherit the kingdom of God."[57] Regarding that point, Wright states,

> Ever since the second century (and increasingly in scholarship during the twentieth) doubters have used this clause to question whether Paul really believed in the resurrection of the *body*. . . . In fact . . . 'flesh and blood' is a way of referring to ordinary, corruptible, decaying human existence. It does not simply mean, as it has so often been taken to mean, 'physical humanity' in the normal modern sense, but 'the present physical humanity

53. McDowell and Wilson, *Evidence for the Historical Jesus*, 266, quoting Pinchas Lapide.

54. McDowell and Wilson, *Evidence for the Historical Jesus*, 267, quoting Sir Norman Anderson.

55. Barker, *godless*, 294–95.

56. Wright, *Resurrection of the Son of God*, 312–17.

57. Barker, *godless*, 295.

(as opposed to the future one), which is subject to decay and death."[58]

Finally, it must be stated that Barker's approach to this topic is one in which he frequently asserts that he is countering the uninformed approach of many Christians who have not examined their beliefs. However, Barker does not approach the subject in any kind of scholarly way. His approach is much more subject to his own criticism than is the biblical view of the resurrection. For the most part, Barker never even offers any scholarly citations that are contrary to his stated views. He simply disregards the arguments of conservative scholars and writes as if there are no views contrary to those of the radical liberals that occupy the Westar Institute and the Jesus Seminar.

Even worse, Barker constantly uses poor logic and absolute deception couched as high-level criticism. One example demonstrates this. Barker hypothesizes how the growth of the legend could have worked in the New Testament. Writing about Jesus's supposed appearance to Paul, Barker states,

> Paul, needing to establish credentials with his readers, tacks onto the list that Christ "appeared also to me," so if we look at the description of appearance, we can see what he means. Paul claimed that he had met Jesus on the road to Damascus, but notice that Jesus did not *physically* appear to Paul there. He was knocked off his horse and blinded. (I know there is no horse in the story, but for some reason I picture a horse—an example of legend making!)[59]

Here, Barker purposely misstates and inaccurately portrays the biblical account and pretends that it is evidence that the writers of the New Testament did the same!

CONCLUSION

Barker's arguments against the credibility of the biblical account of Jesus's resurrection are very weak. In fact, Barker's work is wholly and completely unscholarly. He frequently makes unsupported assertions and cites only the arguments of scholars who agree with him. When he does cite these scholars, he misrepresents their standing by claiming that they represent the broad spectrum of biblical scholarship, when, in fact, they are a small group of scholars on the radical fringe of biblical scholarship.

---

58. Wright, *The Resurrection of the Son of God*, 359.
59. Barker, *godless*, 295–6.

Virtually every objection Barker raises against the historicity of the resurrection has been dealt with extensively, yet Barker almost completely ignores the widely known responses to his criticisms. As a result, we can conclude that Barker is uninterested in a sincere search for truth. He is quite obviously intent on misleading the uniformed. Despite Barker's assertions to the contrary, it is apparent that there is no alternative hypothesis to the biblical account of the resurrection that can explain the facts of the historical record.

BIBLIOGRAPHY

Barker, Dan. *God: The Most Unpleasant Character in All Fiction.* New York: Sterling, 2016.

———. *godless: How an Evangelical Preacher Became One of America's Leading Atheists.* Berkeley: Ulysses, 2008.

———. *Losing Faith in Faith: From Preacher to Atheist.* Madison: Freedom From Religion Foundation, 1992.

Bauckham, Richard. *Jesus and the Eyewitnesses: The Gospels as Eyewitness Testimony.* Grand Rapids: Eerdmans, 2006.

Blomberg, Craig L. *The Historical Reliability of the Gospels.* 2nd ed. Downers Grove: IVP Academic, 2007.

Craig, William Lane. *Reasonable Faith: Christian Truth and Apologetics.* 3rd ed. Wheaton: Crossway, 2008.

Habermas, Gary R., and Michael R. Licona. *The Case for the Resurrection of Jesus.* Grand Rapids: Kregel, 2004.

Licona, Michael R. *The Resurrection of Jesus: A New Historiographical Approach.* Downers Grove: IVP Academic, 2010.

Martin, Michael. *The Case Against Christianity.* Philadelphia: Temple University Press, 1991.

McDowell, Josh. *The New Evidence that Demands a Verdict.* Nashville: Nelson, 1999.

McDowell, Josh, and Bill Wilson. *Evidence for the Historical Jesus: A Compelling Case for His Life and His Claims.* Eugene: Harvest, 1988.

Wenham, John. *Easter Enigma: Are the Resurrection Accounts in Conflict?* Eugene: Wipf & Stock, 1992.

Wright, N. T. *The Resurrection of the Son of God.* Christian Origins and the Question of God 3. Minneapolis: Fortress, 2003.

11

Finding Purpose on the Journey to Nowhere

—Tricia Scribner

If there is no purpose of life, but there is purpose in life, then where does it come from? How can you find a life-driven purpose? You don't find it. In most cases, it finds you. You create it yourself by your intention to keep living your life as fully as possible, overcoming any obstacles in your way.

—Dan Barker[1]

For centuries humans have asked, "What is the purpose of life?" Atheist Dan Barker is here to tell us that this is a silly question, one not worthy of the volumes of ink wasted by philosophers over the centuries, especially when the answer is so simple. During his 2017 debate with Richard Howe, Barker said that at rock bottom, "There's no meaning of life—there's no purpose of life."[2] While this dismal fact may cause angst for some, Barker assures us not to worry: "That's actually a good thing that there's no purpose of life and no meaning of life in the cosmos. The cosmos doesn't care about us. Someday we're all going to be extinct. No one's going to remember us or

---

1. Barker, *Life-Driven Purpose*, 28.
2. God Who Speaks, "Is There a God Who Speaks?," 1:40:15.

this building or even this planet someday."[3] So, why should we be happy in light of our impending annihilation? Barker says, "The fact that there is no meaning of life, or purpose *of* life, does *not* mean there's no meaning *in* life. Instead of top down, . . . meaning is bottom up, life-driven-purpose, and meaning and purpose come in our lives from solving problems. When you have a problem in life that you're trying to solve, that gives you meaning."[4]

There it is. All we need is a problem to solve, and our lives have meaning and purpose. In other words, there is no purpose to our *being*, only to our *doing*. And the purpose of our doing is determined by us.

As in all debates, had there been more time, perhaps more headway could have been made on this issue. On the other hand, while Howe attempted to move the conversation beyond soundbites to fundamental issues, Barker wouldn't step into the ring. So, we'll give the subject the attention it deserves here, to whatever extent a single chapter can accomplish that goal.

Although his discussion of meaning and purpose in life comprised only a brief segment of his debate presentation, Barker has devoted an entire book to the subject, called *Life Driven Purpose*. The book's thesis serves as a foil to Rick Warren's *Purpose Driven Life*, and in Barker's book, "purpose" takes center stage, with the term appearing 212 times.

I agree with Barker that the issue of purpose deserves an entire book. He's not the first to recognize its centrality in any discussion about reality. Over two thousand years ago, philosopher and scientist Aristotle (382–322 BC) examined the ubiquitous feature of purpose throughout the universe and, indeed, of the universe as a whole. Medieval Catholic philosopher Thomas Aquinas (AD 1225–74) expanded upon Aristotle's thought, developing the implications of the world's features known as change and purpose for the existence of the theistic God. The synthesis of Aristotle's and Aquinas's accounts is often referred to as the A-T view ("T" referring to the "Thomas" portion of Aquinas's name). The issue of purpose also receives in-depth treatment by contemporary Christian philosophers, such as Catholic philosopher Edward Feser, who notes,

> A complete account of the universe and of human nature in terms that make no reference whatsoever to purpose, meaning, and design is not within our grasp and never will be, for the simple reason that such an "account" is in principle impossible, and the hope for it based on nothing more than muddle-headedness

3. God Who Speaks, "Is There a God Who Speaks?," 1:40:20.

4. God Who Speaks, "Is There a God Who Speaks?," 1:40:32 (emphasis in original).

mixed with wishful thinking. We can no more eliminate purpose and meaning from nature than we can square the circle.[5]

The issue of whether purpose exists, and if so, what it says about the
nature of the universe, living beings, and about implications for the existence
of God, is the focus of this chapter. We will proceed by addressing several
questions: What does Barker mean by the term "purpose"? Is purpose as a
feature limited to conscious living things? If purpose is an intrinsic feature
of even nonconscious entities, what are the implications for the nature of
reality, and specifically, for the existence of God? Given the constraints of
his materialistic view, what justification can Barker offer for viewing his
life as purposeful? I contend that while Barker may experience existential
fulfillment in his life, given his stated convictions, he lacks justification for
his conclusions about what purpose is and what it says about the natures of
things and the existence of God.

In critiquing Barker's responses to these questions, I will offer the
alternative Aristotelian-Thomistic (A-T) account of reality, drawing upon
Aquinas and contemporary scholars such as Feser, who articulate Aquinas's
views. If the debate between Barker and Howe is any indication, Barker has
not given the view a fair hearing. While he insisted that he had read about
Aristotle, his responses were devoid of any substantive evidence that he had
seriously considered any of these classical arguments, and in particular,
Aquinas's arguments from change and final causality (intrinsic purpose) for
the existence of God.

While the brief length of this chapter entails the danger of exchanging
accuracy for brevity, even this rudimentary presentation of the A-T account
of reality provides a far richer, more accurate view of the world than Barker's
materialism allows. Will Barker reconsider his position? I don't know. But
he should, as I hope the reader will, even if one prefers that there is no God.
After all, as Barker points out, wishing something to be so, doesn't make it
so.

"PURPOSE": WHAT DOES BARKER MEAN BY THE TERM?

In his book, *Life Driven Purpose*, Barker uses the term "purpose" in at least
three different senses. Let's take a look at each of these usages. As relates
to humans, Barker initially defines "purpose" as "striving for a goal, an

5. Feser, *Last Superstition*, 12.

intentional aiming at a target."[6] This striving is for a reason: namely, "surviving or enjoying your life."[7] Note here that Barker defines "purpose" as conscious intentional striving for a goal, an act of will. Thus, in his view, the only entities in the world that exhibit purpose in this sense are living beings who are not only capable of intellectually forming conscious intention, but also are actually doing so. Goals, he says,

> can be to get something you want, or to avoid something you don't want. The purpose of your actions might be the need for food, water, or shelter. It might be to find a mate, repel a threat. It might be physical exercise, to keep fit to meet future challenges. These goals, and others, when achieved by some kind of striving, are pleasurable or positive, because they ultimately relate to survival. . . . Even indirect goals, such as helping others to survive, are enjoyable. . . . They all affect the brain, which is a physical organ striving to control and protect a natural organism in a natural environment.[8]

Problem-solving constitutes our immediate purpose and enables us to fulfill the more ultimate, though temporal, purpose of survival and not just individual survival, but survival of the species. Survival, then, serves as the impetus for all other purposes we intentionally contrive.

A second sense in which Barker employs the term "purpose" is vested with an existential meaning:

> If there is no purpose of life, but there is purpose in life, then where does it come from? How can you find a life-driven purpose? You don't find it. In most cases, it finds you. You create it yourself by your intention to keep living your life as fully as possible, overcoming any obstacles in your way.[9]

He shifts from defining "purpose" as an intentional striving toward a goal to defining it as a feeling or positive subjective experience, as in *sensing* purpose. In doing so, he recasts "purpose" as an existential concept, connoting an internal experience of humans commonly associated with the concept of meaning in life as a subjective experience. Overcoming obstacles or solving problems makes us feel good, giving us a sense that we are accomplishing something of value in our lives.

6. Barker, *Life Driven Purpose*, 21.

7. Barker, *Life Driven Purpose*, 21.

8. Barker, *Life Driven Purpose*, 21.

9. Barker, *Life Driven Purpose*, 28.

Finally, Barker uses the term "purpose" to refer to an attribute of human artifacts insofar as humans make use of them. He says, "We transfer a goal to the method used to achieve that goal. When we ask for the purpose of a hammer, we are not imagining that a tool has any intentions. We are really asking for the purpose in the mind of the person who designed or uses the hammer."[10] He adds,

> The hammer was invented by organisms with opposable thumbs as a way to deliver a large direct force to the head of a nail (not to the opposable thumb), driving it into wood, or to leverage the force to yank it back out. It was designed to help construct things like shelter, bridges, and military defenses, all having something to do with survival.[11]

So, the hammer as an implement is not purposeful, or oriented to an end, in and of itself. Rather, the purpose of the tool arises from a rational being seeking to survive and who uses the implement for the purpose of survival.

To summarize, Barker employs the term "purpose" in at least three different ways throughout his book. These multiple uses must be kept in mind in order to avoid equivocation, assuming that he is using the word with a single definition. In one sense, purpose is the conscious striving toward a goal, and thus, can only be affirmed of humans who exercise will and, thus, exhibit purposeful actions. These purposeful actions, such as identifying and solving problems, enable us to fulfill the ultimate purpose of survival. By survival, Barker is referring not only to individual or family group survival, but also to survival of the species. Barker also uses the term as an existential concept, to refer to how we feel about the value of our lives as we accomplish individual, self-designed purposes. Finally, he applies the term to artifacts, inanimate objects used by rational beings for specific purposes determined by the craftsman. We'll need to keep these varied usages in mind in order to accurately parse what he is saying and respond accordingly.

THE PERVASIVENESS OF PURPOSE

We've seen that, according to Barker, only conscious living beings show purposeful action. We've also hinted at the direction this chapter will take, namely, that he is simply wrong. As we will see, purpose pervades the entire universe, encompassing both consciously willed acts and those not

10. Barker, *Life Driven Purpose*, 22.
11. Barker, *Life Driven Purpose*, 22.

consciously willed, acts of organs, acts of animals and plants, and even acts of inanimate bodies.

While Barker attributes intention only to consciously willed acts of humans, we should note that even humans often move toward ends or goals without consciously choosing to do so. In fact, we rarely mentally formulate our goal as survival of ourselves and our families, much less to help humanity to survive as a species. Much of our day-to-day problem solving focuses on the immediate resolution rather than any contribution the solution makes to survival *per se*. This fact does not negate the reality that some people in the world, such as subsistence farmers, do consciously focus on daily survival. On the other hand, many people go through their day without ever pondering that the small and large problems they have worked to resolve contributed to their and their species' survival. So, intention cannot be limited to consciously willed actions for the sake of survival. Therefore, conscious willing cannot be prerequisite for purposeful—i.e., intentional—behavior, even for humans.

Barker has denied any objective purpose of life, no purpose beyond our subjective conjuring of goals for the sake of survival. But, in a very real sense, he has cast survival in the role of objective purpose. What I mean by this is that Barker suggests that all our purposeful behaviors ultimately proceed toward the goal of survival. So, survival, though it is not normally understood as a transcendental notion, for Barker serves as an objective purpose that transcends our conscious intention. In order to move toward survival, toward our own self-flourishing, we do not have to formulate a conscious intention and often are not aware at all that we are doing so. On a micro level, our internal biological processes are directed toward self-flourishing without any conscious engagement of the will. Further, whatever we call purposiveness—goal-directedness or patterned, predictable movement toward specific ends—is not confined to humans, or even to living things, but is pervasive throughout the universe.

Things in the world, whether hammers, hearts, pumpkins, or planets, whether conscious living beings or nonconscious entities, exhibit a predictable disposition and movement toward a goal, a goal that is unique to the *kind* of things they are. This movement toward a kind-specific goal is so obvious that if I plant a cucumber seed and a squash comes up, I don't add to my mental file that cucumber plants can produce squash as well as cucumbers; I figure I confused the cucumber seed with the squash seed. Why is that? Because cucumber seeds and squash seeds look similar, but cucumber seeds produce cucumbers.

Parts of living things, such as the organs of humans and animals, also evince purposeful action in such a way as to preserve and sustain the whole organism. As a former registered nurse, I find the intricate workings of the human body fascinating. I recently read a medical journal abstract on post-injury peripheral nerve regeneration. After injury, the proximal stump—the injured end of the nerve nearest the center of the body—dies and then starts making new daughter nerve cells, some of which extend through the distal stump—the injured end of the nerve furthest from the center of the body—initiating regeneration. If the process continues unhindered, nerve regeneration continues at a rate of one-to-three millimeters a day.[12]

Nerve regeneration is just one of the numerous intrinsic and inter-locking purposeful processes that characterize all levels of the organism, from the organ systems, down to the tissues, the cells, and the intracellular operations. In fact, I don't think I'd be too far off the mark to say the main focus of my nursing practice was to facilitate and support the body's normal restorative processes that kick into action when homeostasis is thrown off balance during illness or injury. The only reason we could support these compensatory mechanisms is because they are pervasively predictable and specific to the type of organ or tissue being treated. Healing nerves don't produce new digestive cells, much less new cow cells or plant cells.

Even British philosopher, Mary Midgley, one of Barker's contemporaries (and like him, an atheist), recognizes the purposiveness of nonconscious entities:

> Purposiveness itself—persistent, systematic striving till a particular end is achieved—plainly is not unique to us. . . . Seeds that germinate under paving stones go to incredible lengths to grow round or through them, or even to lift them out of place, if necessary. As Aristotle noted, there is a remarkable continuity here that runs from our own fully conscious purposes right through the realm of life. The fact that Dawkins represents the Selfish Gene itself as relentlessly purposive shows how impossible it is to describe the workings of life without using such language.[13]

Midgley is right. Nonconscious entities, of course, evince purposive actions absent an intrinsic will. Barker is careful to remind us that hammers and hearts don't have a will to generate purpose. He's like my physiology professor who mocked the human tendency to anthropomorphize purposive actions of body systems to restore homeostasis, whereby they promote the organism's survival. "When profuse bleeding occurs, the heart doesn't 'try' to elevate the blood pressure by beating faster; it just reacts," he'd say. Granted. But his comments, as Midgley confirms, illustrate how hard it is to talk

12. Sulaiman and Gordon, "Neurobiology of Peripheral Nerve Injury," 100–108.

13. Midgley, "Purpose, Meaning, and Darwinism."

about living things without using purpose-laden language. No matter how we say it, we run headlong into this blatant feature of living things, whether they are parts of an organism as is a heart, or organisms themselves, such as bacteria.

Remember that Barker also says inanimate things only have purposes insofar as humans use them. In this context, the word "purpose" highlights the pragmatic benefits of a thing rather than the purposeful action it displays. In everyday language, "purpose" is often employed to refer to usefulness instead of intentionality.

We don't talk of comets hitting the earth on purpose because they do not possess a will to formulate consciously purposeful action. In a philosophical sense, though, it is proper to speak of purposefulness as the proclivity of a nonconscious entity to act with a directedness toward a goal, specific to the kind of entity it is. These entities act predictably as though there *is* an end-goal in mind, even, most remarkably, when the entities have no mind at all. As Catholic philosopher John Wippel says, "Natural bodies act for the sake of an end. . . . They reach their respective end(s) . . . by intention."[14]

Moreover, while we do not commonly describe natural bodies as acting purposefully toward specific ends, we count on them doing so. We depend upon the regular, purposeful action of the universe, its galaxies, and of our planet, all of which are nonconscious, natural bodies. So, the earth's tilt, in relation to its yearly orbit around the sun, produces seasons. This repetitive, dependable action cannot be explained by chance. As Wippel notes, "Chance can hardly account for the regular and beneficial activity of natural agents, whether we regard that activity as beneficial for the agents themselves or also for nature taken as a whole."[15]

And the truth is, all scientific endeavors presuppose this feature of both living and non-living entities. For instance, scientific studies have shown that lightning's electrical discharge breaks tightly bound nitrogen atoms in the air, which then fall to the ground and combine with soil minerals to form nitrates, which plants absorb.[16] This natural activity meets humans' nutritional needs when we eat the plants, since nitrogen is a component of proteins our bodies need. But we do not *assign* this purpose. Most humans don't know that lightning serves their needs. Given this reality, we have to ask ourselves, why do things in the world pervasively act toward ends specific to the kinds of things they are, even when not consciously intentional?

14. Wippel, *Metaphysical Thought of Thomas Aquinas*, 480.

15. Wippel, *Metaphysical Thought of Thomas Aquinas*, 483.

16. Glass, "Lightning Helps Fertilize the Soil."

THE ROAD TO SOMEWHERE

The nature of change and purposiveness evident across the broad spectrum of both living and non-living things has implications not only for our understanding of their natures, but also for how they came to be and for how their continued existence in this moment can be explained. The question of God's existence enters the picture here. In order to understand why the existence of God is not just probable, but metaphysically necessary (i.e., there can't *not* be a God), we'll need to take a few philosophical backroads through the A-T account of reality. The early part of this journey may appear to be a dead end, but it actually feeds into the larger argument. Unlike Barker's road to nowhere, we *are* headed toward a destination.

It seems obvious that there are things in the world, and we can come to know facts about them. Even Barker does not seem to deny this notion, so we will use it as a starting point. These things in the world Aristotle calls "substances" because they exist in themselves as subjects, not as properties of other things. While technically not everything in the world counts as a substance, as far as things encountered within our everyday experience, this will do. Now, a substance is a composite—a single thing made of two or more components, the components being *form* and *matter*.[17] This view is known as "hylomorphism"[18] (for sticklers, "hylemorphism").

Barker mentions a hammer, actually a human artifact rather than a self-existing substance, but his example will suffice. The hammer is composed of matter—wood and metal—and also has identifiable characteristics, including its shape and propensities that make it the *kind* of object that drives nails with its flat end and pries nails with its pronged end. Aristotle called this aspect of the thing the "form." Neither matter—the metal and wood—nor form—the hardness and shape, etc.—on its own, is the hammer. We see nothing in the world that is just matter; it's always a specific *kind* of thing (a form) that is made up of matter. And, of course, in the physical world, the form is always the form *of* something, so it doesn't exist alone, either. So, both the matter and the form, as a single composite, make the hammer exist as the specific thing it is.[19]

Things in the world undergo change, whether we are talking about human artifacts, substances such as living things, or celestial bodies. Change (what Aristotle calls "motion," which includes any change, not just

17. For a more focused and technical account of form and matter, see Richard Howe's chapter in this book.

18. Feser, *Last Superstition*, 57.

19. Feser, *Aquinas: A Beginner's Guide*, 13–14.

movement) is the transition from a *potential* to an *actual* state.[20] And, as Feser says, "Since a potential is by itself just that—merely potential, not actual or real—no potential can make itself actual, but must be actualized by something outside it."[21] So, the potential to lift my hand must be actualized by muscle movement, which is actualized by neuronal firings, which are actualized by chemical changes, which are actualized by molecular changes, which are actualized by atomic changes. While this is a gross over-generalization of the logical sequence, this is the general picture.

In this kind of series of events called an "essentially ordered series," every member requires for its own current existence and action the *simultaneous* existence of a more fundamental member as cause.[22] So, muscles move only insofar as the neurons fire, which fire only insofar as the chemicals change, and so on. Each member causes an effect by being acted upon by the immediate underlying and more fundamental entity that causes its action. Ultimately, all members serve as instruments of the first member, the only member really causing anything.[23]

Now what distinguishes an essentially ordered series from what Aristotle calls an "accidentally ordered series" is that in the second kind of series, each member can cause its action independently of any earlier member of the series, and so there is no reason that this kind of series must terminate in a first member's existence who has intrinsic causal power. Thus, this kind of series could go on infinitely. For example, say a father has a son. The father doesn't need to remain alive in order for the son to have his own son.[24]

But since in an essentially ordered series, whether biological processes or planetary movements, it is impossible that there be an infinite number of members because no member has its own intrinsic causal power, but rather, for its own causal act depends upon the simultaneous act of another member. For any and all of the members of the series to exist, there must simultaneously be a first member with its own intrinsic causal powers. Otherwise, there would be no series at all.[25] We'll return to this in a moment.

The discussion of change ties into the central argument here, the argument from final causality to the existence of God. Based on the A-T account of reality, not only do we know that things change, we come to know a thing when we understand the four causes that explain its coming into existence

20. Feser, *Last Superstition*, 91.

21. Feser, *Last Superstition*, 91.

22. Feser, *Last Superstition*, 92.

23. Feser, *Last Superstition*, 95.

24. Feser, *Last Superstition*, 92.

25. Feser, *Last Superstition*, 93.

and the changes it undergoes once in existence. Now, Aristotle employed the term "causes" more broadly than we do to refer to four types of explanations or descriptions of a thing. The most common use of the term "cause" today refers to what Aristotle called a thing's "efficient cause," or what brought the thing into existence. The *material* that made up a thing constituted its "material cause." Its *form* and structure that made it the kind of thing it was and enabled groupings of things exhibiting similar defining characteristics, he called the "formal cause." (Remember, we discussed "form.") The unique and specific end or *purpose* the thing fulfilled, he called the "final cause." When we understand a thing's four causes or explanations, we have at least general knowledge about it.[26]

Let's use Silly Putty™ as an example of a thing in the world about which we can gain knowledge. When I was growing up, Silly Putty was the rage (okay, so I'm over fifty). But, honestly, my grandsons even like the stuff. You can stretch it into long strings, roll it into a ball and bounce it, or flatten it a bit, press it onto newspaper, and lift the print. What more could a kid ask for in a toy?

Evidently, Silly Putty was created by accident by a guy named James Wright during World War II when the search was on for cheaper substitutes for synthetic rubber.[27] He dropped boric acid into silicone oil and *voilà*, Silly Putty was born. It didn't make much of a bounce in research efforts to find a cheaper substitute for synthetic rubber, but it was a hit as a party favor due to its unusual features that captivated people's interest, and so someone marketed it as a toy.

Now, what does Silly Putty have to do with a discussion of what it means to exhibit purpose? Though Aristotle didn't have the privilege of playing with Silly Putty, he could have gained knowledge about it just by reading the above paragraph (in Greek, of course). He would have said that we know what Silly Putty is when we answer questions about its causes. When we answer the question of what brought it into being, we understand its efficient cause, which was a human's action. When we answer the question of what it is made of, we learn its material cause, which, for Silly Putty, is boric acid and silicone oil. When we answer the question of what are its form and structure that make it what it is and distinguish it from other things, we learn its formal cause. In this case, Silly Putty can be distinguished from other things, such as synthetic rubber or modeling dough, in that it is not only bouncy, but also malleable and displays an unusual feature identified by a guy who decided to throw a 100-pound ball of the stuff off of

---

26. Feser, *Last Superstition*, 62.
27. "Weird Science."

a second story building. Evidently, it bounced eight feet and then shattered on the second bounce.[28] When we answer, "What is its purpose?" we learn its final cause. In the case of Silly Putty, while its form and structure did not accomplish the original goal of its inventor, namely, to be used as a human tool, it is quite good for bouncing, stretching, and lifting ink from newspaper or comic book print, all of which humans find amusing.

Notice that the Silly Putty's formal cause, its nature, makes it fun for humans to enjoy as a toy, but those features are intrinsic to Silly Putty and would still exist, even if humans did not find them amusing. They make Silly Putty, well, Silly Putty, and not modeling dough. So, as Silly Putty exists in the universe and endures changes imposed upon it from external agents, it consistently acts toward end results that are specific to its nature, its form.

Contrast this A-T take on reality with Barker's materialism. Materialism entails that matter, the material cause, and the efficient cause that brings a thing into existence, are all that exist. In this reductionistic explanation of reality, there is nothing above or beyond the fundamental particles comprising the universe (everything can be reduced down to just particles). Sure, the particles can combine into larger things, but as Feser says,

> The ordinary objects of our experience do not have their own individual "forms" in Aristotle's sense, because there is ultimately nothing over and above the particles that make them up, and the particles are all governed by exactly the same laws of nature. There are no "final causes" either, because none of the behavior of the particles is oriented to any goal or purpose.[29]

Matter just exists with no purpose, says Barker, despite the fact that we can't help but recognize that these conglomerates of material particles called planets, plants, and people demonstrate natural tendencies to act in identifiable ways that fulfill certain purposes and distinguish one kind of thing from another. Despite this, says Barker, we are unreasonable to interpret these unique, goal-directed patterns as indicative of any overarching purpose for any single entity or for the universe as a whole.

Despite his best efforts, though, Barker cannot extricate himself from the reality of formal and final causes. He even tacitly admits a formal and final cause of the hammer, when he says, "If you didn't know what a hammer was, you might be able to reverse-engineer and guess its primary purpose."[30] How is it that someone could figure out the primary purpose of

28. "Weird Science," para. 4.

29. Feser, *Last Superstition*, 178.

30. Barker, *Life Driven Purpose*, 32.

an object just by examining its features? Because the thing exhibits a specific form or nature. Barker admits that a hammer is made up of certain materials and is designed with a certain structure (form) to accomplish a specific goal (final cause or purpose). While he adds the caveat that one might use the hammer for something else, he concedes its "primary purpose" is to drive nails and pry them out of wood.

To summarize, it is true that the efficient cause of a hammer is a human with the ability to act intentionally, or a being with opposable thumbs, as Barker says. And, a hammer's material cause is wood and metal, which is just to say that it is made of matter. But it is also obvious that it is a certain *kind* of thing, that is, it has a particular form (i.e., formal cause). And things in the world inherently exhibit specific potentialities for ends (actualities) commensurate with their forms. This is their final cause. In fact, Feser says, "The final cause of a thing is also the central aspect of its formal cause; indeed, it determines its formal cause. For it is only because a thing has a certain end or final cause that it has the form it has."[31] In other words, the function or purpose of the thing, its end effect, determines parameters of the form to be constructed. This is true because the end must be forecast from the beginning in order to accomplish each of the intermediate steps of change in the process of fulfilling the ultimate function for which it is specifically designed. This is true not only of humans themselves, but also for human-designed artifacts, bodily organs, plants, and for the multitude of other nonconscious entities in the universe that operate relentlessly toward specified goals according to their unique forms.

As far as the hammer, it has a specific shape and structure that demarcates it as a kind of thing distinct from other kinds of things. And the person designing it had the end goal in mind of what he wanted its form to be before the hammer came into being as the kind of artifact that performs the function of driving nails in or pries them out of wood. Now, as Barker notes, a hammer can be used for other things than hammering and prying. But it can't be used for just any purpose. We won't come across anyone trying to ladle soup into his mouth with a hammer.

Another problem with denying formal and final causes and assuming that only material things and their efficient causes exist is that the efficient cause—what brings a thing into existence, which in the case of the hammer is the human will—cannot even fully account for its *own* action. It is true that the efficient cause of the hammer is the human. But Barker doesn't drill down far enough into the deeper matrix of reality.

---

31. Feser, *Last Superstition*, 70.

Remember, in the argument from change, we said that the cause of the essentially ordered series must possess its own independent causal power. Living beings seem to possess their own independent causal power because they appear to move themselves, and they exercise their will to act. But this is only part of the story. For the human crafting the hammer through the use of his arms and hands does not consciously will any of the deeper biological, chemical, or molecular actions we mentioned previously that precipitate the arm-hand movement. These deeper structures act toward a specific end without benefit of the hammer maker saying, "Fire neurons, fire!" And this series of causes depends *each moment* on the existence of all other deeper causes that must terminate in an entity that possesses fully independent causal power, which, as we see here, is not the human, who himself is dependent upon nonconscious micro causes.

Since it is the final cause, the end toward which the hammer shows a propensity—driving nails—that explains the efficient cause's actions from the beginning, and the final cause or purpose must be conceptualized in an intellect before it comes into existence in a certain form, all of the series of causes at the nonconscious level can only be explained by an agent. "A final cause cannot exercise its causality apart from an agent, since an end can serve as a cause only by moving an agent."[32] This is what changes something potential into something actual.

An example is helpful here. Perhaps you've built a house as my husband and I are doing right now. He designs plans, we review them, and then we edit and redesign the blueprints to look like we want the house to look in reality once built—in the end. So, the end result of how we want the house to look is in our minds before the real house is actual. So, whatever the efficient cause is that brings a natural body into existence—whether that entity is an orbiting planet, an amoeba, or a human—before it actually exists, must be *moved by the agent* from the beginning of the causal event so that the thing caused will act the way it must act in order to accomplish a specific end or effect. Therefore, there must be a supreme intellect as the efficient cause of not only the things in the universe, but the universe itself.

In other words, since unconscious things in the universe, such as planets and trees, have final causes, this shows that there must be an intelligence outside the universe guiding them to their purposes. This is because their end goals do not exist in themselves (e.g., an oak tree doesn't exist within an acorn), yet they move toward these goals. Thus, there must be a supreme intellect (itself uncaused and unguided) outside the universe that determines the goals of all things and is willing and guiding them to these

---

32. Wippel, *Metaphysical Thought of Thomas Aquinas*, 220.

goals. The existence of my future house will not be by chance, and so also, the continued existence and purposive behavior of nonconscious things in the universe do not exist by chance either.

Where does this leave us? The implications of these truths cannot be overestimated. Whether we are talking about humans or nonconscious celestial bodies, final causality is an inescapable reality. And while in the example above, the human can be the immediate efficient cause of his own hand movement, when we trace the chain of causes down to ultimate reality, we find that the causal chain must terminate in an ultimate intellect. We call that intellect God.

As Étienne Gilson has observed, it matters not whether we reconfigure the terminology and call the obvious movement of biological things toward ends "adaptations," we are talking about final causality. Renaming it doesn't do away with this inescapable feature. It takes about sixty days, or 1,440 hours, or 86,400 minutes, or 5,184,000 seconds for a cucumber to reach maturity as an edible cucumber. Every moment of every hour of every day, the step-by-step change process ascends from the micro-level through the macro-level. Each miniscule change is not just any change, but a change specific to cucumberness, that is, movement toward becoming *only* a cucumber.

Barker's denial of the existence of formal and final causes arises not from the evidence, as we have just shown. We unavoidably recognize that things are not only made of material stuff, but that they act toward ends in kind-specific ways that distinguish them from other kinds of things. Barker ignores this evidence due to his philosophical commitment to materialism's mechanistic framework, which cannot admit formal or final causes, since they require an explanation of their existence in this moment—namely, an intellect. Once purposeful final causes are eliminated, all that is left is self-contrived purpose in life.

Interestingly, though, Barker unwittingly affirms the point that things exhibit final causes, which presuppose an agent with intrinsic causal powers as the sustaining cause in this moment. For it is Barker himself who has based his entire argument for purposefulness on the contention that only intellects, the ultimate of which he posits are humans, can direct things toward their ends.

In summary, Barker fails to acknowledge the purposefulness inherent in organisms and entities that lack consciousness. Attributing purpose to inanimate things only insofar as humans exploit them does not explain the purposeful behavior of natural bodies in the universe. If nonconscious natural bodies, "things with their own natures but that lack cognition,"[33] do exhibit purpose, this purpose requires an explanation, an explanation that Barker has completely ignored.

Even though the human hammer-maker is the immediate efficient cause of the hammer, a multitude of nonconscious biological micro-systems are simultaneously acting for the human hammer-maker's hand muscles to move the hand, and the neurons to fire to move the muscle, and the chemicals to be released that elicit the neuronal firing, and the molecular changes to elicit the chemical release, until at the bedrock of reality we reach the four fundamental forces, all of which require an agent to orchestrate and initiate each step of change toward the end goal. This conclusion does not reveal that an agent is probable; rather, an agent is necessary.[34]

THE MADNESS OF MATERIALISM

Barker's insistence that purpose can arise from an ever-increasingly complex biological systems reflects a common view among atheists. Jeremy Adam Smith, writing in *Greater Good Magazine*, suggests that "a sense of purpose appears to have evolved in humans so that we can accomplish big things together—which may be why it's linked to better physical and mental health. Purpose is adaptive, in an evolutionary sense. It helps both individuals and the species to survive."[35] Barker must have read from the same atheist scout manual. "Find something more important than you are, and devote your life to it, protecting it, improving it, making it work, celebrating it."[36]

But, in the same breath, Barker also contends that "we are biological organisms in a natural environment and that's all we are."[37] If he is just a biological organism in a natural environment, then the totality of his nature is confined to neuronal firings and chemical reactions completely beyond his control. In this case, Barker's worldview takes one hit after another.

First, the causes of his actions have nothing to do with his appraising options and exercising his will to choose to do one thing over another. He is at the mercy of the biological parameters of his existence. Biological processes *demonstrate* purpose; they don't *create* purpose. Purpose is a feature *of* them, not caused *by* them. If the totality of our being is constituted of biological processes, we cannot give purposes to things; rather, the biological

33. Wippel, *Metaphysical Thought of Thomas Aquinas*, 480.

34. Feser, *Last Superstition*, 115–16.

35. Smith, "How to Find Purpose in Your Life."

36. Barker, *Life Driven Purpose*, 11.

37. God Who Speaks, "Is There a God Who Speaks?," 30:55.

processes determine *our* actions and *our* ends. Molecules in motion don't exercise will to choose purposes. Barker cannot have it both ways. Either we are biological organisms through and through, and our biological processes (even our intentions) are explained by physical phenomena/causes, or not. Barker's mechanistic view of the natural world, which includes man, strips humans of the ability to exercise will in any meaningful way.

Second, Barker also asserts that we really *can* (i.e., "have the capacity to") act with good intentions toward other terrestrial specimens like ourselves. "To be good is to act with the intention of minimizing harm."[38] But on his view, there exists no justifiable reason that any action can be construed as good, bad, or otherwise. There is no moral weight to anything we do. Remember, we are machines hard-wired to survive for the ultimate purpose of species perpetuation. At rock bottom, it is all a matter of mechanistic processes that relentlessly move the organism toward survival. We breathe, think, and act at the mercy of chemical reactions and neuronal firings. Thus, for humans, altruism, and even love, are nothing more than a survival mechanism for the species, certainly nothing laudable as Barker surmises.

Third, Barker insists that his purpose comes from finding a project greater than himself, solving problems that it presents and impacting the world. But on his view, there *is* nothing greater than himself. There are just more selves just like him, who, though currently the top dogs on the food chain, will one day succumb to the fate of all other extinction-bound species.

Fourth, Barker believes his views are scientific, thinking that this gives him an intellectual advantage. But the question of whether we can have purpose without God is not a question of science, but of philosophy. Science can reveal causation. Science can identify patterns in the functions of the universe and entities in it. But science cannot tell us why we seek purpose as humans or why Barker thinks his purpose must be found in "something bigger than ourselves."

THE ANSWER TO EXISTENTIAL ANGST

Despite his materialistic, mechanistic commitments, Barker recognizes that humans naturally seek purpose for their lives, a purpose bigger than and external to themselves. He believes that exchanging purpose *of* life for purpose *in* life allows him to preserve and explain this inherent feature of humanity, while at the same time he rejects its implications for a transcendent reality.

38. Barker, *Life Driven Purpose*, 54.

As far as we know, humans are the only kind of beings in the universe who ask questions about the purpose of their existence. Cats don't; rocks don't. Yet, beings called humans anxiously question, "Why are we here?" "What is our purpose?" "Does our existence matter?" Barker has attempted to explain *how* to find purpose as an existential sense of a fulfillment, but he has failed to ask *why* we seek purpose in the first place. What does the fact that only humans ask these questions tell us about the nature of humans? The question hangs in the air, yet Barker never responds. Instead, he rebukes us as humans for raising such questions:

> Does a raven ask itself, "What is the purpose of my life?" as it finds creative ways to obtain food? Do cats struggle with existential anxiety? Do pandas ask, "Why am I here?" I have read that elephants grieve, but do they wonder what happens after they die? Don't they just live? Why can't life be awesome on its own?[39]

But what is his point when he says, "Why can't life be awesome on its own?" Is he saying that humans need to stifle all existential angst and ignore the inner voice asking "Why I am here?" and "What's this life about?" Will he only be satisfied if the rest of humanity becomes more like the ravens, cats, pandas, and elephants, who don't reflect on the meaning of their own existence at all? It's true they just live. But that is the distinction between humans and animals. What makes us humans and not pandas or elephants is the fact that we possess the capacity to reflect on our own thoughts and the reason for our existence. Animals don't, and not because they refuse to ponder such things in order to enjoy this awesome life more, but because they possess no capacity for self-reflection. It is human *nature* (think "form"), humanity's intrinsic essence, which is reflective of the *kind* of beings we are that makes the existential problem of purpose and meaning real for us.

Perhaps there is something about these conscious human tendencies to seek purpose for our lives in "something bigger than ourselves," as Barker puts it, that signal to us that we are more than sensate, instinct-driven animals. Perhaps this explains why Barker himself felt compelled to address the question of purpose in a two-hundred-page book. The human story, our story, goes deeper than just living the here and now. We suspect that we are something more than what Barker's materialistic view suggests. Just maybe this fact points to the cause of our origin and continued existence in a God that Barker simply does not want.

I say he does not want God to exist because, like many other atheists, Barker's happiness seems at least partially grounded in the belief that he

39. Barker, *Life Driven Purpose*, 46.

doesn't answer to an authority figure beyond himself. While the bulk of his ammunition is aimed at the God of Christianity, he doesn't seem interested in any other kind of external authority figure, either. He likes being free to do what he wants. Barker could've have ripped a page from evolutionary biologist P. Z. Myers's book, *The Happy Atheist*, which preceded Barker's *Life Driven Purpose* by five years. Myers says, "I don't want to live a purpose-driven life. You'd have to be insane to aspire to a life defined by someone else—especially if that someone else was a megalomaniacal alien."[40]

There are other atheists, however, who, instead of blaming their rejection of God on the lack of evidence, honestly admit that at the base of their disbelief in God lies their wish that there is no God in authority. Thomas Nagel describes the deep resistance to the possibility of God's existence prevalent among many atheists as a "fear of religion itself."[41] He says,

> I speak from experience, being strongly subject to this fear myself: I want atheism to be true and am made uneasy by the fact that some of the most intelligent and well-informed people I know are religious believers. It isn't just that I don't believe in God and, naturally, hope that I'm right in my belief. It's that I hope there is no God! I don't want there to be a God; I don't want the universe to be like that.[42]

What Nagel is saying here is profound, but not new. Like Nagel, other atheists have been honest enough to own the fact that their conviction about the nonexistence of God arises, not from an appraisal of the evidence, or at least not primarily from that, but more fundamentally from their wish, their hope, that there is no God. This affirmation is more genuine than imagining that everyone wants there to be a God. Feser is right in his observation that if it is true that many do wish for a God to exist, it is just as true that many people don't.[43] And, honestly, why would people who want to be their own authority want God to exist? As C. S. Lewis says,

> We know that if there does exist an absolute goodness it must hate most of what we do. That is the terrible fix we are in. If the universe is not governed by an absolute goodness, then all our efforts are in the long run hopeless. But if it is, then we are making ourselves enemies to that goodness every day, and are

40. Myers, *Happy Atheist*, 52.
41. Nagel, *Last Word*, 130.
42. Nagel, *Last Word*, 130.
43. Feser, *Last Superstition*, 10.

not in the least likely to do any better tomorrow, and so our case is hopeless again.[44]

By virtue of our human nature, we are the kinds of beings that possess the capacity for happiness and a sense of purpose as we accomplish our self-designed tasks. But we also exhibit an innate desire to invest in something transcendent that exists objectively beyond us and that is of eternal value. This desire is often expressed as investing in "something bigger than myself." We do not have to believe in God in order to *feel* we've accomplished this goal. But if the God of Christianity does exist as the self-existing cause of all being, rejecting this God cuts us off from our ultimate good, the very source of our own being. Thus, our deepest desire can never be fully satisfied, because as Barker notes, in truth, there is nothing greater than me. As Aquinas observes,

> It is impossible for any created good to constitute man's happiness. For happiness is the perfect good . . . else it would not be the last end, if something yet remained to be desired. Now the object of the will, i.e. of man's appetite, is the universal good; just as the object of the intellect is the universal true. Hence it is evident that naught can lull man's will, save the universal good. This is to be found, not in any creature, but in God alone; because every creature has goodness by participation.[45]

So, while Barker's sense of purpose derives from a determined, mechanistic, biologically driven urge, on the Christian view, we are designed to find purpose in our Maker and Sustainer, God alone.

CONCLUSION

For Barker, survival is the name of the game, our ultimate purpose, and the subconscious motivator of all our efforts to conjure purposes at the conscious level. The result is that we live in order to—or for the purpose of—surviving. And since surviving on an individual level is simply another word for living more, Barker is saying that we live in order to live more and survive in order to survive more. It's like playing a slot machine with no place to spend the win. I put money in the one-armed bandit in order to get money out in order to put money back in. As long as I'm feeding the machine, my purpose is to get more money to keep feeding the machine.

---

44. Lewis, *Mere Christianity*, 38.

45. Aquinas, *ST* I-II, q. 2. a. 8. English quote is from Aquinas, *Summa Theologica*.

Barker says we should be satisfied—no, happy—with this Sisphyean existence. At least he is.

Maybe so. But we can't ignore the obvious. Things in the universe are more than conglomerates of matter particles in motion, all caused to act when other particles bump into them. For the materialist view cannot explain the nature of change in entities and why both conscious and nonconscious things act toward goals or ends specific to their natures. The arguments from change and final causality show us that there must be a Being who sustains things in existence through change and has ordered the ends of those things before their beginning. Our coming into being and our continued existence right now depend upon him.

Barker hates the reality that our purpose resides beyond or external to ourselves in the Creator. This Creator, he believes, enslaves and exploits humans for his own selfish glory. Humans are like lifeless hammers in the hand of God. Barker says,

> When we ask, "What is the purpose of a hammer?" we assume that the hammer is lifeless. So asking, "What is the purpose of life?" assumes that life is dead . . . [and the] belief that life, like a tool, has no internal purpose of its own. If you don't have the freedom to choose to strive for your own goals, then you are not really alive. You are a hammer. If you think your purpose must come from outside yourself, you are a lifeless implement or a slave to another mind.[46]

Ironically, as we've seen, it is Barker's materialistic view that casts humans as slaves to biological, chemical, and molecular events orchestrating our thoughts, actions, and emotions every minute of every hour of every day of our motorized, miniscule lives. So, when he urges us to embrace purpose *in* life and discard any hope of purpose *of* life, presenting the Christian view as "bondage" while materialism is "liberty," we have to wonder if he's looking at the same world we are. Because, from my perspective, his hope of giving his own life purpose is a pipe dream. And I don't think he's realized the full implications of his materialism. For if materialism is true—he's the hammer.

BIBLIOGRAPHY

Aquinas, Thomas. *Summa Theologica*. Translated by the Fathers of the English Dominican Province. Benziger, 1947.

46. Barker, *Life Driven Purpose*, 22.

Barker, Dan. *Life Driven Purpose: How an Atheist Finds Meaning*. Durham: Pitchstone, 2015.

Feser, Edward. *Aquinas: A Beginner's Guide*. Oxford: Oneworld, 2010.

———. *The Last Superstition: A Refutation of the New Atheism*. South Bend: St. Augustine's, 2008.

Glass, Don. "Lightning Helps Fertilize the Soil." https://www.indianapublicmedia.org/amomentofscience/lightening-helps-fertilize-soil.php.

The God Who Speaks. "Dan Barker Debates Richard Howe: Is There a God Who Speaks?" *YouTube*, October 18, 2017. https://www.youtube.com/watch?v=LD3-qK-2gu8&.

Lewis, C. S. *Mere Christianity*. New York: Macmillan, 1952.

Midgley, Mary. "Purpose, Meaning, and Darwinism." *Philosophy Now*, 2009. https://philosophynow.org/issues/71/Purpose_Meaning_and_Darwinism.

Myers, Paul Z. *The Happy Atheist*. New York: Vintage, 2013.

Nagel, Thomas. *The Last Word*. New York: Oxford University Press, 1997.

Smith, Jeremy Adam. "How to Find Purpose in Your Life." *Greater Good Magazine*, January 10, 2018. https://greatergood.berkeley.edu/article/item/how_to_find_your_purpose_in_life.

Sulaiman, Wale, and Tessa Gordon. "Neurobiology of Peripheral Nerve Injury, Regeneration, and Functional Recovery: from Bench Top Research to Bedside Application." *The Ochsner Journal* 13 (2013) 100–108. https://www.ncbi.nlm.nih.gov/pmc/articles/PMC3603172/.

"Weird Science: The Accidental Invention of Silly Putty." *Kids Discover* (blog), August 19, 2013. https://www.kidsdiscover.com/quick-reads/weird-science-the-accidental-invention-of-silly-putty/.

Wippel, John F. *The Metaphysical Thought of Thomas Aquinas: From Finite Being to Uncreated Being*. Washington, D.C: Catholic University of America Press, 2000.

Index

P

Paul, the apostle, 150, 185, 190,
    194–95, 197, 199–201, 203–4,
    206–8
Peter, the apostle, 180–81, 185,
    194–95, 197, 199, 201, 204
Plantinga, Alvin, 12, 21, 30, 42
potentiality, 68–69, 102, 144
proof, burden of, 7–9, 14–16, 19–21,
    202
Pseudo-Dionysius, 65–66

R

relativism, historical, 179
Rowe, William, 5

S

Sagan, Carl, 196, 202
Shermer, Michael, 111, 120, 122, 124,
    171

skepticism, 19, 22
slavery, 111, 120, 122–25, 154, 166
Smith, George, 22, 27–28
Smith, Quentin, 78

T

theism, 2, 5, 8, 10, 14, 16, 18, 50, 52,
    58, 70, 84, 111, 113, 116, 120,
    127, 158
    classical understanding, 28, 30, 45,
    64–65, 70, 73, 76, 82–84, 87, 94,
    100, 102, 106–7, 111, 116–18,
    127
three moral minds, 155–58, 162–64,
    168, 172

W

Wenham, John, 198, 205
Wippel, John, 73, 217
Wright, N. T., 188–89, 205, 207